Advanced Praise

A pioneer of healing modalities, such as acupuncture and herbal medicine, Jason Elias now adds storytelling to his talents. In this courageous book, Elias shares his life experiences in the context of storied wisdom from many cultures across the ages and how those experiences shaped his healing journey. It is a touching and compelling story."

—Steven P. Cole, Ph.D., Director of Research, Research Design Associates, Inc.

"Jason Elias's elegant memoir reveals his search for an inner freedom that coincides with the power to heal the self and realize human well-being, and for a spiritual practice that centers on the good of humankind. His example can inspire us all.

—David Appelbaum, Professor of Philosophy at SUNY, New Paltz, former editor of *Parabola Magazine,* and author of *The Shock of Love*

"Through his real life experiences, Jason Elias guides the reader into the deeper aspects of healing, love and grace. His stories are inspirational, entertaining and explore the true meaning of one man's soul journey."

—Marc Grossman, behavioral optometrist, acupuncturist, and author of numerous books

"A fascinating journey of world travels and inner discoveries that made him the great healer that he is."

—Bill Lewis, renowned vocal teacher, composer, and pianist

"Integrating modern practices with the ancient, Jason Elias's book, Kissing Joy as It Flies, *bridges both worlds with expert skill and deep respect. It has something for everyone on a path toward healing."*

—Irving Milberg, M.D, at 97, an internist and dermatologist still in private practice in New York's Hudson Valley

"Jason Elias has given us a wonderful story of his amazing life journey, filled with insight and grace. It will inspire anyone who is on a path of healing."

—Stephen Cowan M.D, author of *Fire Child Water Child*

"Jason's memoir epitomizes a creative journey to the center of the self. Bravo!"

—Vladamir Feltsman, renowned pianist, professor of SUNY, New Paltz, New York

for Kissing Joy As It Flies

"*Becoming a healer one exploration at a time, in* Kissing Joy As It Flies *Jason Elias has created a personal university of the highest order, allowing us to join him on an adventure much like a travelogue that extends across our planet and deep into his soul. Jason's university course is unending..... He has yet to graduate because he understands that the ultimate diploma manifests in his son for whom this book was written.*"

—Bob Duggan, M.A., M.Ac (UK), Director of Traditional Acupuncture Institute
and author of *Common Sense for the Healing Arts*

"*Jason Elias's journey as son of an immigrant stowaway fleeing persecution in his homeland to the relative peace and fulfillment as a shaman-healer in his mature years is a calling more than a career, as if he is chosen rather than choosing. He has done the work to make each struggle a choice to loosen the ties to the past, to convention, to his fear and insecurity. I encourage all those who come within the purview of Jason Elias's* Kissing Joy As It Flies *to read it for its inspiring message and as a standard and model for one's own spiritual path.*"

—Leon I. Hammer, M.D., OMD, author of *Dragon Rises, Red Bird Flies,*
Director of Dragon Rises College of Oriental Medicine

"*In this refreshingly honest odyssey, sprinkled with humorous stories and wise words from ancient (and modern) sages, Jason Elias shares what led him away from the expectations of his male, Greek Jewish lineage, towards expressing his healing gifts inspired by his great-grandmother* Kissing Joy As It Flies *can take you from the periphery to the center of your own life. It provides a mirror to your soul.*"

—Puja A. J. Thomson, author of *After Shock: From Cancer Diagnosis to Healing*
and *My Health & Wellness Organizer*

"*Like Jacob the Baker with whose story Jason Elias ends his book,* Kissing Joy As It Flies, *Jason is one with his efforts. Beyond his acupuncture, bodywork or healing herbs, Jason's work is like a prayer. Inspired by many master teachers, his mastery is his own, a 'soul not restrained by the weight of its own importance.'* "

—Gillian Jagger, world-renowned British artist and sculptor for over 50 years

Also by Jason Elias
Feminine Healing:
A Woman's Guide to a Healthy Body, Mind, and Spirit
Chinese Medicine for Maximum Immunity
The A to Z Guide to Healing Herbal Remedies

Kissing Joy as it Flies

A Journey in Search of Healing & Wholeness

He who binds to himself a joy
Does the winged life destroy
But he who kisses the joy as it flies
Lives in eternity's sunrise

—William Blake

Jason Elias

Published in the United States by:
Five Element Healing Press, New Paltz, New York 12561
Cover design: The Turning Mill, Palenville, New York 12463
All photographs by Jason Elias, except image of Rolling Thunder, and
Elias family photographs.
Graphic images of the Generation Cycle, the Control Cycle, and the
combined image of both are all by Mikio Kennedy.
ISBN: 978-0-9966542-0-3
1. Memoir 2. Healing 3. Spirituality

To all those who seek healing and wholeness, may you pull through the resonant thread from the stories of your lives and celebrate your unique journey on this eternal path we walk together...

CONTENTS

PART THREE:
Around the World
on a Healing Journey 149

PART FOUR:
Five Years of Ashram Life 241

PART FIVE:
Living an Integrative Reality 309

Foreword

Living in Eternity's Sunrise: The Alchemy of a Healer

By Stephen Larsen, Ph.D.

I knew of Jason Elias for many years before I met him. My *Psychology of Consciousness* students at SUNY would tell me, "Hey, you know, Dr. Larsen, all this stuff you're talking about: *Energy medicine, spiritual disciplines, meditation.* This guy really does it!" What they were telling me was that Jason didn't just talk about those ideas; he had somehow come to embody them.

Over the years, we would share patients, and the impression deepened. Each of us provided different services. My office offers biofeedback/neurofeedback for traumatic brain injury, PTSD, and psychotherapy with a specialty in dreamwork, for crises in living. Jason offered Chinese medicine, including acupuncture and herbal support, as well as bodywork. The patients who moved between our offices seemed to find our alternative methods complementary, indeed—but not competitive. I could tell they usually liked us both, and felt understood and supported by their work with each of us.

But our meeting in person didn't happen until about seven years ago when, after a hernia operation by a careless surgeon, I contracted MERSA (Jason mentions in his book that about one fourth of admissions to hospitals are due to *iatrogenic* illnesses: ones caused by doctors). I was walking proof: an otherwise healthy sixty-six year old, terribly infected, and with sores all over his body. Knowing that this disease could be lethal, I felt I needed exceptional help. (My surgeon, when I showed him the ominous red lines and open sores leading from the surgery area, shrugged his shoulders and said, "take Ibuprofen." After the situation got really serious, he finally put me on ten days of antibiotics, which seemed, in effect, like using a pea-shooter on a raging wild animal.) Soon I was in the ER, and then in the hospital, on IV Vancomycin.

I was given a hospital-assigned doctor with a face like a bulldog, which he only partially hid behind his protective facemask as he got close to my bed—after all, I had MERSA! When I asked if I could add colloidal silver to my antibiotics, as I had heard it might help, he glazed over and snarled: "Forget all that crap! It's bullshit! I do this every day, all day!" he added, for emphasis.

"What?" I wondered incredulous, "dismiss people's own efforts to heal themselves?"

After my release from the hospital, five days later, feeling weak, very mortal, and suffering from a terrible restlessness in my limbs from the infection, I still couldn't sleep, and knew something was really wrong underneath.

I headed for the healer my own patients and friends had praised. When I met Jason, we both said, "At last!" and hugged.

I found his office, and its energy, immediately inspiring. The Tibetan chanting he played while I lay on the acupuncture table stayed with me. The sonorous, spirit-imbued, drone said: "*You will heal!*"

After Jason's first treatment I did have the expected healing crisis—sometimes called a *Herxheimer reaction,* or "die-off." I had no choice but to go to bed for a number of days, while my staff ran my therapy office. I took the special herbal decoction that Jason made—tailor made, in fact, to my condition. Gradually my strength and immunity returned, and I began to get better.

If I told him I "owed him my life," he would probably rephrase it to say, "We became good friends and learned to trust each other, and I'm so glad I was able to access your energy and considerable reservoir of life-force." (I like that just a little better than the angry hospital doctor.)

As I delved into this manuscript, I thought of books that have touched and inspired my own life: *In Search of the Miraculous, Meetings with Remarkable Men, Be Here Now, Autobiography of a Yogi*...I could go on, as I love reading how people of integrity have made their way through this perilous and wondrous playing field we call "life," and emerged with an affirmation worth sharing with others.

It's the mixture of biography and living experience that gets my attention, and I can remember my own mentor, Joseph Campbell, saying: "It's not the *meaning of life,* people really need, it's the *experience of being fully alive!* I didn't realize until writing *A Fire in the Mind, the Life of Joseph Campbell,* how the labyrinthine turns and twists of Campbell's life led up to his best-selling *The Hero with a Thousand Faces,* and ultimately *The Power of Myth* series with Bill Moyers, that reached millions of minds and hearts throughout America in the 1990s. My wife

Robin and I began our biography with a quote from Arthur Schopenhauer that was one of Campbell's favorites:

"Looking back over the course of one's own days and noticing how encounters and events that appeared to be accidental, became the crucial structuring features of an unintended life story through which the potentialities of one's character were fostered to fulfillment, one may find it difficult to resist the notion of the course of one's biography as comparable to that of a cleverly constructed novel—wondering who the author of the surprising plot can have been..."

—from *The Inner Reaches of Outer Space* by Joseph Campbell

Over the years of lecturing on Campbell I had almost memorized the above passage, and the words leapt to mind as I read the manuscript of this book in one very intensive weekend. I was working on a book of my own, on dreams, but once I started Jason's book, I could hardly be parted from it: "...an unintended life story through which the potentialities of one's character were fostered to fulfillment!" Schopenhauer's musing fit's Jason's autobiographical narrative like a glove. His aging is not unlike my own; his life is all woven out of the journey of his becoming. And his schooling is not formal, but *informal* education, though there is no lack of discipline and perseverance in its pursuit.

Reading it may help to prepare you for the exceptional healer you will meet if you cross his office threshold. It is also the story of a hero's journey that moves from humble beginnings, through initiation into, in Campbell's words, "a realm of timeless wonder," so that he may return home with that priceless something that makes the journey worthwhile, the "boon" or treasure hard to attain, that he may bestow on his community. In Jason's case it not only explains his wizardry as a healer, but now in the form of this narrative, what the psychoanalysts call the *anamnesis*, "the remembering." It is the story of how an exceptionally talented seeker of our time transformed his very self; the "gross substance" the alchemist starts with—into the "gold." Thus it is a message for all of us, *of how we can become all of which we are capable.*

During the fifties, as Jerry grew up, there was a shadow and a blight of evil that had spent its fury, but left a dark and smoldering trail, in this world. Centuries before, his Sephardic Jewish family had fled the Spanish Inquisition to Kastoria, Greece, which "safe haven" in turn, was now threatened in the 1930s by the terrible genocidal onslaught of the Nazis. Now just some of the family was forced to flee to America—carrying the memory of those who never made it to the promised land—all told some 60,000 of their people from Greece and Turkey alone.

Young Jerry Elias (Jason's birth name) worked for his father in their store in that same Lower East Side neighborhood, but found he didn't fit in with the serious and grim men of his family, determined to make a living at all costs. The only one of them with whom he shared a connection was his Uncle Pincus, a softer, more imaginative man who affirmed the young, shy boy who sometimes stammered as he spoke.

Jerry then identified the truly luminous figures in his family constellation, the women herbalists and healers, his grandmother, Nona, and great-grandmother, Esther, who never learned to speak English. She was called "the little doctor," who could make healing remedies out of plants others considered useless weeds. This was the start of his journey, the magic talisman, and the personal myth that runs throughout the tale.

Young Jerry does the obligatory exploration with mind-expanding drugs, and learns a lot, but doesn't derail his life with them! (As so many of our generation did—"running, starving, hysterical, naked through the negro streets at dawn"—in

Ginsburg's flavorful phrase.) Instead they seem to help pry open his mind and soften it for the sometimes chaotic-seeming and disjunctive learnings that follow. The core of his path is to be a student of whatever draws him most deeply. Instinct pulls him to the Esalen Institute, where the eucalyptus and sage fragrance, and wide-open atmosphere of the Monterey coast breathes a kind of "romance of becoming" into his soul. It is here, at an experiential workshop, that "Jerry" is converted in a single visionary moment into "Jason." The name fits. He changes it, knows it is meant to be, and later finds to his delight that "Jason" means "healer!"

With his new identity now in hand, so to speak, Jason begins the quest for his spiritual "Golden Fleece." And he will have to pass through sirens, and clashing rocks, whirlpools and sleepless dragons indeed! But he will also get to pluck the fruit of the Hesperides, and maybe even marry the princess!

The *Psychology of Consciousness* program, with such luminaries as Robert Ornstein and James Fadiman, now opened up into visionary potentialities. The list of people with whom Jason associates and studies in these years, reads like a "*Who's Who*? of the Human Potential Movement: Michael Murphy, founder of Esalen, Bioenergetics Analyst Stanley Keleman, Joseph Campbell, Tai-chi teacher and dancer Chungliang Al Huang, Bodyworker Moshe Feldenkrais, and Ilana Rubenfeld who becomes a good friend of Jason's.

The reader may join Jason's relatives in asking: "What is the real point of all this growth and becoming? Does it lead to a profession? Does it (as his relatives kept insisting) make good money?

Somewhere, somehow, Jason realized that in order to become what he was capable of, he had to allow himself to be transformed—to change. This would be an unknown alchemy. He didn't quite yet know what it was going to be—bodywork along the lines of F. M. Alexander? (In which he trained for three years, back on the East Coast.) Bioenergetics (Neo-Reichian) and characterological release with John Pierrakos? The "Rubenfeld Synergy" of Ilana Rubenfeld? The liquid-slow, muscle-release of Moshe Feldenkrais? He tried them all, to see if they fit.

Shamanic visions appear and recede along the way. A leitmotiv is a black bird, which, like a true apparition, rushes toward him and vanishes. (The ancient Romans, and many still older shamanic cultures regard such apparitions, particularly black birds, as auguries.)

Jason learns, gradually, to trust the serendipities, or "synchronicities," as Jung and Pauli coined the phrase. A fortuitous series of circumstances lead him into the presence of the legendary Rolling Thunder, the weather-shaman, who was observed by Stanley Krippner and Doug Boyd, literally to create thunderstorms and tornadoes out of the clear blue sky—in fact he does it while Jason is there, visiting. ("Well, that got rid of the curiosity-seekers," the medicine man quips after a torrential downpour.) But Jason stays longer for a personal teaching. Rolling Thunder has a simple heartfelt message for him to trust himself and his own heart, which stays with Jason throughout his entire journey.

Synchronicities multiply into a kind of bibliomancy, when books on "psychic surgery" keep falling off shelves around him in the East-West bookstore of San Francisco, leading him to an encounter with a Philippine healing network of psychic surgeons; some of who connect with him, and some of whom seem pretentious and distant. Jason follows his heart, and is gradually initiated into a wonderful network of simple, but potent healers, who become his "family."

Eventually his worldwide network of friends and seekers on their mutual journeys lead him to the community of Bhagwan Shree Rajneesh. Like many other psychologists, physicians, and talented professionals, Jason is charmed by the wise, wild little guru, and comes to rest in Pune (or Poona), India for five years. At a recent meal in a little, local café, and while talking about this book, Robin and I were astonished to find that we had been in India at exactly the same time as Jason, though we were only there for a year or so, while Robin completed her Ph.D. dissertation on Ritual Art, and we never visited Pune. Still the timeless magic of that journey stays with us, even as India itself breathes an air of timelessness.

When a new, bureaucratic administration took over the ashram, Jason's inner guidance told him to leave. (Less than a decade later, the whole international organization was to self-destruct in scandal.)

I am content here, merely to tantalize you and prepare you for Jason's wonderful book, without going on more. It reads, not only like the tales of the great spiritual seekers I mentioned, but the story of a healer in becoming and how he became who he is. It may speak to other readers as it spoke to me: *Of how we become who we really are.* As our son Merlin (who accompanied us to India in 1975-6) used to sing, softly and sweetly with his seven-year old child's wisdom, as we walked along walls of prayer stones in Nepal: "What will become of us, if we can't find ourselves?...What will become of us, if we can't find ourselves?...

Introduction

"All wisdom is plagiarism; only stupidity is original."
—Hugh Kerr

Stories and their mysterious power have fascinated me from an early age, beginning with listening to stories of the old country from my immigrant parents, hearing some told over and over again, others hidden from me, whispered out of earshot. This fascination led me to listen deeply to the stories I was told and to remember especially those that carried a teaching, a kind of healing essence.

The mystery of healing like those of stories also found me early in childhood. Natural healing happened at home, often in the kitchen, where my grandmother, Nona, passed along the natural remedies that she had learned from her mother, my great grandmother, Esther, known for her healing powers as "the little doctor," in her homeland of Kastoria, Greece.

Having grown up with a very firm, provincial Jewish father with whose energy I could not relate or strive to emulate and a mother with whose healing energy I naturally connected, I realized upon finishing this book that my early seeking nature evolved into a search for balance and healing through self-awareness.

My experiences at the Esalen Institute in Big Sur, California in the early 1970s exposed me to many psychological and spiritual practices of body, mind, and spirit—from psychotherapy to bodywork, such as massage therapy, Rolfing, and the Alexander technique—infusing my desire for personal healing with a spiritual call.

These awakenings and the blessed company of great teachers have guided my journey. When struggling to sustain my equilibrium while upended emotionally at the crossroads of decision-making, my repetitive vision of a Black Bird flying towards me has also guided me, often clarifying a gnawing ambivalence.

The unfolding metaphor of Wholeness, intrinsic to Chinese medicine, the yin/yang that ever challenges us to seek and accept one's ever-changing truth, gave me a roadmap to consciousness that I could share with others as wounded healer.

Though I never met my Greek great grandmother, Esther, she lives through me to this day. As if by osmosis I inherited from her my two essential professional callings: the desire to heal others naturally and complementing this healing by sharing teaching stories.

My seeking has led me to explore healing traditions around the world and introduced me to my lifework as an acupuncturist and practitioner of Chinese medicine. I have come to understand and synthesize the universal, holistic necessity of balancing the life force across body, mind, and spirit. Healing takes many forms: the healing of psychological wounding —of fears, of loss, of trauma— the healing of the wounded body, the healing when separated from the Source of our being. Each of these carries a thread of our life story: the wounded story, the healing story, and the story woven from wounding to healing.

For over 40 years, my private practices and my books have focused on the healing of others. This book focuses on my own healing journey. I am a seeker after meaning, a pilgrim not on the road to Mecca but to the truth carried always within my own heart, my own body, and my own soul.

Like my great grandmother long ago, I often call on the ancient teaching stories of Mulla Nasreddin to impart knowledge through humorous allegory. Nasreddin was a Sufi, believed to have lived and died during the 13th century in today's Turkey. A philosopher and wise man he appears in thousands of teaching stories.

The following story speaks to the age-old tendency to look for the key to freedom, to love, to fulfillment, to meaning, in the light, where one believes they can see clearly, rather than all too often in the darker places, where the key has likely been lost:

> *A man is walking home late one night when he sees an anxious Mulla Nasreddin down on all fours, crawling on his hands and knees on the road, searching frantically under a streetlight for something on the ground.*
>
> *"Mulla, what have you lost?" the passerby asks.*
>
> *"I am searching for my key," Nasreddin says worriedly.*
>
> *"I'll help you look," the man says and joins Mulla Nasreddin in the search. Soon both men are down on their knees under the streetlight, looking for the lost key. After some time, the man asks Nasreddin, "Tell me, Mulla, do you remember where exactly you dropped the key?"*
>
> *Nasreddin waves his arm back toward the darkness and says, "Over there, in my house. I lost the key inside my house…" Shocked and exasperated, the passerby jumps up and shouts at Mulla Nasreddin, "Then why are you searching for the key out here in the street?"*

"Because there is more light here than inside my house,"
Mulla Nasreddin answers nonchalantly.

I invite you to join me as I retrace the mysterious steps and encounters that have created my life's unfolding path toward healing, a story where I trust you will recognize or awaken to your own evolving story and perhaps learn that you held your key all along.

During my final read-through of this book before its publication, certain early parts of my journey, particularly the Esalen years, felt too long. But, though not compact, their shape and content remains essential to the full unfolding of this time. My experiences at Esalen gently and persistently nudged me to persevere toward intensely rich learnings on my path toward healing and wholeness.

"Remember only this one thing. The stories people tell have a way
of taking care of them. If stories come to you, care for them. And learn
to give them away where they are needed. Sometimes a person needs a
story more than food to stay alive. That is why we put these stories in each
other's memory. This is how people care for themselves."
—Barry Lopez from **Crow and Weasel**

When we share our stories, our lives, we belong to each other. I share my story in hope that it will inspire you to tell yours.

PART ONE

Introducing a Life

*"Life must be lived forward,
but it can only be understood backwards."*

— Søren Kierkegaard

1

So Close and Yet So Far

Nan-in, a Japanese master during the Meiji era (1868-1912), received a university professor who came to inquire about Zen.

Nan-in served tea. He poured his visitor's cup full, and then kept on pouring.

The professor watched the overflow until he no longer could restrain himself. "It is overfull. No more will go in!"

"Like this cup," Nan-in said, "you are full of your own opinions and speculations. How can I show you Zen unless you first empty your cup?"

—from Zen Flesh, Zen Bones, compiled by Paul Reps

As I look book, I realize that much of what I experienced in my early life seems today, in my late sixties, unbelievable, or, even as an objective observer, it stretches my "reasonable" limits. I've recounted my experiences from deep reflection but also transcribed my very detailed journals from those days. I can only ask that my readers temporarily empty their cups of preconceived notions and read my story as just that.

In his book *Travels with Epicurus* philosopher Daniel Klein remembers his teacher, Eric Erikson, the renowned developmental psychologist and psychoanalyst. Erikson believed that mature and wise ways of reminiscing precisely offer the essential ingredient necessary to live an authentic old age. We want to convey the essential truths, the learnings, of our experiences—how it felt to us, what it meant to us then and what it means to us now. Memories of Klein's esteemed teacher may or may not exactly reflect the facts, but his memories do express the author's truth.

I too have recalled and recreated the memories of my life's journey, particularly those that establish steppingstones on my path to wholeness. No doubt a professional fact-checker would find errors in my accounts, however, my encounters and my memories are mine alone.

* * *

It was a crisp autumn day, the leaves mostly off the trees, and a sense of excitement in the air. Standing in front of the old tenement building on Orchard Street in Manhattan's Lower East Side, every cell in my body vibrated with a kind of recognition and awareness of a rare but familiar presence. Something old, deep within me, searched for its voice, seeking to be heard and honored. Both my inner knowing and the keen sense of familiarity convinced me that I had been in this exact place before.

As people lined up behind me and followed me into the vestibule of the Tenement Museum, I felt that I could have been their guide. The walls and rooms held a myriad of stories and personal histories, of different languages and cultures, imprints of the old world and the countless immigrants who had flooded to New York from other continents. In the late 1800s and early

1900s, some of those immigrants had found their first American homes in this very building. These hallways once teemed with

daily life, often 12 or more people to a room, all in search of a fortunate destiny.

I recognized the stairway, the layout of the rooms, and somehow knew that my father had lived here, though I had never, in reality, stepped foot in this building. During my teenaged years I had worked in my dad's store, just across the street from where I now stood, and for years in graduate school, lived only a few blocks west. I'd watched my son grow into adolescence only 30 miles north in an idyllic suburb, unaware that my father, Benjamin, had spent his formative years, since age 13, in what had become an important cultural and historical landmark of immigrant history. Now my son was the same age that my father had been when he immigrated.

My wife and I had brought our son to the Tenement Museum that day in 2003 to help him prepare for a middle-school class project—tracing his ancestral roots—that would culminate with a school tour of Ellis Island.

On the train ride from Westchester into the City that morning, I had shared with my son many memories of my parents, who had both lived in this Lower East Side neighborhood after being processed through Ellis Island. I reminisced about going to work in my father's shop on Allen Street every Sunday where he sold women's clothing. The whole area was closed on Saturdays for the Sabbath, but, on Sunday, the main business day, shoppers would fill the streets seeking bargains and haggling over prices.

I wanted to share all of this with my son: show him the restaurants, the pickle merchants on Essex Street, the Jewish way of bargaining for better prices, the atmosphere of the time. He looked at me with little interest, as if to say, "So what? What does this have to do with me?!"— probably the same way I'd looked at my dad when he'd waxed on telling stories of his own. Like me at his age, my son wasn't ready to hear the old stories, so I kept them to the point, but I didn't want what happened with my father to happen to him.

I well remembered those few times when my dad had tried to share his history with me, but my adolescent lack of interest had consistently rebuffed him, until he stopped trying to tell me his stories, his hurt expression clear in my mind.

Just before my twentieth birthday my father died, and it became quite clear that the time had passed for me to listen better to his stories. At first bereft after my father's passing that I would never know the details of my family history, I remain forever grateful to my Uncle Pincus, my father's youngest brother, for filling many of the lingering gaps of my family's history as we sat Shiva together for seven nights (the Jewish family tradition of celebrating and honoring the spirit of the dead), knowing the day would come when I could now share those stories with Adam, my own son.

As I read and reread about the families of origin who had lived, thrived, and often died in these very rooms of this Lower East Side tenement building—transformed, no less, into a museum— I felt my father's presence fully alive in me, there for me and there for my son.

2

The Stowaway

"Our word 'courage' comes from the French word coeur, *for 'heart.' Courage is a willingness to act from the heart, to let your heart lead the way, not knowing what will be required of you next, and if you can do it."*

—Jean Shinoda Bolen, from *Gods in Every Man*

Thousands of people sought passage to the New World in the early 1900s. I knew that my father had emigrated from Greece to New York when he was only 13. He had been very resourceful, the oldest of his brothers, fluent in five languages, and thought to be the best representative of the family to make the journey. He told me he'd been smuggled across the seas inside of a trunk. A stowaway? It began to dawn on me that day at the Tenement Museum how very brave my father must have been!

Our guide took our visitors' group up a dark staircase into the rooms, the worlds, inhabited by immigrants and their families: a Bavarian family on the second floor, next to an Italian family, and on the third floor, a Jewish family from Lithuania, next to the Sephardic Jewish family from Kastoria, Greece—the Confino family. The hallways bustled with excitement as people behind me on line connected to their ancestors' experiences, sharing memories of parents and grandparents. Clearly I was not the only one touched by this experience, but, for me, it was momentous, opening a door within, a door semi-shut, where my father came alive again through me.

I learned from our guide that the Confino family was a successful, relatively wealthy family in the Sephardic community of Kastoria, the same small village from which my father's family originated. Granted asylum by the Ottoman Empire, Kastoria had been a safe haven for the Jews evicted from Spain during the Spanish Inquisition. Though for many generations this relocated community had prospered, Greece and Turkey had fought constantly over which country had dominion over Kastoria. These incessant disputes, even war, had depleted the local economy and severely threatened the Confino family's way of life.

With further study about the Confinos, I learned that Abraham and Rachel Confino and their family immigrated to New York in the very early 1900s and moved into a small tenement building, often referred to as a walkup, at 97 Orchard Street. The large, extended family had lived together in only a couple of rooms yet they openly offered to share their new, meager life with others fleeing the oppressive environment of their homeland.

I remembered that my father had arrived less than a decade later, and I speculated that he had given the Ellis Island authorities the Confinos' Orchard Street address to secure his entry into America. Reading that the Confino family survived by selling "bloomers" off a street-cart on Delancey Street, I recalled that my dad had told me the same story about his first business venture in America. Both the Confinos and my dad later sold dresses and skirts on Allen Street, but as separate businesses. Indeed the 97 Orchard Street tenement where I had stood with my family had been my father's very first home in America!

Both thrilled and incredulous at my father's courage and tenacity, my perspective about my father shifted. He was no longer the boring, workaholic man that I tried so desperately not to emulate, but rather an adventuresome man, full of dreams for a better future. His responsible values and moral compass led him to sacrifice his own desires and raise money to bring his extended family to America, while providing for his own young family.

* * *

Ten years or so after arriving in New York, my father met and married a distant relative, named Miriam, also originally from Kastoria. They had two children: my half sister, Estelle, and my half-brother, Stanley. When Estelle was six and Stanley only two, my father's first wife died of breast cancer at 28. Overwhelmed and grieving, not knowing how to raise his children while earning a living, my father asked his mother to come from Greece to New York to fill the void. Nona agreed and came to the States, taking over the household duties and stepping in as mother to Estelle and Stanley while leaving her other sons, Pincus, 10, and Albert, 13, behind with her mother in Greece.

Meanwhile, Hitler's Third Reich rose to power in Germany by the mid-1930s, and soon Nazi armies moved into neighboring countries, threatening the Jews throughout Europe, including my family's native Greece. Like millions of innocent Jewish and non-Jewish people living in Europe during that time, much of my family's unfolding story is tied to Hitler's horrific rule.

Nona, Alabama Avenue in Brooklyn

Nona fast became a doting second mother to Estelle and Stanley and did all she could for my grieving father. She cooked the traditional Sephardic food, a combination of Spanish and Greek/Turkish dishes, and shared her healing remedies, as her mother had taught her in Greece— diffusing herbal teas, making poultices for scrapes and bruises. Passed down from her mother and probably generations of wise women healers, Nona had a remedy for almost everything! At the slightest hint of cold or flu, she would toss a handful of strange-smelling herbs into a special pot simmering on the kitchen stove and after much tasting and clucking over her treasured recipe, offer her vile-tasting brew to the reluctant "bubba" who needed it.

When a sickness was particularly tenacious, Nona would cover our naked bodies with healing balms and strategically place glass cups called "bankes" on our backs to draw out the "bad" energy, releasing it through the pores of our skin. (I learned much later that the bankes (cuppings) were used and mentioned in the writings of Maimonides and in the Talmud.) Onions were just the things for abrasions; cucumbers worked wonders for bruises and black eyes, and if all else failed there was chicken soup to care for every manner of body, mind, and spirit.

Taking care of everyone in her New York family, while also keeping an ear to the whispered rumors of atrocities in Europe, must have been unimaginably trying for her. No one could confirm the horrific rumors, and Nona lived with her worst fears, waiting endlessly for news of the fate of her sons, her mother, and other family members and friends still living in Greece. Who could believe the increasing talk of mass executions, that human beings could perpetrate such heinous acts upon others? What would become of her relatives, their homes and farms?

The first occupation of Greece came in 1941 by the Italians, but this was relatively benign in part because the occupiers actually had relationships with the Jewish residents. The German troops, however, observed this behavior and believed members of the resistance must be executed. By 1943, the Germans took over the occupation with a vengeance. Within a few months, the rumors of executions and exterminations had grown worse and now were reliable. The German army had by this time invaded and carted off entire Sephardic Jewish families in Greece and, in fact, whole communities.

Nona was a stranger in a strange land unable to speak its English language and always dressed in traditional black garments. She communicated with her American grandchildren by taking good care of them, feeding them her cherished recipes, and tending to their ills with her herbal wisdom. As a young boy I didn't understand her solemn intensity, but I knew she'd have a remedy for whatever ailed anybody. We all trusted her quiet, healing ways. Only as an adult did I realize that she carried the losses and sadness of a lifetime.

My father had met, courted, and married my mother, Betty, in 1940. Fifteen years his junior, she willingly had agreed to raise my father's first two children—my sister Estelle only a few years younger than herself—and moved into the Brooklyn home that his mother, our Nona, ruled. Nona taught my mother how to prepare all of her Greek and traditional Sephardic dishes as well as her herbal concoctions and poultices.

Soon my mom learned to speak Ladino, the Spanish dialect spoken by the Sephardic Jews all over the world as a common language, connecting them to their roots, and slowly my mother became accepted by the Sephardic clan.

The day we visited the Tenement Museum these snippets of memories flooded back to me. I recalled my father's stories about immigrating to America as a young teen. I remembered my mother's many kindnesses and my Nona making a strange herbal remedy to swab my knee when I fell off my bike. Our home had felt solemn and stern, for reasons that my Uncle Pincus had revealed after my father's death. Alive with curiosity, I vowed to refresh my memory, to recover the old stories, to honor my father and mother and the healing powers that my great grandmother had passed on to me through Nona. I had felt her presence, her potent medicinal awareness, when Uncle Pincus had first told me of her. That recollection now again quickened my blood on this momentous day. With the sun setting as we departed the museum for Grand Central Station and home, I looked over at my son. Pieces of broken memories opened into distant ones as the mosaic of our family's history began to gather its pieces to tell this story. One day he too would want to know more and I would share it with him.

3

Pincus's Arrival - When Everything Changed

"Over the entrance to Yad Vashem, Israel's memorial to those who perished in the Holocaust, is inscribed into the stone an aphorism ascribed to Baal Shem Tov: 'Exile comes from forgetting. Memory is the source of our redemption...'"

—Elie Weisel

I knew very little about my Uncle Pincus when I was a little boy. Nona spoke of her youngest son, and my father occasionally mentioned his younger brother, but Pincus lived far away in Greece, and I had never seen him—until he came to visit when I was five years old.

At that age, with my mother and grandmother both doting over me, I thought I was the center of attention. Seven years older, newly a teenager, my brother Butch was always out with his gang, leaving me at home with Nona and my mother. I watched the women cook their time-honored Sephardic and Greek/Turkish recipes, the aromas of spices and herbs greeting everyone who walked in our door.

Nona's healing remedies, a potion or liniment, was always at the ready for any ailment. She would soothe my father's chronic back pain by dipping a cloth into a salve laced with fragrant spices, mashing it first with her strong hands before taking the cloth and wrapping it around my father's back. She created a similar tonic wrap for a sprained ankle or injured arm. I would imitate her by collecting grass clippings and flowers from the yard, mixing them with pebbles and dirt to make my own "medicines," a family member or neighbor humoring me, when I tried to tend to their ailment or wound.

My father and brother often chided me that I was playing "girls' games," and that I should think more about sports or playing soldier. Regardless of their harsh judgments, Nona's treatments felt right to me and I remember those carefree childhood days fondly. Still, a tension rumbled beneath the daily routine. I felt it but didn't know quite how to speak about it.

Suddenly one day frenzy overtook the house as we prepared to welcome our Uncle Pincus and his family from Greece. I didn't understand my family's odd mix of profound sadness and tears of happiness. Unbeknownst to me, my father and grandmother had been trying to bring Uncle Pincus to the States for some time. A few years after the war ended, my father had heard that Pincus had survived the camps at Auschwitz and been released by the Russians, but lost his wife and three children to the horrors of extermination. (I learned many years later that the Nazis had also killed my father's middle brother, Albert, and his entire family.)

Sitting me down at the kitchen table, my parents told me that my Uncle Pincus, his second wife, Sulica, and their two young children, Bonita, who was my age, and Izzy, a boy a little younger, would be living with us, and I must share a bedroom with my older brother, Butch. Even at five, I willfully made it known that I didn't like this news one bit. I can only imagine how much Butch, at 13, hated the idea of sharing a room with his bratty, little brother. Our guests would live in my bedroom along with part of the living room, and we would share the rest of the house.

My mother and grandmother became solely focused on the pending arrival of Pincus, Sulica, and their children, and how they would help them adjust to the American way of life. My father worked constantly. He would leave the house at seven in the morning every day *except* Saturday for Shabbat and would not return home until seven in the evening. He then ate his dinner, threw back a shot of ouzo, and either sat down to watch television or to discuss the logistics of the "coming event" with the other adults. They always talked in Ladino, the traditional Sephardic language, and my brother and I could not fully understand them.

On Saturdays my father would spend the mornings in shul, religious Jewish services at the synagogue, sometimes later in the day taking us on a family outing but more often to visit with other relatives. He never seemed to want to talk with *just* me, leaving me lonely and dejected. Thankfully, my mother reassured me that once our relatives arrived things would be all right again, but I did not fully believe her. Already I felt like no one had time for me and sensed, even though so young, that I was losing something that I could never reclaim.

When Uncle Pincus and his family finally arrived, I was certainly no longer the center of the universe. I once locked myself in the bathroom and refused to come out. Through the door, I heard my parents and Nona talking about how selfish I was behaving, having no idea what Pincus and his family had suffered. All I knew was that I felt very alone, isolated, and teased.

Adding to my feelings of isolation and alienation, no one spoke English. Pincus, Sulica, and Bonita all spoke fluent Greek and Turkish, and everyone, including my mother, spoke Ladino. My brother and I simply did not exist for those first few months after our guests had arrived. I no longer had a room of my own, and Nona and my mother had others to dote upon. Still, the fragrances of their cooking and herbal preparations soothed and consoled me.

Things did settle down again, as my mother had promised, and our fractured family became a little more whole again. My relationships with our cousins deepened as they learned English. Bonita and I walked to school each day, and we played together in the afternoons.

About a year after their arrival, Uncle Pincus and his family found an apartment of their own, above Red's Toy Store, that always smelled like the plastic and rubber that toys were made of. To this day if I pass a toy store, I'll think of Red's for a brief moment before my mind travels back to the narrow stairwell that I climbed hundreds of times to the tiny apartment, only one block away, that became home to Uncle Pincus, Aunt Sulica, and their children, our cousins.

* * *

Losing my Nona hit hard. For quite awhile I had noticed that she spent more and more time in bed, and received many visits from Dr. Ginsberg with his leather doctor's bag. I knew that she was ill and very much missed her cooking and caring for us with her many remedies, but now the healer was in need of healing. When I saw my father's tears, I knew that Nona had died. My mother's mom had passed the year before, but I had not felt close to her. But Nona! She had always been there with a hug when I was needy.

Only seven years old when she died, I didn't remember how I felt when my grandmother Nona died until I began to write about it. She had been my surrogate mother—tending our wounds, serving us delicious food, but forever refusing to learn English. She ran the house with strict rules, Jewish "kosher" rules, which I resented. Who can live without bacon?!

Although Nona cared for us, it was my mother's warmth that carried each day, but she could never speak against Nona. When my grandmother died I felt numb, became depressed, being in the house felt so empty without her presence. More than grief, I felt a conflicted mixture of fear that her omnipresence was no longer there to protect us and a kind of liberation, for my mother was loving and permissive, clueless about boys being boys.

I discovered my oasis on the corner lot. Brownsville had no parks or green land nearby, but my little corner lot became my world. I'd pick wildflowers and grass and pretend to feed the grasshoppers and mend their broken wings. I'd pretend to be Superman or a Viking king. In my lot, everything was possible.

* * *

Living in Brownsville, Brooklyn was in many ways like village life in Kastoria, Greece. Relatives and friends who had fled their homeland occupied most all of the homes on our street. Everyone took care of and supported each other. Each household had an open-door policy, and everyone knew each other's business. Uncle Sol, a distant relative, lived next door to us, and aunts and uncles lived all around us.

By the time I was eight or nine years old, Izzy, Bonita, some friends, and I would play together outside. Our favorite game was Billy the Kid, complete with toy guns and holsters, to fight the bad guys. I'm told that I always chose to be Billy the Kid, the greatest cowboy. One day when Uncle Sol was observing us playing and shooting at each other, he asked, "So who are you?" I told him that I was Billy the Kid, to which he retorted, "Billy the Kid was an okay cowboy, but he was nothing compared to Kid Schmutz. Kid Schmutz was the greatest cowboy of all time!" And from that day on I was always Kid Schmutz. It took me awhile to learn that "schmutz" was the Yiddish word for "dirty." My cousin Izzy has never let me live that one down.

Brownsville surely lived up to its reputation as Hell's Kitchen, with its gangs and turf battles, but our few square blocks felt relatively safe because a few members of Murder Incorporated, the Jewish Mafia, still lived there. When I was only six or seven years old, I used to rub one of those men's shoulders from time to time, earning a rare two-dollar bill for my efforts—my first experience as a massage therapist. Years later, I learned that this neighbor was a hit man for Murder Incorporated. Nonetheless the community felt safe with them there and everyone got along splendidly.

While Jewish families and black families had coexisted in Brooklyn for years, most of the black population lived in other neighborhoods or a huge housing project across Linden Boulevard that we referred to as the "pink houses." For well over a year, all the adults in our extended family had been whispering about our deteriorating Brooklyn neighborhood. The exit began slowly when the first black family bought a house within a few blocks of our community. After that, the residents of our small, two-block radius refused to sell their homes to black families, allegedly to keep the neighborhood "safe and to protect the value of the homes." When a resident on our block sold a house to a middle-class black family, a mass exodus ensued.

A common insidious prejudice remains prevalent toward both African Americans *and* Jews, projections all based on fear veiled as anger. As we witness in today's brutal strife around the world, any such racism perpetrates divisiveness and hatred that denies the essential truth that life is a generative interconnected, interdependent whole. Perhaps this fact instills the quest in us to realize our unified potential.

4

Leaving Brooklyn

Struggle

*A man found a cocoon of the Emperor moth
and took it home to watch it emerge. One
day a small opening appeared, and for
several hours the moth struggled but couldn't
seem to force its body past a certain point.
Deciding something was wrong, the man
took scissors and snipped the remaining bit of
cocoon. The moth emerged easily, its body
large and swollen, the wings small and shriveled.
He expected that in a few hours the wings
would spread out in their natural beauty, but
they did not. Instead of developing into a creature
free to fly, the moth spent its life
dragging around a swollen body and
shriveled wings.
The constricting cocoon and the struggle
necessary to pass through the tiny opening
are God's way of forcing fluid from the body
into the wings. The "merciful" snip was, in
reality, cruel. Sometimes the struggle is
exactly what we need.*

When I was ten years old, my whole life living in a close-knit community of family and friends, changed drastically. In 1957, when we moved from our home in Brownsville, Brooklyn to Long Beach on Long Island, Butch and I felt like it was the end of the world. Even though our new home was across the street from the Atlantic Ocean and only an hour from the old neighborhood, we left behind the familiar back streets and our core group of friends, along with a strong sense of rootedness and belonging. Our parents tried hard to convince us that moving from the noise and frenzy of the city to a quiet, suburban neighborhood, only an hour away, would be as wonderful for us, as they thought it would be for them. We would have none of it. Butch especially had been angry and belligerent ever since we'd heard the news.

I vividly remember that drive to Long Island. My brother sat brooding and silent while the tension in the car bristled with unspoken angst. To fill the void my parents turned on the radio, when suddenly a news bulletin reported a violent incident at Thomas Jefferson High where Butch attended school. A disgruntled student had thrown lye acid at his teacher, which also severely burned many of the students in Butch's class. My brother and I were no happier about the move, but we were all relieved that he hadn't been in school that day!

As much as I wanted to be disenchanted about our new community, there was no doubt that Long Beach was much cleaner and brighter than Brownsville. Certainly a step up from our Brooklyn house, our new Spanish-styled house had a terracotta-tiled roof with a clear view of the ocean, just as our parents had described.

Though I did make friends, everyone teased me about my thick Brooklyn accent. Long Island schools were far superior to the ghetto school I was used to, and I began to fall behind, feeling increasingly like I didn't belong. The more I felt lost and insecure, the more I acted out. My mother encouraged me to share my feelings with her, but I felt too old to go to her with my problems.

Butch hated all of it and refused to attend the Long Beach schools. He drove to Brooklyn every day to his old Brooklyn high school, where he led his teenage street gang, the Garrisons, so named because they wore studded Garrison belts that doubled as weapons. He repeatedly advised me to be a man and to handle my problems by myself, not to be a sissy. But my affected swagger felt fraudulent, at odds with my empathic and intuitive nature.

Even though I didn't share my feelings with my mother during those young teenage years, she knew something was very wrong. My poor school grades and acting out greatly concerned her, and she sought advice at my middle school. The guidance counselor recommended that I take an aptitude test to determine my natural proclivities and to set me on course.

At the time, the results seemed totally out of character, but now I realize how amazingly accurate they were. The test revealed that I had the highest aptitude for becoming a doctor, with priest, a close second, followed by persuasive salesmanship! With my minimal math skills and poor grades, I knew becoming a doctor was improbable at best. Already detached from my own Jewish religion, with no interest in *any* religion, much less Christianity, becoming a priest seemed a ludicrous result. Finally, sales, meant going into the family business—exactly what I wanted to avoid! I assumed that the absurdity of these results confirmed the stupidity of the system and the fallacy of such testing. Today as a healing arts practitioner with a strong spiritual foundation, I realize that the old test was quite accurate. And, because my work truly reflects my passion for healing, "selling it" evokes sharing something that I love with others.

Even after this encouraging guidance for my future, I continued to act out, including the usual early teenaged pranks and practices: drinking at 14, breaking windows in abandoned houses, and so on. I often got in trouble in school as well and continued to do poorly in class.

I particularly hated attending Hebrew school, every day after school. I would much rather have been with my friends and not spending another two hours indoors. I can hear myself saying, "But why do I have to learn Hebrew? If God is all-knowing why can't I pray to him in English?"—the exact words my son said to me at that age. My dad retorted, "Until you're 13 and become a Bar Mitzvah, you will do what I say, no questions asked. When you're a Bar Mitzvah, you're a man and then you can choose."

I hated the coursework, but I enjoyed the final year, when I worked individually with Rabbi Abitan, a humble and learned man, who took a special interest in me. He taught me to read the Torah, of course, but also connected Judaism with seeking spirituality. He understood how I could be critical of the hypocrisy that I witnessed in my family as well as in the general congregation, where people came to temple, but didn't live the teachings in their daily lives. I repeatedly challenged how people could go to shul and pray and then cut each other's throats the next day. Rabbi Abitan heard me and understood how I felt.

After finally completing my Hebrew studies, I had my Bar Mitzvah and celebration. As people came up to congratulate me, Butch whispered into my ear, "I don't care how many times you get Bar Mitzvahed. You ain't a man till you get laid." There was only one way to live this down after such a statement from my older, and much more worldly, brother!

Soon after my Bar Mitzvah, Butch and our cousin Marty arranged for me and Marty's brother, Steve, to lose our virginity, our private rite of passage. They gave us the money and instructed us to take the train from Long Beach into New York City and to hail a cab to the corner of Fifth Avenue and 65th Street, bordering Central Park. When we arrived at that infamous corner, an attractive, light-skinned black woman in a fur coat was waiting there and joined us in the backseat of the taxi. She gave the driver a downtown address and sat back "to relax" with us boys. Within moments, she opened her coat to reveal her totally naked body. I could barely speak. She took us to her apartment and gave us our first lesson in sex. I was too young and too overwhelmed to truly perform but she satisfied us nonetheless. The next day I went to Long Beach Hospital, convinced I had contracted venereal disease.

After my liberation from Hebrew school, my Bar Mitzvah, and my introduction to sex, I felt proud of my accomplishments, like a real man, and my time after school became my own again. But, my relief and joy didn't last long. Now that I was a man, at 13, my father informed me that it was time to start going to work with him every Sunday and to begin taking on "true

My Bar Mitzvah (I'm on the far left)

responsibility." Though I tried hard to escape it, my father made clear that this was the family tradition, and I must uphold it.

Every Sunday morning my father and I left our house at seven in the morning to either drive into the city with Butch or take the Long Island Railroad into Manhattan and then a subway to Delancey Street. I was always disgruntled on those Sunday mornings and often a tense silence permeated those trips. I hated the work, but my father told me I must start at the bottom and work my way up. I worked in the basement, pulling and boxing orders for Monday shipment, making a bit of money. I tried to persuade my father to at least allow me to interact with the public and sell, but he wouldn't hear of it.

Only on Sundays did the wholesale stores open to the public. Like a big carnival, all the shops hung their wares outside

on the street and bargaining was the order of the day. (Many years later when I moved to India I felt at home with the market bargaining because of this experience.) I learned quickly that the first price a salesperson offers is always inflated. The buyer is wise to respond with a low-ball price and haggle until both parties are satisfied. Although I disliked the business and hated working on those Sundays, I enjoyed the busy shopping scene on Orchard Street. I'd walk the streets during lunchtime and browse other shops, stopping for a pickle at Gus's Pickle Shop or lunch at Ratner's Dairy Restaurant on Delancey Street, where the waiters literally threw your order onto the table! Though I felt ambivalent, I realized that this neighborhood held the roots to my immigrant parents' connection to America. If we had a good day, we might go to Sammy's Romanian Steakhouse for dinner or walk a couple of blocks from Delancey to Chinatown for Chinese food. Though my father and I said little to each other, I felt more connected to him when eating together in the neighborhood that felt so close to our roots.

By the time I reached my mid-teens, I knew I wanted to devote my life to something more meaningful than selling clothes. Even though I knew it wasn't for me, I feared that if I didn't meet my father's expectations, I'd never make it on my own. Self-doubt and feelings of inadequacy ate away at my self-confidence. I began to sabotage any ability to break free from the perceived safety of the family business by socializing with a group of misfits and using fake identification to drink with my "friends," frequenting a bar/disco called The Silver Knight where we listened to the band while drinking whiskey sours or beer, occasionally trying to pick up girls.

Conflict colored my teenage years with many highs and lows. In my senior year of high school, my grades remained poor, yet I scored high on my SATs. While many of my friends had begun applying to colleges, I surrendered to the forgone conclusion that I would remain in "the business." But, the freedom of college intrigued me, and I applied to a few schools. Unexpectedly, Long Island University's C. W. Post College accepted me into their Directed Studies Program (DSP), to which those with intellect but in need of academic direction were accepted on a probationary basis. I welcomed this opportunity and actually convinced my parents of the same.

I began college as a Business major, but I never took a business course. I took Psychology 101 during my first semester, and it was as if all the lights had gone on. The coursework drew me in, and I wanted to know more and more about human behavior and all of its subtle intricacies. I came to believe that if an individual could become aware of the impetus for his behavior, as he matured, he could identify the factors from early life that could establish defining behavioral patterns. I learned that our past helps to define and determine our future, and suddenly William Wordsworth's words "the child is father to the man" made perfect sense. I decided to follow a psychological path of study and pursue an education in healing but without going to medical school. I absorbed all I could, reading psychological texts voraciously, and became a regular Dean's List student as well as a member of Psi Chi, the National Honor Society for Psychology.

Life finally started to gel for me, affording me a nearly lost opportunity to focus on what I was naturally good at and to further develop my natural gifts. This launched the professional life that I now feel I was meant to live. In keeping with my feminine forbears, I sensed a call to healing. Looking back I feel I also channeled by mother's beloved gentle and generous nature.

*　*　*

My mother's family descended from a long line of intellectuals rather than business owners. Her paternal family members were primarily Polish writers and teachers, and her mother came from a long rabbinical lineage. Rebelling against an arranged marriage, her mother, our Grandma, took her only child, my mother, and escaped her Polish family and her husband by taking passage on a ship to America. Only two years old at the time, my mother had no memory of the event, only of growing up on the Lower East Side, never allowed to speak of her father or who he was. Only Tillie, my mother's great aunt, knew all of the Polish family, and after her sister's death, my grandmother, she shared several of these family stories with my mother.

I remember this one: when my mother was still a young girl, her mother married again and eventually gave birth to a son, my mother's half-brother, named Joe. My mother's stepfather was not a kindhearted man and hated the fact that my mother was not his own child. He often treated her badly and withheld gifts and affection, paying more attention to his own son. I can only imagine how this deeply wounded my mother as a child. She could have grown into a bitter adult, but instead she became the quintessential nurturer to everyone around her. I imagine that she married my father, fully 15 years her senior, seeking the "good" father that she never had.

My mother had a very generous nature and would always give food and small amounts of money to those in need, much to my father's irritation. She could be very naive as well, as she always assumed the best in people. She was no doubt taken advantage of at times because of her ever-constant goodness and her belief in others, but she overlooked it and moved on to the next person who might need her help.

I realize that I'm like her in many ways, sharing both her generous spirit and her gullibility. I remember taking a trip to Florida with my parents and my brother when I was 11 years old. My father had bought a very large and expensive box of chocolates. We had just boarded the airplane when my father gave me the chocolates to put underneath my seat. I had never sat next to a stranger before, and as I began speaking to my fellow passenger I thought it would be a kind gesture to offer her a piece or two of chocolate. I didn't know that the chocolates were intended for someone else; I only knew that my father had entrusted me with them. I not only offered my fellow passenger some chocolate, I offered the box to everyone!

My mother had fallen asleep and when she woke up and found out what I had done she was bothered, but, when my father said, "That's something your mother would do!" I felt I was really "my mom's son." For me, being just like my mother was the highest compliment.

5

A Loss and a Gift

A disciple asks the rebbe, "Why does Torah tell us to 'place these holy words upon *our hearts'? Why does it not tell us to place these holy words* in *our hearts?"*

The rebbe answers, "It is because as we are, our hearts are closed, and we cannot place the holy words in our hearts. So we place them on top of our hearts. "And there they stay until, one day, the heart breaks and the words fall in."

"No one is as whole as he who has a broken heart."
—Rabbi Moshe Lieb of Sasov

The call came to my college dorm, to the one pay phone on my floor. It was my mother. I felt my stomach pitch; she never called late at night. Choked with emotion, she told me my dad had been rushed to Long Beach Hospital and needed emergency surgery for an obstructed colon, could I come right away.

As I drove the hour to the hospital, my mind flooded with images, but strangely I didn't feel much of anything. I was driving the British racing-green Olds Cutlass 4-4-2 speedster that my dad had given me as a going-off-to-college gift. He gave me things when he could afford them but never gave me much emotional support. With this awareness, I remembered the last time I'd seen him in a hospital, five years earlier, when he'd barely survived a heart attack. The scare had left him very vulnerable. As I sat with him that day, tears came to his eyes, as he told me, "The doctor said I came very close to dying." We actually looked deeply at each other and connected—within an awkward silence. He told me he'd realized that life was too short, that we had a lot to talk about. I was excited about getting closer, but when he got home and felt better, the door closed tight again. It hurt me that we never had those promised talks. In my disappointment, I adamantly decided to no longer wait for his approval.

The next few years passed, and I was still a young man who was psychologically knowledgeable but still immature. Intellectually I understood that my father's fear and inability to express his emotions was a result of his buried vulnerability. In my heart I felt rejected and angry, and my conflicted feelings created a dissonance within me, that, looking back, I handled with apathy. I continued to see my father as a man who could only open his heart when he was sick and scared. As I drove along the expressway late that autumn night, I already knew the pain that comes with loss. Even if he died, I thought, I'd lost him long ago.

When I got to the hospital, I made it to my father's room, just before they wheeled him toward the operating room. He called me close and whispered that he was ready to die.

"But the doctor said that this is a simple procedure. You'll be just fine!" I tried to assure him, but he looked into my eyes in a way I hadn't seen since his heart attack, and said, "I'm sure it will turn out okay, but I want you to know that if I don't come out of it, I'm content. My family is taken care of; the business takes care of your brothers and sister, and I know in my heart that you'll do fine. I accept that the business isn't for you, and I see that you are studying hard. I trust you will find what you seek."

Tears welled up in both of us, and I gently touched his hand. He grasped mine tightly and pulled me toward him. We embraced... and said goodbye... for the last time.

As the immediate family—my mother, brothers and sister—huddled in the hospital waiting room, the wall clock ticking persistently, we anxiously awaited the surgeon's report. The operation lasted many hours, much longer than expected. Finally, the doors swung open and the surgeon greeted us with a somber look on his face. We all knew it meant bad news. He told us that my father had massive cancer in his colon, and it had invaded his surrounding organs. If Dad came through the surgery, he said, it would be a slow, painful death. He told us to go home and rest and to come back in the morning that, at best, Dad would be unconscious for some time.

It came as little surprise when, at three in the morning, the phone rang; my father had never regained consciousness and died in the middle of the night.

I felt cold inside, torn between grief and anger—grief that my father was gone for good, angry with him for rarely being there for *any* of us emotionally, and never truly listening to me when I needed him. Confused and empty, I vacillated between tears and resentment, ultimately left numb, oddly devoid of any feelings at all.

As I sifted through my memories I realized that he had softened a bit in the last year of his life with a sense of urgency about him. On my own by then, it was too late; I had detached, was no longer truly available to him.

That first day after his death, as our family sat Shiva, I realized that many gaps existed in what I knew of my father's early life, and I regretted not better listening to his life stories and experiences when I was a boy. What had he been like as a teenager and young adult and as a young man struggling in a new country? I felt a deep loss knowing I would never be able to recapture those stories—if only I'd listened better.

During that week of sitting Shiva, Uncle Pincus, stayed up late with me, night after night, long after everyone else had gone to sleep. We cried and laughed together as Pincus surprised me with story after story about the very past I thought I'd lost forever. Often into the earliest hours of daylight, my uncle vividly described his childhood growing up in Greece, raised by his grandmother, my great grandmother, after his own mother, our Nona, had come to America to help my widowed father care for his young children.

Pincus told me about his family's decision to smuggle my fearless 13-year-old father aboard a Greek cargo ship destined for New York, where it was hoped he would make his fortune and send for the rest of his family to join him. But, World War II intervened, and eight members of my father's family were killed in the ovens at Auschwitz, among them Uncle Pincus's wife and children.

When the next night's stories began, he went on to tell me about his reunion with his brother, my father, when he and his new family had come to live with us. Although I was only five years old, I did clearly remember that.

* * *

My family's history, and all that they endured, was never revealed to me as a child or even as a teenager. Early on I got the clear message, though unspoken, never to ask any questions.

However, my parents, my father, in particular, insisted we watch every World War II television documentary about Hitler's regime, its war crimes, and the war's aftermath, including the Nuremberg trials. While growing up, I did not literally know how the war had tragically impacted our own family, although loss, hardship, and pain were tangible if unspoken.

After my father's death, as I listened, riveted, hour after hour to my Uncle Pincus telling his stories about the family, a historical world opened up to me. I began to grasp the intense suffering and courage that had preceded me, truth hidden for decades in order to protect us children. It became my duty to keep these stories alive. They carry essential truths not only about my family but also about a lost generation. They must be told and remembered, for future generations, and, especially, for my son.

l. to r., Uncle Pincus and Dad

* * *

"'Memory' is the key word. To remember is to create links between past and present, between past and future. To remember is to affirm man's faith in humanity and to convey meaning on our fleeting endeavors. The aim of memory is to restore its dignity to justice.

...But you may ask: Isn't there a danger that memory may perpetuate hatred? No, there is no such danger. Memory and hatred are incompatible for hatred distorts memory. The reverse is true: Memory may serve as a powerful remedy against hatred."

—Elie Wiesel from *The Kingdom of Memory*

"Yes, this is what good is: to forgive evil. There is no other good."
—Antonio Porchia from *Voices*

Uncle Pincus gave me the great gift of his memory, filling in the missing pieces of our family's history, the hidden, untold, or unlistened to stories. Not only did we bond, uncle to nephew, our natures so similar, but also he connected me to my father in a way that had eluded me. Our shared loss in the wake of my father's passing evoked a deep empathy for what had come before: the unimaginable suffering that Pincus himself had suffered and the suffering that my father had experienced and carried to his death.

While I had the opportunity to say goodbye to my father, Pincus never said farewell to his beloved wife and three children, ripped from him in a senseless agony. For the first time, during those nights with Pincus sitting Shiva, I realized, in body and soul, the depth of these brothers' pain and the pain of a people, the people from whom I'd come.

Uncle Pincus told me about his childhood, how his father had left home and was never heard from again, how his mother and grandmother had raised him with his older, middle brother Albert's help. (It was rare for Pincus to mention his father and, in fact, *my* father never spoke of their father, my grandfather.) When Albert married and moved to Romania, only Pincus remained with his mother and grandmother. At only ten, his mother and our Nona had left him when my father had summoned her to America.

Pincus told me also about his marriage and the birth of his three children, two boys and a girl. He had witnessed the emptying of his village by the invading German army, his family and friends carted to the nearest big city, Salonika, where they were herded into cattle carts and transported in unthinkable conditions to Auschwitz concentration camp. Tears streaming down his cheeks, he recounted the last time he saw his wife and children.

His second wife, Sulica, who too had lived through the horror of that time, later revealed to me that, until those late nights of intimate sharing with me, Pincus had never spoken of his concentration camp nightmare, never since the Russian army had released him from the camp.

He and Sulica, liberated at the same time, were left to fend for themselves and to find their way back home to Greece, two of the only 20 survivors of the 1,200 taken from their village by the Nazis. They had been friends as children in Kastoria, Pincus told me, but their ordeal at Auschwitz had bonded them. Coming to America, to their only remaining family, to us, had established a sense of belonging, and they slowly found their paths forward. With the grief of his brother's loss, the last member of his immediate family, Pincus could release some of his feelings, and, I think, eased the burden he'd carried since 1945.

Uncle Pincus revealed the unconscionable things he was forced to do to survive in the camp and the terrible things that he had witnessed. Not long after his liberation, he heard that Albert, the middle brother, along with his wife and children had been killed. Albert had married a wealthy Jewish girl from Romania, where they owned and operated a hotel during the war. When I asked Sulica if they too were in the camps, she told me that no Romanians arrived at the camps. To save the expense of housing and feeding them, the Nazis put the Romanian Jews on ships to be sunk at sea.

My great grandmother loomed large in these remembrances, a welcome relief from the sad stories, for she was Kastoria's much-loved island healer, a tiny woman with astonishing resources of energy whom the islanders called "pia stechi" meaning "little doctor." She was one of three sisters, all of whom looked alike and practiced the healing arts. But, according to Pincus, it was his grandmother to whom everyone came for advice and healing. She took care of them all, he told me, sometimes neglecting her own family. He described the herbs drying in almost every room of their home, the little bottles of remedies on shelves, and the pungent fragrance of herbal brews permeating the air. How this captured my imagination!

The stories Uncle Pincus told me of his childhood, growing up as he did with women, echoed my own experience. Though "the Pashas," the men in the family involved with the garment business on Manhattan's Lower East Side, would appear to carry my most obvious family connection, it was the feminine side, the women, who most definitively influenced me. I had come to emulate their practices, particularly my great grandmother's, as Nona had shared her healing ways, likely traceable back for many generations. How ironic that my father's acceptance on his deathbed of my individual path and the stories Uncle Pincus had told me after his death brought me full circle to the root of my life's work in the healing arts.

While I was reflecting on my family's past and the atrocities of the war, my niece sent me an article about a recently established memorial in Athens to commemorate the tens of thousands of Greek Jews killed in the Holocaust: "Greece lost more of its Jewish population in the Final Solution, proportionately, than almost any other country in Europe during the Second World War. Around 65,000 men, women, and children were dispatched to their deaths in Auschwitz between 1941 and 1944."

The sculpture in the form of a Star of David acts as a compass, pointing to cities and villages across Greece where tens of thousands were gathered and deported to extermination camps. The marble monument is set in an herb garden, symbolizing the healing from our wounds.

From our wounds begin the healing...in the greater world... and in my family.

6

The Little Doctor

Mulla Nasreddin was sitting in a teashop when a friend came excitedly to speak with him.

"I'm about to get married, Mulla," his friend stated, "and I'm very excited. Mulla, have you ever thought of marriage yourself?"

Nasreddin replied, "I did think of getting married. In my youth in fact I very much wanted to do so. I waited to find for myself the perfect wife. I traveled looking for her, first to Damascus. There I met a beautiful woman who was gracious, kind, and deeply spiritual, but she had no worldly knowledge. I traveled further and went to Isphahan. There I met a woman, both spiritual and worldly, beautiful in many ways, but we did not communicate well. Finally I went to Cairo and there after much searching I found her. She was spiritually deep, graceful, and beautiful in every respect, at home in the world and at home in the realms beyond it. I felt I had found the perfect wife."

"Then did you not marry her, Mulla?"

"Alas," said Nasreddin, as he shook his head, "She was, unfortunately, waiting for the perfect husband."

I first heard of my great grandmother, affectionately known as "the little doctor," when I was only 20, during those priceless, late-night discussions with my Uncle Pincus, just after my father had died.

Esther Elias, "the little doctor,"
and her grandson, my Uncle Pincus, at age 9

Twenty plus years into my own journey into alternative healing modalities, in the 1990s, I began writing books on healing and made the overwhelming connection between my own calling and "the little doctor," my great grandmother, Esther Elias, from the village of Kastoria, Greece. Aunt Sulica, Pincus's wife, has continued to bring her to life for me. Sulica is the only one alive today who had many personal experiences with Esther before the Nazi invasion.

I've come to believe that "the little doctor" has not only influenced my work but also invisibly guided me. I'd been "trained" by the knowledge passed down to her daughter, our Nona, through her consistent and myriad use of medicinal concoctions, poultices, and remedies—this and her intuition.

My great grandmother Esther had been a wise woman healer in Kastoria with legendary abilities to heal the sick. The old stories tell that she often took the sick into her home, tending to them with herbs that she would gather in the hills, brewing them into compounding salves, poultices, and infusions. People travelled long distances seeking her services as healer and midwife.

Esther was known to lock herself in her small cottage where, according to Uncle Pincus and Aunt Sulica, she often prayed, chanted, and talked with her patients as she administered her herbal potions. In time they would emerge from her cottage healed and ready to begin their journey home, carrying packets of remedies with them. Aunt Sulica noted that even a small book had been written about her in Greek, for she had quite a reputation—as legend has it, she allegedly performed many miracles.

To treat a headache, she made her patients, Sulica included, curl up their tongue, and with a golden instrument she would slice a vein under the tongue and bleed it, giving instant relief to her patients—ironically, a procedure taught in acupuncture but not in our modern day culture.

When someone came to her with tonsillitis, she would wash her hands and put lemon on her fingers before manually squeezing the pus from the tonsils, instructing her patients to follow this procedure by consuming and gargling with an herbal brew for a few days afterwards.

Aunt Sulica's favorite story about "the little doctor" took place when Sulica was a young girl. One day, while climbing along the cliffs, Sulica fell and split her knee open on the rocks. Blood gushed from the wound, and she knew she needed medical attention. She hobbled home, and her mother immediately took her to see "the little doctor." My great grandmother greeted them, telling Sulica and her mother to take a seat inside, as she promptly disappeared. In a short while she returned, carrying what looked like a large vegetable pod.

She bit off the tip and squeezed the white powder over Sulica's bleeding wound, immediately ceasing the bleeding.

Sulica braced herself for what she thought would follow, since she'd heard that my great grandmother rinsed infected wounds with salt and lemon. To Sulica's pleasant surprise, "the little doctor" explained that her injury was not infected, so there was no need for the dreaded salt-and-lemon remedy.

My great grandmother also often told her patients stories, not only to distract them from their pain but also to teach them something. These were Jewish and Sufi teaching stories, most notably revolving around Nasreddin, a wise fool. The stories were the same for the Jews as well as the Muslims, but the Jewish community prefixed Nasreddin with "Hoja" instead of Mulla. Mulla refers to an Islamic holy man, Hoja to a *pasha*, the Turkish word for an important person. This information astounded me! For 40 years, since beginning my practice, I have shared Nasreddin stories with my patients, in hope of assisting with their healing processes.

I had assumed that "the little doctor" had only worked with members of her own Jewish community, but Aunt Sulica assured me that she had left no one out. Everyone came to her for treatment, Muslims and Jews alike—a healing practice in itself.

On one of our late night talks, my Uncle Pincus had told me of Esther's Greek/Sephardic version of the Native

My great grandmother Esther, the little doctor

American ritual of smudging. If she sensed bad spirits lingering in someone's house, she would visit the person's home and, together with the resident, burn various herbs to purify the space with their fragrant aromas and healing properties. With all the windows and doors closed, Esther would chant or pray over the bad spirits, and then open the windows and doors to liberate the negative energy.

* * *

I well remember sitting at our the kitchen table in Brooklyn and watching diminutive Nona, dressed in traditional black garb, tending to everyone. She flitted here and there, reminding me of a little black bird, a comforting image that would come to visit me repeatedly in my future.

The two photographs that I have of Esther look nearly identical to how I remember Nona—the threads to the roots of my healing heritage.

PART TWO

Discipline and Delight: Finding My Own Way

"In the books of wisdom Jacob had studied as a boy, it was said that every time a door shut, somewhere another door opened. Now, feeling not so much pushed as pulled, Jacob walked through the day, watching it move from dark to light to shades of gray. Behind him the distant outline of his village lost form and then flattened. What was dissolved into what would be?"

—Noah benShea from *Jacob's Journey: Wisdom To Find the Way, Strength To Carry On*

7

A Psychiatric Aide to Esalen

"They will say you are on the wrong road, if it is your own."
—Antonio Porchia from *Voices*

I graduated from college in 1969 with a BA in Psychology but realized right away that I must secure my Ph.D. to have full credibility as a psychologist—with focuses on psychopathology and psychotherapy. Committed to my own analytically-oriented therapy at the time, my call to study psychology was essentially motivated by my desire to understand myself—not only how I came to develop my own neurotic patterns and insecurities but also to become more whole by expanding my knowledge and awareness. Working in parallel with my own deep therapy, I felt that if I studied diligently, I could heal myself, and then concurrently help others find themselves and their own freedom—meaningful work that I could truly love to do.

The study of different theories of psychopathology mesmerized me, as did the variety of therapeutic modalities developed to support individuals through their healing transitions. I came to believe that if we could learn what makes us behave as we do and identify the defense mechanisms (a la Freud) that we typically (and atypically) create to grapple with our pain and insecurities, we could, in time, potentially free ourselves from the emotional chains that bind us.

Though The New School for Social Research accepted me into their Masters program in Clinical Psychology, upon graduation from Long Island University, I decided to help fund my education by working and got a job as a psychiatric aide at The South Oaks Psychiatric Hospital on Long Island. I'd heard that Judy Garland had stayed there after one of her breakdowns. Although the grounds were like an elegant estate with rolling hills and garden, the hospital's healing modalities at the time seemed quite primitive, reminding me of Ken Kesey's novel *One Flew Over the Cuckoo's Nest*. I wore the same white uniform as those orderlies, and my duties included taking blood pressures and temperatures but, fortunately, I also related with the patients and assisted in group therapy sessions. In a few unfortunate cases, I was sent with other psychiatric aides or orderlies to bring people to the hospital against their will, often using a straitjacket.

Although there was no Nurse Ratched at South Oaks, the system itself seemed to take on a similarly harsh role. I vividly remember walking into the rec room where the patients sat, zombie-like, all heavily medicated, watching TV or playing table tennis as if in slow motion. I was intent on engaging them and felt it was my duty to give them the attention they deserved.

In those days electro-convulsive therapy (ECT) was the order of the day. We secured the electrodes to the patient's head, placed a tongue protector in his or her mouth, administered an anesthetic agent, and initiated the shock. The patient's body convulsed for a few moments. My job was to hold them down, to support them, physically and emotionally, and to be present when they regained consciousness. The patients never remembered the procedure, and it seemed only to help elderly depressive patients, who often forgot what had been troubling them. It bothered me that these treatments were used across the board—whether schizophrenic, manic-depressive (now called bi-polar) or even, I suspected, for punishment. Surely, I thought, this treatment could not constitute constructive or even humane psychological or psychiatric practice. Effective alternative treatments must exist along with therapists to administer them!

As I stood with my hands on each patient's head, I imagined generating love and empathy and flowing this energy into them to offset the cold and unfeeling act of ECT. I strongly believed that a compassionate approach could be found, but in those moments the most I could do was hold the person's head and talk to them while they received the anesthesia.

Some patients were not mentally ill, but in the hospital for drug-related charges. They were often from wealthy families, having chosen psychiatric hospitalization over jail time to address their drug addictions. Some even admitted, as I escorted them to the shock therapy ward, that they intentionally behaved badly to get the high from sodium pentothal, the anesthetic administered before the shock treatment.

My thoughts wouldn't rest. I found myself identifying with many of these patients and found fault with "the system." How could such a barbaric treatment be healing? I felt that true healing must emanate from the heart. Although the staff was well meaning and well educated, it seemed to me that they could not relate to the patients, treating them with their therapeutic theories, but not with a deeper, more empathic, emotional intelligence. Many of these patients, who I'd come to know through our interactions at the hospital and through shock therapy, would benefit most, I was certain, by being heard and nurtured. When I listened to them and they came to trust me, together we realized that we had much more in common than would appear on the surface. When any of us are left unseen or unheard, we make waves to win acknowledgment, even negative attention. We would often rap for hours and brainstorm about how they might reinvent themselves when they were released from the hospital rather than returning to using or peddling drugs. I wanted to awaken them to avenues of constructive, life-affirming rebellion.

I remember Rob who was hospitalized for drug addiction. He had also been dealing drugs. He reminded me of myself and wanted to relate with me as a peer.

"What does the drug give you?" I inquired gently. "I've experimented with some drugs myself, but what drives your obsession that's led to addiction?"

His answer surprised me. "I feel stuck in the muck. I know there is more to reality than this bullshit I see all around me. When I'm high, I have a sense of meaning, that there is some crazy purpose in life, but when I come down, it hurts!"

I understood how Rob felt. He wanted to feel connected, as if, like me, he wanted to experience a more spiritual nature of things, where he could open his senses and freely live his sensitivities. I tried to relate with him empathically and encouraged him to seek meaning in less self-destructive ways.

Patients not at South Oaks for drug-related issues were typically severely depressed or suicidal. I also related with these patients—sensitive people, often deemed weak in Western culture, crushed by those they loved. Again, I saw little difference between us, except that I had perhaps been given more choices and made better decisions that had encouraged me to accept my sensitive nature. Feeling impotent to change my self-perception, or the men in my family's belief that I'd never make it on my own, I could have easily fallen into a world of drugs and alcohol. But, my desire to move beyond my family and make a difference in the world motivated my inner reserve to forge ahead, to attempt college, although no one in my family had even graduated from high school. I knew that a mentor would have helped me immensely and, in lieu of that, having mentored myself to some degree, I committed to being that mentor for others in search of themselves.

These early psychiatric hospital experiences helped form my therapeutic philosophy: disturbed individuals can best be served, first, with compassion, and then by nurturing each individual's transformative process as they discover how life wants to be expressed through them.

I'm reminded as I reflect on this time that the Indian guru Meher Baba (1894-1969) often spoke of the spiritually insane, noting that seekers on the spiritual path could evolve to a point where super-consciousness transcended and blurred ordinary reality causing them to lose their way and to exhibit psychotic symptoms. Meher Baba went to the psychiatric hospitals in India and released approximately one in ten whom he considered "spiritually insane." He took them to his community and instead guided their spiritual journey. He claimed very good results in grounding these patients on their path so that they might serve society. As the Buddhist proverb says and the Donovan song asserts, "first there is a mountain, then there is no mountain, then there is a mountain again."

When it became clear that the bureaucracy at South Oaks would not embrace the more preferable caring approach of many of its nurses and staff, I left for Long Island Jewish Hospital, where they practiced a more experimental approach, short-term psychiatric hospitalization with an open-ward scenario. There by their own free will and initiative, patients had three months to process what had led to their hospitalization. It was an unlocked unit where only staff nametags revealed the difference between patients and staff. Although the hospital used drugs and shock treatments, these were ancillary to more therapeutic modalities. Human elements ruled here, and I felt in tune with the more nourishing quality of care where staff took time to listen to the patients and empathize with their struggles and feelings.

Considered a psychiatric assistant, a designation for graduate students, I was essentially a glorified aide. I took blood pressures and temps, but my fundamental role was to lead and/ or assist in group therapy and relate one on one with patients. I spent lots of time talking with the patients about their lives and could do so in the open, even being acknowledged for it.

Violet, the head nurse and my closest ally and confidante, ruled the roost by accommodating the psychiatrists and the psychologist and delivering the "meds," but she still encouraged me to be myself and to connect with the patients. She felt I could model for them how their lives could be if they followed their dreams and passions rather than coping in destructive ways. Sean, for example, labeled schizophrenic, was a brilliant boy of about thirteen whom the staff loved. However, at least once each day, Sean would pass out, his eyes rolling up into his head. When he came to, his whole persona had transformed. He spoke fluent French but called this language Quagian, an imaginary men-only world. In this world, he became an alternate persona named Gerry, strong and omnipotent, who could become aggressive and even violent, especially against women, requiring active constraint. Gerry knew about Sean; in fact, his mission on Earth was to kill Sean, but Sean knew nothing of Gerry and his hatred for all women.

Violet convinced the psychiatrist to prescribe mild medication for Sean hoping this and connecting one-to-one through talk therapy would help resolve his affliction. We wanted to educate Sean about his alter ego and progressively reveal to him how his behavior was hurting him. We encouraged him to stand up to Gerry, his adversary, by embracing his own strengths and brilliance, to consider his affinity with men as acceptable, though his family was indeed homophobic. His episodic outbursts decreased until they occurred infrequently. On my birthday he made me a beautiful card, thanking me for my support, and signing with, "In the breadbox of your affections, regard me as a crumb." His family promised to continue his therapy and, remembering him, I do hope Sean found comfort in himself.

Many of the patients at Long Island Jewish were in their twenties, a bit older than Sean. They'd been deeply hurt in relationships or felt that no one understood them, thus intensifying their loneliness and alienation. I was often amazed at how similar I felt to them. In turn I believe having a twenty-something therapist in training gave them hope that their sensitivities could actually be beneficial and constructive rather than reflecting weakness and evoking shame.

Tripping into the Past

"Those who cannot remember the past are doomed to repeat it."
—George Santayana

During this time I shared an apartment in Queens with my old high school friend, Donald, and his friend Alan, who was finishing one job and searching for what he wanted to truly do with his life. Alan and I were both in psychotherapy and sincerely attempted to reflect upon our pasts. We intended to free ourselves from early-childhood traumas, believing it important to relive some of what we'd left behind.

Those were the days of drug experimentation, and we both used marijuana and some psychedelics as mediums to go deeper into our therapeutic processes. Knowing I had a Monday off, we dropped LSD on a Saturday night and braved the journey out to Coney Island, Alan's old neighborhood in Brooklyn. We visited his old playgrounds, his old school, and the beach, talking all the while, "reliving" scenes and events from his past. At dawn we returned to our apartment and slept the day away.

The next evening it was my turn, again using LSD to enhance our experiences, we drove in my car to my old turf, the Brownsville, East New York section of Brooklyn, still a dangerous neighborhood, especially at night. We went to my old school, my old house, and even "*my* corner lot," that little plot of nature where I'd play and retreat from community life. It was so small and straggly, I couldn't imagine what I had seen in it, but it had been a haven in hard times, especially after Nona died.

By dawn, driving back to our apartment in Queens, we both noticed how depressed and angry all the people in their cars looked on their way to work on a Monday morning. I remember Alan and I agreeing we never wanted that to be us, off to work only to make a living, without purpose and meaning. As we approached our apartment, we observed the many people herding down into the subway, a hole in the ground, like a colony of ants. This further affirmed that we wanted our work to mean something, to bring healing and joy to ourselves and to the lives of those we touched.

After our somewhat reckless and naive adventures, we were fortunate to return from the old neighborhoods unscathed and somehow richer for the experiences.

Shortly after this, Alan, my cousin Izzy, and I attended a music festival promoted as that year's Woodstock, in the town of Mountaindale, a much smaller event than the original Woodstock Festival held the previous year but also in upstate New York. We dropped acid again but this time I had an ecstatic trip and Alan had a bad one. He left the festival before Izzy and I were ready to go and got a ride from a friend. Later, when, Izzy and I arrived back at the apartment, the first thing we saw when we opened the door was Alan lying on the couch in his skivvies, one of his ties noose-like around his neck, his head tilted to one side and his hand lifting the tie over his head! Horrified for a split second, it turned out he was fooling around, but on a deeper level I knew the most recent "trip" had been too much for him. That night he told me he would be returning to his job and moving back to Long Island. He told me that this was not the life for him. I couldn't help but feel he was "choking" on his new life and simply couldn't handle the freedom and inner questioning.

We remained civil until Alan moved back to Long Island but we were never close again. Shortly after, I moved to a place alone in Greenwich Village near The New School.

Wolpe or Perls: Choosing the Path Less Travelled

"I do my thing and you do your thing.
I am not in this world to live up to your expectations,
And you are not in this world to live up to mine.
You are you, and I am I,
and if by chance we find each other, it's beautiful."
If not, it can't be helped."

—Fritz Perls, considered the "Gestalt prayer," from *Gestalt Therapy Verbatim*

Prayer Is a Path Where There Is None

A child was filled with a question, which like an itch demanded to be scratched.

"Jacob, what I don't understand is how you are to decide whether to follow what you feel is right or what you think is right?"

Jacob touched his own chest and said, "My heart knows what my mind only thinks it knows."

The answer pushed the boy to another question.

"What if neither my heart nor mind can help me find the way?"

And Jacob answered, "Prayer is a path where there is none."

—Noah benShea, from *Jacob the Baker*

I worked days at Long Island Jewish Hospital and attended graduate school at The New School at night. My psychology studies enriched my knowledge and expanded my awareness. Although The New School focused on a behaviorist orientation and my interests leaned toward the therapeutic, they offered informative courses on Freud and Jung, psychopathology, humanistic psychology, theories of learning, theories of memory, and many more.

Though behaviorist in nature, the work of Joseph Wolpe from Philadelphia intrigued me when I heard him lecture at Long Island Jewish, particularly his process of curing phobias and intense fears through a technique he developed called "systematic desensitization." This involved two essential steps: first, teaching the patients a form of relaxation called The Jacobson Relaxation Method, where every major muscle group of the body is invited, slowly and methodically, to relax until the entire body is heavy with a general state of relaxation. Secondly, the psychologist creates a series of fear-inducing stimuli, from the least fearful to the phobic object itself. Step by step, from least to most fearful, the therapist guides the patient to relax within each fear-inducing stimuli, until the patient confronts his or her greatest fear, such as holding a snake or public speaking.

Though intrigued, my connection with depth psychology led me to question how such a fear or phobia could be cured without facing the root of the fear, not only the phobic object.

A fellow psychiatric aide at Long Island Jewish told me about a new type of therapy called Gestalt and suggested that I research it. While walking the aisles of The Strand bookstore, one of my favorite New York pastimes, I found a book that changed my life: *In and Out of the Garbage Pail*. It was an autobiography of Fritz Perls who along with his wife Laura created Gestalt therapy, that is, psychotherapy derived primarily from Gestalt psychology, psychoanalytic theory, and existential psychology.

Perls's autobiography, a free-flowing record of his thoughts and remembrances, and how he related to them, revealed and established a new Gestalt framework. It spoke to me, and I continued my study of Gestalt therapy with Perls's more theoretical text, *Gestalt Therapy Verbatim*, as well as his first book, *Ego, Hunger, and Aggression*.

Gestalt is the German word meaning "whole." The foundational principle of Gestalt therapy asserts that we can only truly relax when we've created closure, that is, when we are no longer carrying unfinished business. Perls taught that we could only truly be present in our lives when we come to full rest, well illustrated by the simple philosophy made famous by Ram Dass, "Be here now," not in the past, nor in the future. Perls taught that many of our problems and even our neuroses stem from unfinished business from our past—from relationships with our parents, teachers, siblings, partners and actions that have remained figurative thorns in our sides. Perls's therapeutic model focused on the patient confronting various fragmented aspects of himself and creating inner dialogues to resolve these conflicting inner processes.

Long Island Jewish Hospital was willing to contribute to my continuing education and I was torn between training with Joseph Wolpe in Philadelphia in "systematic desensitization," or journeying to The Esalen Institute in Big Sur, California to further my knowledge of Gestalt therapy with an instructor trained by Fritz Perls, the great teacher himself having died earlier that year. The staff at the hospital considered Wolpe's work *real* science, but I opted to train where I felt brought alive, with Perls's work at Esalen.

I easily sublet my West Village apartment for the summer, and the hospital provided a stipend to further my education, giving me a full two months to explore the Gestalt therapy that called me. By May of 1970 I was ready to head cross-country and begin my first adventure at Esalen.

Summer of 1970: Expansive Possibilities

My cousin Izzy and I decided to drive out West together and camp our way across the country. We would go our own ways after we reached California, but first we wanted to rekindle our closeness. He appreciated all that I was learning and seemed endlessly curious. We shared a sense of alienation from the family, felt grateful to have each other, and looked forward to getting to know each other again, on a deeper level, as we traveled.

We took my Volvo station wagon and began heading north from New York City. We planned to travel across Canada, and then south into North Dakota through the Badlands National

My cousin, Izzy, summer of 1970

Park and in to South Dakota to Mount Rushmore before Yellowstone National Park in Wyoming and finally through Nevada before reaching California. We gave ourselves two weeks to complete the trip in time for my training to begin at Esalen.

In Niagara Falls, I threw my watch into the Falls as I'd seen in *Easy Rider*, symbolically transcending time, refusing to be a slave to the clock. We camped wherever we found campgrounds at the end of each day. The trip brought us closer, as we'd hoped. We enjoyed each other's company but also relished our own solitude: Izzy, an aspiring playwright and musician, would play music on guitar or write, and I would read texts on humanistic psychology, Gestalt therapy, in particular. My intuition told me that this trip marked the beginning of a transformative time that would direct the course of my life.

First Taste of California Life

Izzy and I parted company in Los Angeles, but before I headed north to San Francisco to visit friends, I'd promised my sister Estelle that I would look up a best friend of hers. When I arrived at her friend's door, her son answered the doorbell. He was about my age and invited me in. (I wish I remembered his name.) I told him the reason for my stopping by and that I was on my way to Esalen. He was a vegetarian and into health food, which to a meat-eating New Yorker at first seemed strange, but, after deciding to stay over since his mother wasn't due back until the next day, we found much in common. Both of us were seeking more meaning in our lives, something deeper, a philosophical reason for being in the world and our purposes in it. He introduced me to some of his circle of friends, and our discussions felt relevant and spirited, unlike conversations with my New York friends. I realized that it had taken courage to embark on my journey, alone now that Izzy had gotten where he was going, and I felt compassion for myself.

The following day my new friend's mother, a widow, returned with a couple from the San Francisco hills, and we all had dinner together, aware that I would be heading north the next morning to visit friends. The couple kindly suggested that I call their daughter when I arrived in the Bay area and that they would let her know I'd be calling. Everyone's warmth welcomed me to California.

The next morning I drove the slow route up the Pacific Coast Highway through Santa Barbara, hugging the coast, relishing the natural beauty of sea and sky. I passed the entrance to Esalen, just south of Big Sur, noting, with anxious excitement, that I'd be back in only four days.

After two days with old college friends in San Francisco, I decided to call the daughter of the warm couple I'd met in LA. She invited me over to their house and gave me directions over the Golden Gate Bridge. Driving through forest with lush vegetation and large homes down long driveways, I finally found her home, a multi-million-dollar estate, parked, and rang the doorbell. After a few tries, she came to the door in her bathrobe and invited me out to the swimming pool where she said she was entertaining a few friends. I followed her through the house and out to the patio, a lush paradise with a swimming pool, water cascading down into it like waterfalls, two men and two women—all very attractive and pleased with themselves— sitting around and in the pool, stark naked!

Though I knew that people at Esalen enjoyed the hot springs naked, and I had been slowly harnessing my confidence, I was self-conscious about my body and not ready for this. If I hadn't followed suit, I would have been the odd one out and, without much thought, wanting to belong, I began to peel off layers of clothing until I was naked too. The day passed uneventfully and I stayed for dinner, but, except for the shock value of the nakedness, there had been nothing else memorable about the experience. I found the environment and the company snobbish and boring, simply not my place nor my people. That evening I drove back to the Bay area and spent my last night with my friends before leaving for Big Sur.

8

First Encounters: The Black Bird & Arrival at Esalen

"There is only one journey. Going inside yourself."

—Rainer Maria Rilke

I was quite nervous driving down the coast back to Big Sur. I sensed that spending a whole month at Esalen, a full cycle of time, would have a profound influence on me, but I was moving into the unknown and felt frightfully anxious. As I got closer I realized I was bracing myself, when, just passed Carmel, as I'd begun contemplating my breathing to calm myself, in the distance I saw a big black bird flying toward my car. I remember thinking, "how beautiful," as the bird drew closer and closer. Suddenly, it was so close I feared it would crash into my windshield, when as suddenly as it came, it disappeared! My heart was racing. I knew this experience held meaning for me. This would be the first of many encounters with the Black Bird.

Turning off Route #1 into Esalen's long driveway, the Pacific Ocean beyond, it felt like coming home. As I entered the grounds, smiling faces nodded greetings as I found a place to park my car. A staff member guided me toward the office where I would check in for my workshop and pick up my cabin assignment. The folks at Check In explained that while at Esalen I would be part of the Esalen family. This meant helping out with cooking and dishwashing, but since the residents, guests, and paid chefs shared the duties it only took a few hours twice to three times a week to manage mealtime. My Gestalt therapy training began that evening and would be led by Frank Rubenfeld.

I found my cabin and met my roommate, Tom, a Catholic priest, who was also signed up for the Gestalt therapy training. I told him right away that I didn't believe in religion, particularly Catholicism, and that I didn't want him to try to convert me. He laughed and assured me that we were both there for the same purpose: to learn therapeutic skills to help those who we had been called to help. He warmly shared that he too sought a unified approach to religion, universality, and laughed again saying we might have more in common than our different backgrounds might suggest. Indeed by month's end we were like brothers in our journeys toward self.

Gestalt Therapy Training at Esalen

It is obvious that an eagle's potential will be actualized in roaming the sky, diving down on smaller animals for food, and in building nests.

It is obvious that an elephant's potential will be actualized in size, power and clumsiness.

No eagle will want to be an elephant, no elephant to be an eagle. They "accept" themselves; they accept them "selves."

No, they don't even accept themselves; for this would mean possible rejection. They take themselves for granted. No, they don't even take themselves for granted, for this would imply a possibility of otherness. They just are. They are what they are for that's what they are.

How absurd it would be if they, like humans, had fantasies, dissatisfactions and self-deceptions! How absurd it would be if the elephant, tired of walking the earth wanted to fly, eat rabbits, and lay eggs. And the eagle wanted to have the strength and thick skin of the beast.

Leave this to the human to try to be something he is not, to have ideals that cannot be reached, to be cursed with perfectionism so as to be safe from criticism, and to open the road to unending mental torture.

—Fritz Perls, from *In and Out the Garbage Pail*

The Gestalt Therapy training not only involved learning therapeutic skills to enhance our ability to help those in our work, it provided a safe space for us to address our own personal issues. Each day consisted of inner work as we learned therapeutic skills and meditations to support our ability to focus on the "here and now." In addition to group work, each participant was required to undergo a series of at least ten Rolfing sessions, deep individual bodywork devised by Ida Rolf. These treatments intended to systematically free the body of tendon and muscular blocks through a very deep and often painful holistic, massage-like process of soft-tissue manipulation along with movement education. Rolfing's ultimate intention is to re-organize the whole body in relation to gravity.

On that first night of the Gestalt Therapy training about 15 of us gathered in the Great Room, where Perls had taught, for a short meditation. We were instructed to use our names as a mantra and to simply repeat our names as chant. At the time my name was Jerry, and I repeated, "Jerry, Jerry, Jerry," but I felt nothing. In that moment I changed the mantra to another name and repeated, "Jason, Jason, Jason…." My whole body tingled with electricity, and I blurted out, "I'm Jason!" The group looked at me nonplussed, but I apparently did not need outside affirmation. Though I wondered if this would be my Esalen name, Jason felt like my true name. A few years later I legally changed my name and in the process looked up the meaning of "Jason," finding to my delighted surprise, it means "healer."

The first night continued with introductions and sharing

intentions for our Esalen time while connecting with each other. We finished the evening by walking together down the paths to the hot tubs overlooking the Pacific cliffs, disrobing and submerging ourselves in the natural hot sulfur water. It induced an instantaneous meditative state. I thought to myself how ironic that I prepared for this experience with the wrong people that I might be ready when I shared my nakedness more naturally with the right people—these loving, accepting, and open people at Esalen. We made friends easily. The more each of us opened up and revealed those parts of ourselves hidden by shame or self-loathing, the more accepting we became, experiencing the refreshing reward of authenticity. Our group work continued into our individual relationships outside the group. We began to practice individually the therapeutic skills we were learning to help others. As we explored our inner worlds together, we also explored new ways of relating with each other, both emotionally and sexually. Rather than acting out the rampant hedonism, sexual abandon, and avoidance of commitment that characterized the late 1960s and early 1970s as a time of rebellion and rejection of authority, at Esalen we explored our relationships with a sense of balance and awareness of each other's feelings. If discomfort arose, we tried to process our feelings before we pushed them away, back into the shadows, or behaved without regard for our selves or others.

After a few short days I realized that most all of the group members had exposed their weaknesses via the Gestalt work and had received unconditionally positive support, allowing me the safety I needed to work in the group on my own issues. Fear of humiliation and the symptoms of stammering had plagued me for years, and, for the first time since I was seven years old, I cried deeply, remembering my brother and his gang's ridicule when I wanted only their acceptance. To feel good about himself, my brother, Butch, had needed to diminish me. I experienced my tears as a sign of strength rather than weakness. Rather than being called "sissy," the group embraced me for my courage.

I had grown up with excruciating body shame! Everyone in our home walked about fully clothed. I once went into the bathroom and startled my mother, feeling horrible about it as if I'd done something terribly wrong. Even after my expansive experiences at Esalen, when I made love, I sometimes needed both my partner and myself to remain clothed or under the covers.

I also worked in the group on my occasional feelings of sexual inadequacy. This essentially entailed working "on stage," in front of the group, while dialoguing with the opposing aspects slugging it out within me. The instructor, Frank Rubenfeld had me inhabit two chairs, one for my "top-dog," and the other for my "underdog." My top dog might say, "What's wrong with you? She's gonna think you're a pussy. What would Butch say?" from one chair, and I'd change chairs to play the underdog, who might say, "But I tried, and I didn't do any harm. If she thinks less of me, that's her problem. We're all imperfect, so leave me alone!" This process continued, albeit painful, until I came to the realization that what is, is; no explanations needed.

As Fritz Perls so astutely wrote in *Gestalt Therapy Verbatim*, "… anybody who wants to hold onto the status quo will get more and more panicky and afraid. It's just concern with the role we want to play, it's stage fright. 'Will my role come off?' 'Will I be called a good boy?' 'Will I get approval?' 'Will I get applause, or will I get rotten eggs?' So that's not an existential choice, just a choice of inconvenience. But to realize that it's just an inconvenience, that it's not a catastrophe, but just an unpleasantness, is part of coming into your own, part of waking up."

I had realized that when I slept with women that I was not particularly attracted to or with whom I had no interest in a long-term relationship, sex came easily, but with those women who I wanted to impress, I experienced premature ejaculation, bringing with it shame and fear of ridicule. It tickles me to remember that after having the courage to share these intimate details about my sexual performance, almost every woman in the group tried to help me overcome these fears!

Rolfing Release

Often quite physically painful and likely to release emotional memories, the intensive Rolfing that we all had to experience created grist for the therapeutic mill, adding to the wealth of material to work with both individually and within our training. Ida Rolf trained her students to manipulate the body to break down adhesions made of fasciae, connective tissue, that bound muscle to muscle, or tendon to muscle or tendon to bone. She theorized that trauma, both physical and emotional, could cause such blockages and adhesions. We considered terms such as "shouldering responsibility," "sitting on anger," eating one's pain," swallowing one's pride," and so on. The body carries emotional memories, and Rolfing can expose such blocked energy and allow it to release.

During my Rolfing sessions, I realized that when the Rolfer worked on my thighs and my buttocks, encouraging me to allow sounds to express my pain, anger coursed through my screams. When I addressed this later in therapy, it became clear that rather than directly expressing my anger, even rage, toward my father, teachers or other authority figures, I literally sat on these feelings. When I began to release these muscles and tendons, the feelings and memories re-emerged. When the Rolfer worked on my jaw the pain carried a profound sadness with forgotten memories of my grandmother's death. My shoulder revealed a bad fall off my bicycle when I was only five years old. I remembered too my Nona's soothing poultice, reminding me of my healing lineage—and now, the direct experience of parallel healing of body and mind, psyche and soma as one.

The summer of 1970 at Esalen expanded my awareness, personally, professionally, and spiritually, one to the other, leading me to deepen my self-awareness and to awaken and nurture a divine connection, all the while leading me to seed a unique practice in the healing arts.

Esalen Luminaries

Living in the midst of and studying with a myriad of Esalen luminaries that summer offered me the opportunity to explore many educational and therapeutic modalities of the human potential movement.

Al Huang, a Tai Chi master, offered a weeklong workshop open beyond its registrants to those who could attend in their spare time. This man emanated peace, and I practiced with him each day on the deck overlooking the cliffs. He taught the importance of embracing our core, the *dantian*, our center, and, from this place of centeredness, of oneness, to invite  and allow the Tai Chi movements to fully integrate our bodies.

 I also sat in on Joseph Campbell's weekend workshop called "Hero with a Thousand Faces," based on his seminal book of comparative mythologies of the same name, that focuses on the journey of the archetypal hero found in most all world mythologies.

His enthusiastic and inspiring lectures introduced us to the mythological world. They guided us to envision our personal myths while noting that each culture has created a mythology but all of them point to very similar symbols and insights. Campbell was a lovely man but rather intellectual for my tastes at the time.

That summer I met Alan Watts, the philosopher, writer, and speaker, best known for his interpretation of Eastern philosophy for the West. I had read some of his books, particularly *The Wisdom of Insecurity*, and held him in high regard. He was giving a workshop on Taoism with a focus on developing an observing consciousness, cultivating a witness within that simply observes, without judgment. He asserted that the importance of Taoist thought lies in its "...great emphasis on the balance between our human awareness and our natural being, as an integral part of the web of life..." I also read his book *Psychotherapy East and West* that summer and would meet Watts again the following year in one of his New York workshops.

I delight in remembering his claim that the belly laugh accompanies enlightenment. We spent many workshop hours exploring our deep belly laughing. All around the Esalen grounds that weekend, people tried to laugh, its sounds and humorous intonations naturally leading to real laughter.

Having put Watts on a pedestal, to my surprise he was what my mother would call a "mensch," an unpretentious and somewhat awkward man, who I could easily relate to. Our time together reaffirmed my budding belief that we are all connected and encouraged me to take back my projection, for the truly wise are also vulnerable. This helped me immensely to overcome a longstanding tendency to stammer when speaking in public.

Mescaline Madness to Be Here Now

I knew that Watts had tried psychedelics and found them useful but ultimately he considered them a tool for awareness that once experienced need not be repeated. Not long after the Taoism workshop with Watts, my friend and workshop-mate Ron, a fellow therapist from Pennsylvania, and I decided to try mescaline, a hallucinogenic component contained in peyote cactus. We thought if we used it to meditate, it would give us deeper insights into our psyches. We expected to vomit first before the "trip" came on and had arranged for a friend to drive us down the coast to a secret beach, where he would also pick us up four hours later.

Ron and I sat on the sand in yogic posture meditating on the ocean, the waves, the cliffs, the rock formations, the clouds, and the sea lions playfully poking their heads up and diving back down. I was feeling an ecstatic oneness with these incredible surroundings, when Ron began to repeat, "I'm grokking." He was also apparently basking in it all, feeling at one, but his experience went beyond mine. "Grokking," is a term popularized by the book *Stranger in a Strange Land* by Robert Heinlein, where the main character, Valentine Michael Smith, a baby lost on Earth's first mission to Mars and reared by Martians, is recovered 20 years later and brought back to Earth. This unique being creates a cult around him through his ability to become one with whatever and whomever he connects. "The sea, the sky," Ron mused, "I'm grokking. It's all one thing, even death!"

My "trip" now included trying to prevent Ron from literally "grokking" death. He repeatedly walked into the surf, and I had to drop myself down from my high to explain that each moment was a mini death, that we could experience dying before we actually die. But Ron was determined to experience *real* death.

Finally Marc came down to the beach to fetch us, and he helped me escort Ron up the path and back to the car.

When I got back to my cabin, my whole body began to shake uncontrollably, and my roommate wrapped me in a blanket, got me some hot chocolate, and stayed with me until the effects of the mescaline began to wear off.

Ron came to me later that evening and thanked me for sacrificing my "trip" to protect him. He gave me a newly published book called *Remember Be Here Now* by Ram Dass. It recounts the author's introduction to meditation and spirituality. When a professor at Harvard, then known as Richard Alpert, he and Timothy Leary experimented and devoted intensive research to the potentially therapeutic effects of hallucinogenic drugs such as psilocybin, LSD-25, and other psychedelic chemicals. They felt that hallucinogens opened the doors to consciousness, and Leary's famous statement: "Tune In, Turn On, and Drop Out" became very popular at this time.

Later, when visiting friends in India, a sadhu (a devotee of a particular guru), originally from the States, asked to introduce

Alpert to his guru. (Alpert was still using drugs to illuminate consciousness at the time.) Upon their first meeting the guru asked Alpert about the hallucinogenic substances, and he told the guru that just a tiny amount created an intense eight-hour experience. Alpert took a handful of doses from his pocket to show the guru. Without hesitation the guru ingested the entire handful. When Alpert responded with alarm, the guru silenced him, asking how long it took to be effective. Alpert told him approximately 30 to 40 minutes, and they waited... and waited. After a few hours the guru claimed to feel nothing but the same bliss he had felt before ingesting the tablets. Alpert knew he had found his teacher and became Ram Dass, claiming in his book never to have taken drugs again, as he came to believe that the only true *samadhi* (bliss) could be attained by meditation.

For most people who've used LSD, the experience has been "psychedelic," dramatically exaggerating their sensory awareness. A person may see blood coursing through his veins, "groove" on the colors and light patterns present, or simply experience the experience. As in Alpert and Leary's research, others have used LSD to reach deeper into their unconscious as a therapeutic aid to healing. I have known a few psychiatrists who used LSD in their practices, but it is largely scorned due to the danger of "bad trips," that may evoke fear and paranoia. For those under supervision, the experience may also reveal hidden internal processes, and, as when Alpert (Ram Dass) found with his guru, if one can reach a state of deep meditation, LSD may have no effect whatsoever.

Be Here Now was a most fitting gift after "the trip" with Ron. I appreciated his thoughtfulness and devoured the book within a few days. It deepened a bubbling awareness that, though confronting our inner demons through psychological work can free energy and further emotional growth, true healing seeks consciousness, communion with the source of one's being, and requires a committed spiritual practice.

I read voraciously while at Esalen that first summer and also well remember my initial introduction to J. Krishnamurti's work through his book *Freedom from the Known*. I soon after also attended his annual discourse at Carnegie Hall. I admired his erudition, his deep and abiding allegiance with truth, and his earnest, articulation of his convictions that became the heart of his teaching.

Second Chance Family

While preparing to leave Esalen that summer of 1970, I heard that Ida Rolf would soon be conducting Rolfing training. I had such profound release during the Gestalt Therapy training and had realized through experience how we store emotional holdings in our musculature. I also sensed that learning some Rolfing techniques would strengthen my psychotherapeutic skills. With the buzz throughout the community that "Mama Rolf" would soon be arriving, I decided to stay for another four weeks to participate in part of Ida Rolf's training.

At the first session she asked, "What is the first thing you do when a patient walks through the door?" Many answers flew back, and she clarified her conviction, "You look at him or her, see them and observe how they present themselves to the world. Do they lead with their head, with their belly? Are they rooted or do they seem lost in the clouds without roots? So much about a person is revealed in the way they carry themselves." Participants volunteered to be worked on during training sessions, and we also had opportunities to practice on each other as well. Ida Rolf was a powerful woman with clear perceptions, but her pragmatism left out the psychological implications of the Rolfing bodywork, the part that most intrigued me.

I had grown immensely over the summer and as the four weeks came an end, I began to mourn the loss of my new family. Some years later in an article in the *Journal of Humanistic Psychology*, Dan Malamud, who taught at G.R.O.W., referred to this type of connection as a "second chance family." Most of us, he asserted, come from very dysfunctional families and have never been known and accepted for who we truly are. Imagine a huge auditorium with hundreds of empty seats, only one seat occupied, and the banner in front of the empty audience reads "Annual Convention for Non-Dysfunctional Families." Malamud's group process invited participants to choose their own family members, people likely more loving and accepting than their actual family. We may choose to accept and love our family as they are, Malamud asserted, and we may also choose a new family of friends where we can consciously avoid re-creating the patterns present in our birth family. Though I was unfamiliar with Malamud's work at the time, my encounters and experiences at Esalen had created just such a "second chance" family for me and knowing that I would be leaving soon, going back to friends and family who saw me in a different way, as Jerry, I worried whether they would accept and love the emerging Jason that I was becoming.

Eager to secure a New York State massage license so that I could continue the Rolfing training the following year, I had only a week to get back to the East Coast. Ron and I drove cross-country together, he to Pennsylvania and me back to New York. We both wanted to try to meet Ram Dass where he was in residence at the Lama Foundation, a spiritual center in San Cristobal, New Mexico, essentially an intentional community, or commune, where individuals came together to live in accordance with nature, with a foundational sense of spiritual direction.

We drove to Taos and headed into the mountains to locate the center. When we arrived the people greeted us warmly and invited us to stay as long as we'd like, but Ram Dass was traveling and would not be returning for some time. Ron and I spent meditative time in the geodesic dome, a space dedicated to spiritual communion, whatever one's spiritual orientation. We enjoyed dinner with the residents and spent the night but chose to continue our journey home the next day.

9

Creating a New City Life

"We are what we pretend to be, so we must be careful about what we pretend to be."

—Kurt Vonnegut, Jr.

Lifted up by my expansive experiences over the summer—learning new therapeutic and personal skills and relating more authentically—my re-entry, coming home to New York City, was less awkward than I'd imagined, though my friends wanted the old Jerry back. "Hey man," one of them would say, "you were always the class clown. You joked about everything. What's this shit about feelings?"

My life direction had taken a different turn in the road from all but a few dear friends, and there was no going back. I knew they would never understand. I got along playing some of the old games with them, getting stoned and partying, but it felt empty and a waste of energy and time. I wanted to get involved with the local community of the human potential movement to meet like-minded people. Although my work with hospital staff and interactions with patients felt richer, I felt like a fraud in my social life.

I decided to begin a private psychotherapy practice in my West Village apartment, walking distance from The New School where I continued my graduate studies, and cut back my hours at Long Island Jewish Hospital to half-time. I found an educational center in the Flatiron District called Anthos, founded on a similar philosophy as Esalen's including many of the same group leaders, such as John Pierrakos and Alan Watts. In addition to its special events and trainings, they held ongoing encounter groups. I joined one led by one of the Anthos cofounders, Marty Shepard M.D., and felt instantly at home. These were my people, all interested in personal growth and authentic relating, and I slowly developed a new Manhattan family. With his many years of expertise as an analyst, Gestalt therapist, and encounter group leader in prisons, Marty led my ongoing encounter group of usually 10 to 20 participants. He created a safe environment to express our feelings—anger, jealousy, lust—and to process them in front of the group.

Developing a private practice, working on my massage license at the Swedish Massage Institute, studying for my Masters in Psychology, and working half time at Long Island Jewish Hospital, filled my life to the hilt, plus my practice was growing by word of mouth. It reflected those modalities that spoke to me, particularly the empathic listening work of Carl Rogers and Gestalt therapy. Plus I'd begun to introduce bodywork as a means to access deep feelings. I trusted my therapeutic approach to evolve as intended. This kept the process alive.

In a film in which Fritz Perls was interviewed, he states that Gestalt therapy itself is a living organism, evolving just as each therapeutic relationship creates an evolving, living organism. Perls asserted that the therapist's approach and techniques also evolve as his expertise grows. He added that if a therapist trained with him at a certain point and continued using only the techniques of that time, it could freeze that therapist's approach rather than allowing him to evolve along with the therapy.

Within six months and with my practice quite full, I terminated my job at the hospital. Massage training came quite easy to me, and I developed a close relationship with the director at the Swedish Massage Institute, Sid Zerinsky. Graduate school study and exams were another story, as its research and diverse coursework required a linear focus that challenged my expanding therapeutic outlook. I managed somehow to handle it all and even enjoyed my social life.

A profound healer, Sid completed a chiropractic degree in the fifties long before chiropractors were professionally recognized in the U.S in the 1970s. To substantiate his validity as a healer, he completed a doctorate in both physiotherapy and naturopathy. In the early 1960s, he turned to teaching anatomy and physiotherapy at the Institute, the first massage training program in the U. S. and also his alma mater, eventually becoming its director, a post he held for close to 20 years.

Sid's true passion was acupuncture, and as our friendship grew and he noticed my dedication and enthusiasm, he invited me to apprentice with him, for at that time there were no schools in the United States and no licensure. He learned the art of acupuncture by training in Chinatown with experts in the field who had studied in China. Immersed in the work, Sid spoke fluent Cantonese but looked like a nebbish Jewish man with a distinctly Chinese face. He took me to Chinatown and introduced me to his teachers and friends. I was drawn to the philosophy of acupuncture, opening blocked energy in the body, *but* I loathed needles myself and couldn't imagine a daily routine of subjecting others to the same.

After I finished my massage training and got my New York State license, Sid and I remained friends. But, having gotten friendly with Ilana Rubenfeld that spring (we had met the summer before at Esalen when I studied Gestalt therapy with her husband Frank), I felt called toward her practice of the Alexander Technique and passed on Sid's invitation to learn acupuncture.

Ilana had separated from her husband and was developing her own therapeutic style based on her Gestalt Therapy training with Fritz Perls and her Alexander Technique practice that she intended to integrate. She led groups in her Manhattan townhouse. While working with Ilana I became increasingly intrigued by the subtlety of the Alexander Technique and applied for the three-year, four-hour-a-day training to begin that fall.

At a fortuitous meeting with Buckminster Fuller, he advised Ilana to call her work "Rubenfeld Synergy," to integrate touch and talk, and by 1977 a formal "Rubenfeld Synergy" training program had been launched.

Through Ilana I met many people involved with the human potential movement in the New York area, tempering my good-byes to old friends and opening doors to many new and exciting relationships based on authenticity, honesty, and a commitment to personal development. Re-reading my old journals from this time, I've been struck by my heightened level of awareness, only in my twenties, in fact, how all of us involved with the human potential movement tried to confront our discomforts and work with and through them.

As the summer approached, looking back over the year's accomplishments I felt pleased with my evolving bodywork/

psychotherapy practice and my group work and staff roles at
Anthos. My social life too, particularly my sexual freedom,
had become intensely rewarding after releasing so much
blocked energy at Esalen and elsewhere. However, even though
I maintained a B+ cumulative average in my graduate work
at The New School, my heart had long since vacated the
academic world.

10

1971, A Short Summer of Wonder

"Events can, so to speak, bunch together in time and space, not because one is causing the other but because their meanings are linked."
—Carl Jung

With my practice building, I decided to curtail my time in California in the summer of 1971, so as not to interfere with the continuity of my clients' processes. I planned to visit my college fraternity buddy, Howie, who lived in Berkeley, and to take a few weekend workshops at Esalen to stay attuned to my own inner work and the latest therapeutic skills.

With only three weeks of vacation, I made the drive cross-country to Berkeley in five days. Howie was also looking for more meaning in his life and had left New York, feeling the city lacked the growth opportunities that he sought. He'd spent a year traveling around the Southwest and Mexico on his own pilgrimage.

We had both embraced the times, wore our hair long, and cultivated a natural lifestyle. Howie introduced me to tofu, tempeh, and the best Monterey Jack, avocado and tomato sandwiches on whole grain bread! White bread and sugary snacks had gone out of favor. A combination of psychology and spirituality had been guiding my path, but in California the definitive connection between a healthy mind and a healthy body began to take hold.

One night Howie told me the story of finding his dog, Pup, after the taxi he was riding in hit a pedestrian somewhere in the Mexican desert. According to Howie, the driver parked the car, ran around the car three times mumbling to himself, and ran off into the desert, leaving Howie with a wounded man, a taxi with no key, and total confusion. While he was sitting on the desert floor wondering what to do, a white German shepherd approached him, and, from that moment, remained glued to his side. When police finally arrived some hours later to sort things out, Howie mentioned the dog and how such a beautiful and obedient creature must belong to someone. The police inquired in all the nearby villages but nobody knew of this dog, so Pup and Howie found each other.

After a few days of catching up, we went to Telegraph Avenue to meet some of Howie's friends. Telegraph Avenue runs in front of the University of California at Berkeley, the center of American anti-war movements in the late 1960s and early 1970s and a congregating place for hippies of all ages. While standing outside of Cody's Bookshop, I heard the florist next door responding to a customer who asked about a particular type of flower, "What kind of flowers, lady? Just touch them, hold them to your nose and smell them. Look at them and let their colors talk with you. Who cares about the name, do you love them?" Shocked but intrigued, I started a conversation with a beautiful woman set up next to the Zen Florist who made and sold her candles on the Avenue. Becky, the candle-maker, laughed, "I love working next to him, he's such a trip." We introduced ourselves and felt mutual electricity. I agreed to meet her later. Our connection ran deep and for the rest of the week I spent my evenings with her at her place or Howie's and many days just sitting with her outside of Cody's Bookshop.

On weekends and some weekdays I'd drive down the coast to Big Sur, meet friends, take enriching workshops at Esalen, and usually stay in Berkeley during the week. While training in Esalen Massage on my first weekend of the summer, some friends and I met an obviously inspired group of individuals who'd recently returned from Chile where they'd been studying with a mystic named Oscar Ichazo. The work was called Arica, after the name of the mystic's village. They excitedly shared about the school for spiritual awakening that Ichazo had developed and felt his work teaching attainment of higher consciousness had the potential to change the world. We attended their brainstorming session about launching the first complete Arica training in New York City.

Ultimately the organizers rented the elite Essex House for the two-month training, but the fees for the program were exorbitant. However, a friend from the Gestalt Therapy training, a professor of Shakespeare at the University of Chicago would be the facilitator, so on many evenings, I'd meet Bill and the group at the Essex House and hear about the work from that day. The Enneagram philosophy, which Oscar Ichazo had introduced to the West, particularly caught my attention, specifically, how each of the nine components of the psyche had a corresponding color and temperament. The group reinforced these psychic "colors" by embodying them through a wide variety of self-development exercises. Bill provided me with copies of the Enneagram class study notes that gave me a thorough introduction to this fascinating personality system. The Enneagram was one of the first maps for understanding human consciousness that I encountered; however it was Traditional Chinese theory that most intrigued me.

Psychic Surgery Synchronicity

"There has been a great tendency in the Western world to build up religious or semi-religious cults around the work of healing. Each cult or sect claims that its cures and healing is the result of some special creed or metaphysical belief, notwithstanding the fact that the other sects make cures in about the same proportion. ... (To the Eastern mind) there is as much mystery and awe about electricity as about psychic force— in fact he sees them as but varying forms of the same thing, and he respects them both."

—Yogi Ramacharaka from *The Science of Psychic Healing*

One night out with Becky in San Francisco, while hanging out at City Lights bookstore, sipping coffee around the tables with plush chairs, I searched for *The Science of Psychic Healing* by Swami Ramacharaka, recommended by a New York friend. They didn't have it but suggested East West Books in Palo Alto, a popular metaphysical bookstore. I felt determined to find this book, intent on driving down to Palo Alto the next day while Howie and Becky worked.

East West Books was located in a small house, each room devoted to a particular subject: Western Philosophy, Eastern Mysticism, Meditation, Whole Food, Psychic Healing, and others. I felt like a kid in a candy store. I craved knowledge, imagining that while standing in the midst of such wisdom that enlightenment could filter into me by osmosis.

I began my search for *The Science of Psychic Healing*. Soon I pulled a book out of its shelf and another fell down. I reached down to grab it, noticing the title: *Wonder Healers of the Philippines* by Harold Sherman. "Interesting," I thought to myself and put it back. A few minutes later I heard a plunk and over my shoulder saw that the same book had again fallen off the shelf. I picked up the book again, this time opening it and glancing through numerous pictures of a man supposedly reaching into people's bodies with his hands and pulling out what looked like blood clots or tumors. "This is weird, but fascinating, probably sleight of hand," I thought, again replacing it on its shelf. Again the book fell on the floor. I read a few pages about Tony Agpaoa, the psychic surgeon, finding it intriguing, perhaps more credible than I realized, but having found the book I'd come for, I put the "psychic surgery" book back where it belonged, purchased *The Science of Psychic Healing,* and drove back to Berkeley.

"You have to be kidding!" Howie and Becky exclaimed in unison when I told them the story. "You mean you left it there?"

I felt foolish for ignoring the book's insistence and the next day Becky, Howie, Pup, and I journeyed back to Palo Alto to get the book, but Howie's Volkswagen broke down on the way and we never got there.

That Friday I was due at Esalen to meet Ilana Rubenfeld and to begin a weekend workshop with John Pierrakos, an Introduction to Bioenergetics Therapy.

Driving south along the coast on Route #1, from Berkeley toward Big Sur in a state of reverie, I couldn't keep my mind on the road, as if the car was driving and my awareness hovered above it, watching the scenario. Suddenly the Black Bird appeared, flying directly toward the windshield and, just as suddenly, disappeared, jarring me back to the moment. My heart raced from the shock, and I stopped the car just outside of Carmel to ground myself.

In those days picturesque Carmel attracted both artists and New Age seekers. Walking along a quaint street I noticed a bookstore called The Pilgrim's Way and wondered if they might have the book on psychic surgery. Inside the warmly decorated and welcoming store, I walked to the back where the proprietor sat behind the desk/counter. Repositioning his glasses, he looked up at me.

"I know this may sound a bit crazy," I said, "but I'm looking for a book on psychic surgery called…" He interrupted my sentence straightaway and asked if I knew Tony Agpaoa. My body tingled, as I told him that I'd never met him, but relayed the story about the insistent book in Palo Alto and our unsuccessful attempt to retrieve it after I'd left it behind. A big smile spread over his face as he reached under his desk and handed me the book. "When you get to the Philippines, please tell Tony that I send my regards. He's expecting you," he said, handing me his business card. He had been to the Philippines and met Tony the previous year. Needless to say, I bought the book. The proprietor and I embraced and I continued down the coast to Big Sur.

Esalen had become a home away from home, my "relatives" coming from all walks of life but on similar inner journeys. I loved California and the consciousness of the people and places, but I felt my roots remained in New York—not a cool thing to express back then.

Ilana Rubenfeld was also leading a workshop. We embraced when we met and walked down to the hot springs for a dip. Later that evening she showed a film of her work with Fritz Perls, "The Making of an Orchestra," where Perls had Ilana act out an assortment of instruments until she could integrate them into a cohesive whole, each instrument an aspect of herself. (She had studied at Julliard as a musician before studying with Perls.)

Shortly afterwards we saw another film that evening. Someone had recently returned from the Philippines, and many people were excited to see home movies of Tony Agpaoa doing psychic surgery. I couldn't believe the synchronicity and its pull on me to psychic surgery.

The film displayed Tony Agpaoa praying and laying hands on some part of a patient's body, usually the abdomen, as the patient lay quietly on a table before him. A force seemed to move his hands, his fingers appearing to penetrate the flesh, while an assistant wiped blood away from the wound. The discrepancy between the rapturous look on the patient's face with the viscerally invasive procedure created an incongruous juxtaposition, what seemed a totally invasive act evoked a harmonious look of peace. My body tingled all over as I watched mesmerized, intuiting that I was destined to visit the Philippines and witness this form of healing.

Unbeknownst to me this was the beginning of a path that remains to this day a great enigma. At that time no exposés or studies existed to debunk its validity. Still I cherish this journey because I learned about the tremendous power of energy and belief.

Being Seen: Body and Soul

The weekend with John Pierrakos, M.D., a co-creator with Alexander Lowen, M.D. of Bioenergetics Therapy, introduced us to active bodywork that could directly breakthrough defensive obstacles to personal freedom. Drawn from the work of Wilhelm Reich, a student of Freud's, who applied "defense mechanisms" to the body. Reich believed that people with emotions and thoughts untenable on a conscious level stored them as "body armoring." Each individual, he asserted, has different patterns of storing unacceptable experiences or thoughts in the musculature, and when these muscle groups are enlivened and released, the suppressed memories rise to the surface, ripe for therapeutic attention.

Pierrakos began by closely observing and analyzing each of our bodies to identify our holding places, for example, the way one held a neck or head, how shoulder height or curve forward reflected how one embodied emotions, frozen or free movement in the pelvic area as reflection of where an individual may store trauma. Such "frozen zones," he explained, reveal to the Bioenergetics therapist where to focus and employ certain bioenergetics exercises to open up the blocked areas and free a client's repressed memories and locked emotion.

Bioenergetics Therapy echoed similar principles of Rolfing, Gestalt, and Alexander practices though the bioenergetics approach directly targeted problem areas. It seemed at times that Pierrakos was psychic; he was so skilled at locating the issues held and even frozen in our bodies. Though the prospect frightened me, I respected him and sensed that I would work with him in therapy (his practice was in New York City). Pierrakos was a therapist I could never hide from.

The three weeks seemed to fly by and leaving California was difficult for me. My relationship with Becky had deepened by the day, and I'd rekindled a solid friendship with Howie. We knew we would stay in touch, but waiting until the following summer seemed too long.

After my summer at Esalen, I was invited to apply for a unique, month-long program that would be offered the following summer of 1972 to only 20 people. It was called "The Psychology of Human Consciousness," a joint collaboration of Stanford University and The Esalen Institute. The participants would live on the Stanford campus in Palo Alto. During the course of the four-week intensive, multiple teachers, well schooled in human consciousness from various perspectives, mostly psychologists or psychiatrists would present their research into altered states of consciousness in both didactic and experiential formats. Other presenters included Dane Rudhyar on the astrology of consciousness and Claudio Naranjo, a Chilean psychiatrist, on the use of psychotropic plants and the psychotherapeutic process as well as the Enneagram. Naranjo was very close to Oscar Ichazo and responsible for bringing Arica to Esalen that summer. Elizabeth Kubler-Ross would lecture on the psychology of death and dying, Murray Korngold on meditation and psychotherapy, and Robert Ornstein on the use of teaching stories as transmitters of knowledge from numerous ancient traditions.

I knew this would be a particularly unique experience because the program would be a communal affair, where the instructors would live alongside the participants, sharing equally with cooking, dishwashing, and play. It would be a once in a lifetime opportunity, and I sent in my application immediately.

Through it all, the pull toward the Philippines and the exploration of psychic surgery continued to bubble within.

11

Back to New York City - For the Love of Alexander

"This very body, the Buddha."
—from *Hakuin's Song of Zazen*

Back in New York, I almost seamlessly resumed my busy schedule in New York, juggling finishing up my Masters program, doing the Alexander training and maintaining a private practice. In September I began teacher training at the American Center for the Alexander Technique (ACAT) across the street from Lincoln Center. The only certified Alexander Technique training program in the eastern United States, it attracted people from various modalities from across the country and Canada. Most of the students came from the fine arts: professional dancers, singers, and actors; others of us came from the humanistic psychology movement, and some even from the equestrian world. The twelve of us would be spending a lot of the time together, four hours each weekday, for the next three years. In addition to each morning's training, various instructors shared how Alexander worked in their modality: Rubenfeld brought a therapeutic quality to the training; Deborah Caplan shared her perspective as a physical therapist; Eileen Crow, a professional dancer and dance therapist, focused on movement through her artistic lens, and Barbara Kent, a professional singer, taught voice using Alexander principles. (Alexander is a required course for all students at the Julliard School; we assisted ACAT cofounder Judy Leibowitz who taught at Julliard.)

Alexander Technique leaders in 1972, l. to r. Illana Rubenfeld, Judith Leibowitz, and Deborah Caplan

We all called Judith Leibowitz "Mama Alexander." She had learned the technique in England with F. Matthias Alexander himself, having sought his help to resolve pain and movement restrictions due to her polio as a child. Though she had little if any muscle strength in her buttocks or thighs, she walked with barely a detectable limp.

The Origin of The Alexander Technique

"Habits! Habits that are built on habits, habits we've learned since childbirth and habits we've been born with, remnants of our evolution. We spend so much of our lives crystallizing the habits so that we can run like a well-oiled machine.

But there is something untouched by automation, something deep within us which cries out to be heard—

We have learned many ways to suppress the cry—
Your cry, my cry...
Yet it remains crying out, even if we perceive it not.
It is that which is beyond habit, that which lies beneath
conditioning in the untapped reservoirs of 'our' mind. "Our" used
not to imply multiplicity, but union, not to imply 'individual' but
'individuality,' not to imply understanding causal relationships, but
beyond cause and effect...
Freedom in the ultimate sense of the word: freedom of choice, not
bound by habit.
As with everything, we have to go through many layers, peeling the
onion, layer by layer.
With each layer peeled, the coarseness gradually fades into
sublime subtlety."

—From my journals while in Alexander training, 1974

F. Mathias Alexander was a Shakespearian actor in Australia at the turn of the twentieth century. He suffered from chronic hoarseness when performing, causing him to occasionally lose his voice entirely. He could find no healing for his condition in his native Australia and began his own experiments including meditation. He went into solitude and began reciting Shakespeare in a three-way mirror while observing his habits.

It struck him immediately that he threw his head back and down, compressing his neck, tightening his shoulders, and creating tension around his vocal chords. He noticed that not only when he orated did this pattern of habit emerge, but also when he spoke with a friend. On close observation, the same patterns associated with the end (goal) of this talking, displayed the identical physical habit. Even when thinking (talking to himself), he noticed how he compressed his neck and tightened his shoulders as his head went back and down.

In order to remedy this damaging habit that had over the years severely inflamed his vocal chords and caused his ultimate voice loss, he "inhibited" his speech habits. Instead of compressing his neck he would imagine his neck lengthening, as if his head were like a balloon floating off the tip of his neck. This allowed the body to open to a perpetual state of gentle lengthening, as the head, became a buoyant object, rather than a great weight carried at the top of the spine. The image of the string invited the head to lift naturally, lengthening the spine.

He no longer needed the old ingrained restrictive habits, even though they felt natural to him. He learned to allow the discomfort of the new dispensation and over a few months increased his awareness of his other habits while speaking that could perhaps impact his voice. Very methodically, Alexander observed each physical habit and addressed those that caused compression or tightening in the body, meeting each debilitating habit as naysayer: "no," there's no need to compress your neck or tighten your lower back or pull back your pelvis." He found that the body relaxed and moved naturally if present to itself and not focused on a goal, such as getting out of a chair or speaking. Attention on the goal rather than the body caused the negative pattern to re-emerge.

Returning to the stage, his vocal chords healed and he became dedicated to, some say obsessed by, the healing power of self-observation. Eventually he receded again from his acting and returned to his solitary experiments, sitting before the three-way mirror and exploring the unconscious habits when sitting in a chair, writing at a desk, and walking up stairs. He further developed his practice of "inhibiting the habit" by again saying, "no," this time to compressing his neck back and down, arching his back, and leading with his rear to sit in a chair. After intense and repeated experiments and careful observation, he discovered organically that when he stopped interfering, **the body became a vehicle for energy.** He felt light and buoyant while simultaneously grounded and solid. He tried to put words to this experience and called the body's natural response, "primary control," in my mind an unfortunate label. I believe that grace takes over and gravity becomes irrelevant.

Alexander realized that he could best communicate what he had learned through his hands, using words to invite the body to find its own natural flow, saying what became the Alexander mantra: "Torso lengthening and widening off the legs," to suggest that the head float forward of the neck and up in space. In cooperation with a teacher's consistent guidance, this kinesiological (bodily felt sense) could be conveyed and experienced by the student. The individually determined Alexander mantra became the student's tool for reconnecting with the bodily felt sense and taking that experience into life thus potentially remedying the underlying affliction. Alexander stressed the importance of this "re-education," reorienting the body to respond naturally, as it was intended to from birth, before conditioned to respond otherwise, often in a damaging manner. Alexander taught that the mantras prompted the buoyancy necessary to open the body's natural flow of energy. He followed a Buddhist approach, carefully mindful to shift patterns that did not flow naturally through the body. Alexander discovered through his personal observations that energy naturally moves up through the human organism's spine, encouraging weightlessness with a simultaneous awareness of the root of one's being and its relation to solid ground.

As Alexander himself clearly stated: "The habits we form when young, unwitting though they may be, in standing, walking, and lying down, tend either to promote or interfere with our wholeness, thus affecting our efficiency—cramping our style—because the spontaneity of natural action is checked.... Now if the habits we form when very young, or during the changes of adolescence, or even in the earlier stages of learning a trade, business, or craft, are bad, they will not only effect our bodily functioning. They will affect our mental functioning in reverse, as it were."

And quoted in *The Creative Advance of the Individual* by George C. Bowden, published in 1965, lauding the Alexander Technique, "The point is made also by Aldous Huxley, a student and tireless apostle of the Alexander teaching, in one of his later essays, written for *Esquire* magazine: 'There is ample evidence that many undesirable mental states have their primary source, not in some traumatic event of childhood or more recent past, but in what the late F. M. Alexander called *the improper use of the self*—in bad postural habits, resulting in impaired physiological and psychological functioning.'"

The first year of the Alexander Training focused primarily on "the uncommitted hand," learning to touch someone without any intention of changing that person, simply making contact with one's undivided attention. Once establishing this touch, the teacher could direct energy through his hands to allow a student to sense the buoyancy and grounded state so unique to the Alexander work.

While we worked on our students, our teachers worked on us, so that every spine was in continuous process of lengthening with each and every act of movement.

My friend Ellie, who had come to study Alexander from San Francisco, said that she wanted to teach others to feel like

Alexander helped her feel, like a princess with their head in the clouds, yet her feet deeply rooted into the earth.

G.R.O.W. (Group Relations Ongoing Workshops)

That fall I also learned about a new school housed in a few brownstones on the Upper West Side called G.R.O.W. that specialized in teaching group therapy skills not only to psychotherapists but to populations in need, such as ex-convicts, ex-drug users and those living in depressed areas to take back into their communities. Word about the quality of their training programs spread, and they attracted teachers from New York University and Columbia as well as some of the most respected therapists in the New York area. Many of my friends either taught or studied at G.R.O.W.; some did both. G.R.O.W. offered courses in creating encounter groups, Bioenergetic groups, Gestalt, family therapy, race relations, and so on. Having received a traditional Master's degree and matriculated toward my Ph.D. at The New School, very research oriented and theoretical, this program felt like a breath of fresh air.

As the school became more popular, G.R.O.W. developed a graduate program offering both a Masters and a Ph.D. in group psychotherapy and psychology. The teachers who taught the group skills agreed to also teach the more didactic and academic work required for graduate programs, and Indiana Northern University worked in conjunction with G.R.O.W. to develop the graduate program.

In January with the semester finishing at The New School, I decided to withdraw and move my credits and course-work over to G.R.O.W., feeling relieved that I could get my degree by studying what I was truly interested in—primarily psychopathology, schools of psychotherapy and theories of neurosis. I had years of Statistics and many courses on Skinnerian and Pavlovian behaviorism and knew that course of study was not for me. I would never become a research psychologist, for I loved working with people and supporting their healing processes.

At G.R.O.W., I felt totally at home. The coursework was intense and as time consuming as my study at The New School, but I was learning from what called me and now I could apply it.

India Calling

At a gathering of friends on Long Island in early spring with my childhood friend Alan, I was introduced to Antonio Balzano, a man of unparalleled passion and depth, and the two of us, feeling a deep spiritual connection, spent the evening talking about psychology, philosophy, and spirituality. We both believed we had known

l. to r., two friends along with me, Mutka, and Antonio

each other for lifetimes and though our paths had been quite different, we were heading in the same direction. My experiences at Esalen and my quest for inner knowing, in general, appealed to Antonio, who was seeking inner meaning and a real sense of spiritual connection. A well-known artist working in oils and sculpture, Antonio's recognition in the art world had convinced him that outer success lacked an essential ingredient, and his desire for that missing ingredient aligned with my own search for meaning. We agreed that our journeys collided toward that end.

Antonio and I together created pure energy and fire but with no hint of sexuality. Passion and sexuality had, until this relationship, gone hand in hand, but ours was a spiritual bond that could support our individual paths toward what we called our "goal-less" goal. Our brotherhood grew deeper the more we got to know each other.

One night during one of our existential discussions he mentioned that an old flame was in New York for a short visit and invited me to join him at a small party that she was having. Antonio told me that she had gone to India with a friend to study yoga and met a man, named Acharya Rajneesh, who had totally changed her life. He had a small following of devotees who met nightly in his apartment in Bombay, India, who listened to his discourses and asked questions. He had given his friend the disciple name Mukta. She had become so enthralled that she decided to discard all of her possessions in New York and to move to India permanently. This was a farewell party to the home that she had just sold in Rye, New York, and a celebration for the beginning of her new life in India.

As we were driving to Rye, Antonio shared that Mukta had shown Rajneesh a picture of Antonio and he had subsequently given Antonio the disciple name Dharmananda, meaning "the blissful state of finding your spiritual path in this life." Although he joked about this name and the concept of discipleship, I felt that something about it moved him deeply. Mukta had shared her transformative process with him and, according to Antonio, the massive changes she had been through were undeniable.

Indeed, when I met her at the party, the light and energy that she and her friends radiated was palpable. Warmly welcomed, I felt at home at the party, but Mukta cajoled Antonio throughout the evening about coming to India, taking the plunge into what they referred to as "sannyas." I soon learned that *sannyas* refers to disciples who surrender their individual egos to a larger whole. It is a common Indian custom for a man or woman (although most typically men), to leave their family responsibilities and to honor their own spiritual journey after raising children. They traditionally take up a begging bowl and wear robes of the *sannyas*, devoting the rest of their lives to attaining spiritual fulfillment. In India it is culturally acceptable and respected for such holy men to walk the streets, and, if one knocks at your door, it is your duty to feed and house them for the night. A *sannyas* also refers to an individual who finds a teacher who has attained enlightenment, where that individual chooses to follow the path of that particular teacher.

Note: Though an aside, it is important to note that holy women were not then, nor are, for that matter, now culturally accepted. Misogyny lingers in India, particularly as it relates to the "dark" association of the feminine as tainted, beneath, even dirty. Such archaic practices and beliefs still plague the globe, more notably in the East but also in the still predominantly patriarchal West. Goddesses are revered in India, but there are very few female gurus, though all the Hindi gods have male and female counterparts: Krishna and Radha, Rama and Sita, Shiva and Paravati. Still, in practice the feminine is discarded.

With our robust yet insecure Western egos, both Antonio and I considered the concept of *sannyas* and surrender as signs of weakness and determined that this was not our path. Still, Mukta's cajoling continued. We played *kirtan* music, Hindi hymns, and danced like I'd never danced before, abandoning restraint, with everyone in the group in abandon, no separation from the dancers and the dance. We finally collapsed in exhaustion and lay on the dance floor while Mutka put a recording of Rajneesh's discourse in the tape player. His voice was melodic and meditative, the information he shared transporting me into a very deep place, amplified by my sheer exhaustion and the implied meaning of his words.

Rajneesh was brilliant. The questions that he answered for his followers could have been written or spoken by any of the great intellects and spiritual masters that I had read or was aware of. I could understand his devotees' attraction to him, but, at that time, following a guru opposed all of my training and what I thought was my very nature.

On the way home Antonio was deep in thought and somewhat agitated. I knew that he was in conflict about Mukta's urging him to accept Dharmananda as his disciple name. Like me, he avidly believed that each of us is the master of our own destiny and must find truth within not by surrendering to an outer master. I knew when I dropped him at his apartment and drove downtown to mine that this evening had been a turning point for both of us.

The next weekend at Antonio's studio I noticed that he had the papers signed by Rajneesh hanging on one of his walls with his given name swami Dharmananda crossed out and above it he'd written "salami." He joked about "swami salami" on the outside, but I knew that he had been somehow transformed within. He told me that he was practicing dynamic meditation each day and that it was having profound effects on his energy and awareness. Dynamic meditation is a term that Rajneesh used for a technique that encourages a meditative state. In the Western world Rajneesh claimed, our minds are so noisy and full that meditation could find no place to reside within us. He devised a technique to exhaust the Western mind and allow meditation to enter.

I agreed to try dynamic meditation with Antonio, and we practiced together.

The first stage took only the ten minutes we timed with an egg timer. We breathed rapidly through the nose to hyper-oxygenate the body which led naturally to the second stage, another ten minutes of self-expression—jumping, screaming, crying, laughing, or dancing—in order to release whatever needed full expression, with the exception of hurting oneself or physically engaging another. The third stage, another ten minutes, consisted of loudly chanting a simple Sufi mantra: "hoo, hoo, hoo," from the lower belly with arms extended over the head. Rajneesh claimed this freed latent sexual energy possibly trapped in the root chakra so it might flow toward the higher chakras. The final stage was to come to rest, to stop all our doing, and to relax, be quiet, allowing meditation to happen naturally.

A few months later, Mukta wrote to Antonio saying that Rajneesh had seen the photos of our little party at Mukta's house and that I too would be coming to India. He had sent along a signed photo with my *sannyas* name, Ramananda, meaning "the blissful state of the Hindu god, Rama."

We learned of a few other people in New York City who followed Rajneesh, and we agreed to support them in their desire to sustain a safe and welcoming space to offer the meditations to the public. Two Americans, Swami Christ Chaitanya and Ma Satya Bharti, their *sannyas* names, ran the Rajneesh Meditation Center on 28th Street, and we became quite close. That spring, I was scheduled to attend an Association for Humanistic Psychology (AHP) conference in Florida. Chaitanya and Satya asked to come along to provide meditations at the conference and also for my support distributing pamphlets of Rajneesh's discourses. Everyone at the conference connected with his philosophy, and we all wanted to bring Rajneesh to the West, perhaps to Esalen.

At the AHP conference I met Bonnie Cousins. She lived in Florida and became my friend and long-distance-lover for many years. She also began to practice the dynamic meditations and eventually received her disciple name, Rupa, from Rajneesh.

12

Summer of 1972: Altered States of Consciousness

"It is the polarity and the integration of these two modes of consciousness, the complementary workings of the intellect and the intuitive, which underlies our highest achievement."

—Robert Ornstein, from *The Psychology of Consciousness*

I continued to believe more and more strongly that psychotherapy could take an individual only so far. One's inner journey ultimately led, it seemed, toward consciousness or spiritual awakening. However, my basic inner conflict remained: to what extent must I confront my demons and to what extent might I move deeper into meditation and learn to transcend my destructive, habitual patterns? The answer kept eluding me, and I hoped that the coming summer would help me clarify this fundamental issue. Having been accepted into "The Psychology of Consciousness" program at Stanford, knowing that we would be living/studying with luminaries in the fields of psychology and research on human consciousness, I trusted that some revelation would come to me.

I prepared for my annual journey to the West Coast knowing that I would be gone for nearly two months. I gave my clients referrals to other therapists, if they needed someone, and sublet my apartment from the middle of July until the first week of September. The weeks leading up to my departure were full of excitement and dread. I feared returning to and examining more dark, internal places within and at the same time remained hopeful that this journey would expand my spiritual path. I wish I'd heard the Sufi story then about looking for the key in the light. We all too often forget, avoid, hide from the darker stuff, tuck it out of sight, where only we know where it is rather than sharing, revealing, letting ourselves be seen as we are. Isn't that what we want after all? To be seen, heard and known, simply as we are? (Refer to page xi in the Introduction to reread this Sufi story.)

I knew that the Psychology of Consciousness conference in Palo Alto would prevent my lounging on the comfortable surface and require all its participants to explore the subterranean reaches of our consciousness or lack thereof. Visits to Esalen this year would be only to connect with friends.

Antonio joined me on my cross-country journey that summer, and we agreed to deliver some Rajneesh pamphlets to a few California bookstores. At each campground, Antonio felt the need to practice dynamic meditation, which, at first, I totally resisted. I felt self-conscious about breathing through my nose and releasing emotionally in silence...but eventually I conceded. We used our trusty egg timer to time our ten-minute intervals through the stages. Invariably when we had finished curiosity seekers surrounded us as we explained what we were doing and why. Within the first week of our travels, we had distributed many of our small Rajneesh books and pamphlets to those interested in learning more.

Antonio and I wanted to spend some time at the National Parks, so we drove as quickly as we could through the Eastern states and within three days were driving through the Colorado mountains. Suddenly, I saw a black bird in the distance flying toward our car. Excited, at first, thinking it might be an eagle or a large hawk, but it kept coming directly toward the car. I suddenly pulled the car to the side of the road, and the bird disappeared. My heart racing, I explained to Antonio that this had happened before. He suggested that I might be shedding my ego to attain *satori* a glimpse into enlightenment. At the least, I sensed that this bird carried an important message meant especially for me.

This incident stayed with me as we drove up through Wyoming to Yellowstone National Park and spent a few days camping there before moving on toward Yosemite in California. The majesty of the country filled me with reverence for the immanence of nature, the deep mystery that throbs through us. Walking in the National Parks and driving through the deserts and mountains elicited a deeply meditative state. Antonio and I would occasionally look over at each other with simple acknowledgment of the great depth of silence that held us.

When we finally reached California, we went immediately to Becky's house in Oakland. Antonio, wanting to give Becky and me time to catch up, excused himself and walked the quarter mile to the beach. Sitting and talking at the kitchen table, we could see Antonio on the beach, arms flailing, doing his dynamic meditation. A few minutes later we looked again and saw three police cars surrounding him. We immediately ran out to the beach to intervene.

Amazingly, by the time we reached them, Antonio sat cross-legged on the sand, chatting with the police officers. They were shaking their heads in agreement. One of them said, "If more folks could get their shit out before it exploded, doing harm to themselves and others, it would make our work much easier." They asked that we not practice on the beach, because it might upset the neighbors but otherwise gently bid us farewell. Later, we all had a good laugh.

The next day, we delivered the remainder of our books to the Oakland Police Department—to the officers who'd showed interest in them—and called Chaitanya and Satya to tell them we'd shared all of the discourse materials, and they'd need to fill the California bookstore orders directly. Such peace with the police felt gratifying, and we had a good laugh over it.

I had to admit that I was nervous about the upcoming conference in Palo Alto to meet my latest "family" for the next four weeks. It helped to remember that when we had time off I could go to Berkeley to reconnect with Becky and Howie, and, when possible, bring them back to Palo Alto to join us for supper or to schmooze after the day's conference.

Psychology of Consciousness Conference

"Almost always it is the fear of being ourselves that brings us to the mirror."

—Antonio Porchia from *Voices*

Driving into the Stanford campus felt like a maze and asking people how to get to Guthrie House (a fraternity house on campus) led me to every part of the campus. By the time I finally found our summer residence, I felt quite agitated, but excited to be there.

The people lounging about seemed nervous too. We made informal introductions and met the coordinators of the weekend, one of whom was David Sobel. After getting our room assignments and chatting a bit, we had our opening session with Jim Fadiman, the author of *Personality and Personal Growth*. He explained that we were all there, students and teachers alike, to explore the realms of human consciousness. We would be intellectually studying the research of many people at the forefront of the exploration of human consciousness as well as working experientially through techniques such as meditation, psychological and group therapy skills, and even metaphysical realities by experimenting with crystal balls and other divination methods.

Fadiman then led us in a guided meditation fantasy into a cave, where we were to imagine finding someone or something hidden inside the cave that would tell us something important. I imagined slowing entering the cave, its big, cold, rock walls surrounding me. It was very dark. I had a flashlight and slowly traversed a long corridor until I came to an empty room with only a glass case in the corner. Something gold glimmered from within it, and, as I got closer, I realized it was my father's keychain. It felt important that although my father was no longer alive, we nonetheless needed to communicate, essentially to reconnect me to my ancestral roots.

I proceeded further into the cave for other clues and entered a large room with light coming in from a hole overhead. I wondered if I should climb up to the light or remain down in the cave searching… I decided to climb to the top, and when I stood up, I was on top of a mountain, arms outstretched, at one with the light, in total ecstasy. Concerned that I'd missed something important down below, I climbed down again into the cave and continued my search. I entered another large chamber, this one wet and colorful with all sorts of stalactites and stalagmites reflecting off my flashlight as well as glimmering down from the hole at the top of the cave. I realized I had to climb up again and that seemed to be my message: the search is not for something within the cave but above it. My familiar internal conflict, confront or transcend, presented itself again at the start of this new adventure. I wrote in my journal shortly after this experience: "I expect to traverse many untrodden caverns in my mind."

For the first few days we explored accessing consciousness utilizing Roberto Assagioli's model of "psychosynthesis." As Fadiman explained it, Assagioli published his book, *Psychosynthesis* in 1965 as his response against psychoanalysis. Assagioli asserted that re-synthesizing the individual was more effective than analyzing his component parts. He dealt primarily with the cultivation of man's higher (spiritual) needs (a la Jung and Maslow) and lower needs (a la Freud). He contended that one type of need was not more important than the other, but rather to be healthy individuals we must learn to synthesize and balance the two. The work included guided meditations, work on dreams, and group work where we processed our feelings. This approach felt gentler and more contained than the encounter groups that I had previously attended at Esalen.

During the next week we continued the work with our seminar leaders, both experientially and intellectually. Robert Ornstein, author of *The Psychology of Consciousness* and other books, posited two basic types of consciousness: intellectual and intuitive, representing two sides of the brain. He asserted that Western culture rewards left-brain development, the rational side (yang—masculine) and looks down upon the more intuitive and receptive side (yin—feminine).

Gay Luce and Eric Pepper presented for a few days on their use of biofeedback technology and hypnotic trance states as methods for exploring consciousness. We all experienced self-modifying our brainwave patterns and our muscular holding using their biofeedback equipment.

Our deep inner work challenged us to reflect upon our inner selves with special attention to those aspects that created obstacles in our lives so that we might uncover our core inner issues. As I recall these experiences, I'm reminded of Colin Wilson's book, *The Mind Parasites* that gives form to this psychological/spiritual concept of bringing our shadow material to consciousness, in Jung's language. Using allegory to posit his theories, Wilson tells the story of an ancient extraterrestrial civilization, existing in pre-history, in which an advanced civilization used human beings as slaves. In order to maintain their supremacy over humans they implanted what Wilson called "mind parasites" into human consciousness, activated when individuals reach within themselves. Wilson believed that if the universe is as vast within as it is without, we as a civilization have only brushed the surface of the study of consciousness. And, in fact, humanity could be in peril, if, when turning inward through meditation or the like, the mind parasites activate a sense of dread and fear, thus forcing human beings to stay clear of their inner power, causing them instead to focus only on the external world for their nourishment.

Sasha Shulgin, a psychologist who specialized in the study of inducing mystical experience through the use of drugs and the study of such experiences within drug-induced indigenous cultures, used guided meditations as we explored various drugs and hallucinogens such as psilocybin and mescaline. Though the experiences were profound, when rereading my gibberish notes taken during these experiences, I remembered Aldous Huxley's assertion in his book *The Doors of Perception* that drugs may open the door to a profound reality, but such cannot be penetrated with drugs.

In spite of our awareness of drugs' limitations, a group of us decided to take LSD at a Grateful Dead concert in Berkeley with our designated driver. My scribbled journal notes after that experience read: "We took the acid in a park not far from where the concert was being held, with the intention of creating a meditative state."

We all found our nooks within the park and "merged" with nature. Resonating with the plant vibrations, the pulsating energy of the essential life force, I became keenly aware of the same pattern of aliveness in my body and indeed in the very body of planet Earth. The mystics have taught that the sound of Earth moving through space makes the sound of OM. As we sat there together, we began to make the OM sound, and, as we merged our sounds, I felt my body dissolve into All That Is or... Nothingness. All boundaries dissolved, yet no fear emerged, only a pervasive sense of gratitude and well-being.

When it was time to go in to the concert, the Dead had already begun to play as they often did before the audience had fully gathered, creating a sense of heavenly chaos as people tripping or stoned tried to find their seats. Walking into the auditorium I felt a strong magnetic pull. When I trusted this pull and followed it, I experienced a state of ease, even bliss, but when my mind took over with its own agenda, even just sending me to my seat, an intense tension would grip me, moving me to relinquish my agenda and "go with the flow." My body felt free from all sorts of conditions of my everyday programming. The back of the auditorium drew me to a particular spot, as if not quite forced, but sent. Resisting the pull felt wrong, and when I followed it I met Ingrid, a woman I knew from New York. We had even *planned* to meet in San Francisco! We embraced and honored the synchronicity of the moment, but the energy pulled me back into the auditorium and up the center aisle toward the stage. Making eye contact with Jerry Garcia I continued to the front and climbed the steps to the stage, where the guard seemed to let me through, and there I was, on stage, not knowing how I got there or why, still gazing into Garcia's eyes, until a waft of self-consciousness took over, and I walked down the steps and again to the back of the auditorium, guided to the same spot as before, bumping into another friend, and then again drawn back to the stage. A college student who must have been watching me asked what kind of drug I was selling. I told him I wasn't selling anything to which he replied, "I just want some of what you're on."

When I arrived safely back in Palo Alto at 6 o'clock the next morning, I wrote in my journal: "This trip has broken my programs. I now know I've simply got to flow with it, even if the trip gets bummed out, (I must) stay with it and ride it through. Here, There and Everywhere—it's all right here—at-one-ment, no-thing-ness. If you try to grasp it, you lose it; so long as there is nothing to grasp, (I can) tune in to the ever-changing flux. Don't hold on, (permanence) doesn't exist. Let it flow…flow is love!"

For the Sport of It

One of the participants in The Psychology of Human Consciousness program was David Meggyesy, who had been an outside linebacker with the St. Louis Cardinals for seven years. His memoir, called *Out of Their League*, exposed the underbelly of "win at all cost" professional football, revealing the fraud, racism, drug abuse—especially the dangers of performance enhancing drugs and pain medications—and accepted violence. Meggyesy's outrage and courage to speak out put the fight for players' rights on the map, but it had also blacklisted him from professional sports.

Mike Murphy, the founder of the Esalen Institute, wanted to create a sports center at Esalen, devoted to pure sport, not sport merely for competition, but for realization of excellence. Mike and David worked together that summer to birth the concept of creating an Institute for Sport and Enlightenment. For them sport held the lure and potential for peak experience. As expressed in such books as *The Inner Game of Tennis* or Mike Murphy's book, *Golf in the Kingdom*, they believed that whether striving for personal excellence in running, baseball, tennis or golf, that sport had the potential to attain a taste of higher consciousness.

Based on this idea, for the duration of the program, the residents—students and teachers alike—divided into two teams: the "Yogis" and the "Sufis." We played volleyball or touch football and strived for excellent teamwork, but we never kept score. It was the game that was important, not winning. Experiencing this concept in action forever changed how I play and view sports.

Working with Moshe Feldenkrais

When one of the Psychology of Consciousness presenters, Stanley Keleman, introduced us to his form of Bioenergetic therapy he brought along an elderly man who he introduced as his father. As Keleman presented his work, his "father" would share a few words of wisdom. Someone soon recognized the elderly man as Moshe Feldenkrais, a distinguished scientist, physicist and engineer, not Keleman's father. According to the

Feldenkrais training (Moshe is left of center with arms crossed.
I'm on the front row, sencond from left)

Feldenkrais Institute what came to be called the Feldenkrais Method "synthesizes insights from physics, motor development, bio-mechanics, psychology, and martial arts to develop a powerful, effective, and practical application, that reconnects learning with human health and function."

The following summer I would spend a few weeks participating in an introductory training with Moshe Feldenkrais, at the invitation of Ilana Rubenfeld. Upon her invitation, though honored, I laughed out loud remembering my first encounter with him. At his training, in Berkeley California, Moshe referred to me as "Ilana's protégée" rather than by my name, but his good humor encouraged me to take it in stride. The Alexander Technique had clearly influenced his bodywork technique and I later learned that he'd studied Alexander in London with Walter Carrington, one of Alexander's protégées.

* * *

My Psychology of Consciousness peers and faculty did indeed become a family, but we trusted our paths would cross again. I drove up to Berkeley after the program ended to spend a few days with Becky before departing for Honolulu, Hawaii, for the Association for Humanistic Psychology's (AHP) annual conference.

AHP always tagged their conference onto the tail end of the American Psychological Association (APA) conference. My friend Bill Kaukeano who I'd become close with through G.R.O.W. and Anthos, the personal growth center in New York, was a native Hawaiian. He had met Marty Shepard, the founder of Anthos, when Bill had been in prison at Riker's Island, and Marty had conducted weekly group therapy sessions there. Upon his release he trained with Marty for many years and continued conducting therapy work himself in prisons and other institutions as well as at Anthos.

Also planning to attend the AHP and APA conferences late that August in Hawaii and to visit his family, Bill not only offered his house to me in Honolulu but also to help pay my airfare.

He and his girlfriend met me at the airport with a warm welcome to paradise with leis and kisses. Hawaii's fecund beauty astounded me, but I was not there to vacation, as much as my mind and inner seeking needed a break, but rather to participate in these two psychological conferences that I had intuited I was meant to attend.

The next day at the APA conference, Carl Rogers, one of the primary founders of the humanist approach to psychology, was the keynote speaker. He shared his passionate conviction that an empathic relationship was essential to the therapeutic process between therapist and client, a hallmark of his "client-centered psychotherapy." Recent studies supported his thesis, positing that the effectiveness of therapy had much less to do with the type of therapeutic modality or psychotherapy, but much more directly related to the empathy bond between therapist and client.

He lambasted the APA audience who he held responsible for attempting to pass the Biando bill, legislation that would limit the practice of psychotherapy to Ph.D.s and M. D.s at the clear expense of the people who needed help and those who provided that help. Rogers claimed that psychologists were so afraid of losing control over the psychotherapeutic domain, with its potential financial and egotistical gains, that they were willing to be fraudulent in the name of preventing fraud. The bill appeared to assert that it would protect the public from disingenuous and inexperienced therapists by restricting the field to only those with academic degrees and licenses. However, Rogers made clear that this was the greatest fraud of all. He believed that extensive academic training often diminished one's empathy, in favor of theories and diagnoses. Many therapists without doctorates, he contended, were deeply empathic and effective, some trained as clergy, others in a variety of specific therapeutic modalities. He went on to remind his audience that with or without academic credentials and licenses, good and bad therapists existed in this known buyer-beware market.

As I listened, riveted, by Rogers's passion and deep regret over the possible passage of the Biando bill, I identified with almost everything he said and felt a strong connection to him. He was a giant in psychological circles yet had the courage to speak his mind and heart with conviction and clarity to this influential professional audience. When he stepped from the podium there was a stunned silence in the auditorium until, very slowly the applause rose, but not from those who had been called on the carpet for their complicity with power.

A few days later at the Association for Humanistic Psychology conference, again Carl Rogers was the keynote speaker, but this time, knowing that he had an audience of empathic listeners, he began to speak about his own experiences—his years of coming fully into himself and through his own process, how he came to the awareness at the root of his person-oriented theories. He shared snippets of his difficult childhood and at times there was not a dry eye in the room. How different these two speeches, I thought to myself, the first full of outrage at psychologists' potential egoism, the second an intimate glimpse into what made this great man.

In an effort to make their mark as a premier professional organization, the APA, in addition to promoting the Biando bill, were attempting to close teaching institutions that were training psychotherapists. They chose to make an example of G.R.O.W.

(Group Relations Ongoing Workshops) and attack it they did. Having come to connect personally with G.R.O.W.'s mission, APA's lies and innuendos pierced my heart. APA circulated petitions signed by psychologists demanding the immediate closure of such "sham" schools, accusing them of selling diplomas and sanctioning individuals with no training and false papers to dupe the vulnerable public out of their money, and worse, potentially deepening their psychopathologies. Though many of us knew it was fabricated, we also knew a huge battle was at hand. Would G.R.O.W. be able to stay afloat?

At the AHP convention we busily signed our own petitions, determined to negate the lies of the much more powerful APA. Although the AHP workshops and the conference energy as a whole were positive, even joyous, a foreboding lingered, a sense that Big Brother had chosen its prey.

When I returned to New York I found G.R.O.W. in sheer turmoil. They had hired an expensive, influential lawyer to defend the organization's credibility, clear among its instructors and students that it issued no diplomas for sale, but rather offered exceptional coursework lauded by all those who knew and benefitted from G.R.O.W.'s good work, but how to prove this?

They continued to offer group training for group work within communities, training therapists to work with drug addicts and alcoholics, ex-cons, and minority groups. These populations desperately needed leadership and therapeutic skills, but the faculty began to drop away, afraid to involve their name in controversy. After many months it became apparent that even the best lawyers in the world could not win back the lost faculty, and, without their exceptional and committed faculty, they could not continue to function. Ultimately, in defeat they closed their doors forever.

The Biando bill thankfully did not pass and, as of this writing, in 2015, psychotherapy is not solely in the domain of the "doctors." Public awareness, however, can always be strengthened: a good therapist may not be the best educated, have the most training, even years of experience and a track record with references. But, good therapists listen empathically, as Carl Rogers so wisely reminded us. Good therapists care about their clients and have also done the personal therapeutic work themselves. The client too must take responsibility for choosing that therapist and their work together.

13

An Irresistible Invitation from India

"Things happen—people come—events stack up. When you're least aware of it, purpose happens."

—Rainer Maria Rilke

Though very disappointed in G.R.O.W.s demise, I felt energized by my summer experiences and settled back into my practice with a greater focus on healing through bodywork, turning to psychotherapy to process and explore the feeling life. My Alexander training also continued that fall, and I became dedicated to my dynamic meditation practice, the call to meet Acharya Rajneesh growing within me.

My Alexander work and my practice kept me grounded in New York, but Antonio had left for India after Mukta's constant nudging, "He's waiting for you!" Upon his return he was aglow. We embraced, and right away he shared that Rajneesh had told him to tell me to come, that he expected me to be part of a new commune. If I could have jumped on a plane in that moment I would have, but the trip to Bombay had to wait until December.

Contemplating a trip to India rekindled a bubbling excitement about visiting the Philippines to learn more about psychic surgery and perhaps see it for myself, wondering how being in Tony Agpaoa's presence might influence my own healing work, personally and professionally. Was my pull toward the Philippines an ego trip, or was I meant to go?

I decided that I must answer Rajneesh's invitation to India and decided to travel to Bombay over my Alexander training's long holiday break during December and January. My mother agreed to give me a loan to make it possible. I would visit him, as suggested, at his apartment in Bombay and hopefully attend Rajneesh's meditation retreat in the forests of Rajasthan, in the holy village of Mount Abu.

My friend drove me to Kennedy Airport to catch my flight, and, while drifting into reverie, my Black Bird flew toward the car. Suddenly jolted fully present, I asked myself if this was a dark omen, but my intuition said no, her presence felt like an affirmation of my decision to travel to India.

Looking back in my journal at that time, I wrote on the plane headed to India, "The beginning, always new beginnings. The beginning of a new diary, the beginning of a new pilgrimage, the beginning of new deaths and rebirths…

Love is in the air, somewhere over the Atlantic Ocean…to be…to be.

Projections pop up, but through awareness, watching them as they come, burns them into nothingness. Take the leap and let go."

Arriving in Bombay

Descending the steps onto the tarmac, the thick warm air enveloped me, my nostrils filling with the intermingling of scents and smells—sweet incense, spices of curry, and a lingering septic odor from the numerous shantytowns surrounding the airport. Somehow, India was familiar, the honking, the mayhem and outside the airport beggars everywhere with hands outstretched, crying "Baksheesh, baba, baksheesh."

I pushed through the crowds and found what looked like a legitimate taxicab. We left the airport and snaked our way

through Bombay, passing more shantytowns, small shopping areas, and the occasional polished neighborhood. We shared the road with  thousands of pedestrians, beggars, peddlers with wooden stands, people-propelled rickshaws, gas rickshaws, trucks, goats, chickens, bicycles, and scooters. The chaos did not rattle me but rather filled my whole being with joy.

The taxi stopped in the Breach Candy section at the tip of Bombay on the Indian Ocean. I paid my fare and surveyed my surroundings—people everywhere in front of Mukta's building.

Laundry hung from all the windows. Children ran through the streets. Multiple beggars looked with smiling eyes into my own, their hands outstretched, playfully begging for rupees. Jiggling my change, I heard my name, "Ramananda, come in, we don't have much time!" Mukta called out from her third floor window.

Arriving at her apartment with only my backpack and a bunch of books that she told me Rajneesh wanted, we hugged. It was a small place, relatively bare, and humble, a far cry from this Greek shipping heiress's affluent home in Rye, New York. Her beaming smile told me she had attained the true wealth of inner joy. "Take a shower. Bhagwan is expecting us. Hurry," she urged me.

Rajneesh's apartment on Peddar Road was modest as well, larger than Mukta's place but barely a two bedroom. Mukta said that often more than a hundred people gathered in this space to listen to Rajneesh's evening discourses. Mukta introduced me to Laxmi, Rajneesh's secretary, who sat at a small desk outside his bedroom. Smiling she acknowledged that they had been expecting me, before quietly announcing my arrival to "Bhagwan," meaning "Enlightened One," and ushering me in to his bedroom.

Rajneesh sat cross-legged in the chair alongside his bed. He wore a white robe, his beard long, head bald, and a radiant smile across his face. The scents of sandalwood and camphor filled the room. (I soon learned that this scent was unique to Bhagwan, as his disciples came to call him. Many had tried to reproduce it but failed. It is said that when a master attains enlightenment, they manifest a scent—frankincense for Christ, sandalwood for Buddha. The master's scent is said to induce meditation.)

I bowed without thinking and sat down in front of him.

"So, Ramananda, you've come. Welcome home," Bhagwan said.

He asked about my work in New York and elsewhere. I told him of my travels, Esalen, the Alexander training, and my practice in the healing arts. I also told him about my pull to the Philippines. He listened patiently and then declared that I had arrived on my path, instructing me to settle in Bombay, participate in the meditations on Chowpatty Beach near his residence, each morning at five AM, and to attend meditation camp at Mount Abu. We would continue to meet privately for *darshan* and speak of general issues about meditation and ego, but discussion of the Philippines would be discussed later after the camp at Mount Abu.

Each morning I would walk the few blocks to the beach from my tiny flat, sometimes alone, sometimes with other *sannyas* passing many people sleeping on the pavement and under the bridge, rats running around them, as they had for hundreds, perhaps thousands of years.

The trip to Mount Abu took 24 hours, a full day-and-night train ride from Bombay. The train felt like a carnival, its cars bursting forth with people and animals. We travelled in a Third Class sleeper, the least expensive fare. People initially competed for a slat of wood, the sleeper "bed," each compartment with three slats, one over the other, pulled down at night for sleeping, two or three people sharing a slat. Once decided who would get which slat, the families took out their *thalis*, tiered aluminum containers containing a variety of Indian foods. They ate with their right hands (left was for toilet use) and all shared their bounty. Laughter and talk of America with those who spoke English filled the air, but the black smoke from the coal engine eventually created a dark film over our bodies.

We rode the hour up the mountain by bus to Mount Abu, surrounded by the silence of the place, as we stepped down from the coach, birds chirping loudly and nature teeming all around us. Known as a holy place, temples populated the mountainside—Jain, Hindi, Zarathustran—and in Rajasthan in the village of Mount Abu was a tree inhabited by thousands of Chiropteran bats, infamously known as the "bat tree," and considered holy.

I had booked a room in a private home that provided lodging for meditation camps. I luxuriated in the large wooden tub at the back of the house, overlooking a stream where Indian women hung laundry on lines between palm trees. Two women wearing saris kindly brought me warm water from inside the house, grateful as the soot from my trip washed away.

The camp took place at an old palace high atop the mountain. We began each morning with laughing meditation, awakening at six, likely still cold under the covers, trying to laugh. I would sheepishly begin with a few "ha, ha, has…" As most participants attending meditation camp rented rooms in homes throughout Mount Abu, within moments I'd hear a similar half-hearted laughing attempt from a nearby house, then another, and another. Within minutes genuine laughter emerged everywhere in the village, and our morning had begun.

* * *

At 7:30 sharp, Rajneesh began his discourse, a banner reading, "I have come not to teach but to awaken. Surrender and I will tranform you. This is my promise," hanging behind him. Dynamic meditation followed, that he personally conducted, accompanied by a small band of drummers. After our exertion and thorough relaxation, we took silent walks in the mountains, and at 11 began a gibberish meditation. This entailed finding a quiet place and only looking at the sky, allowing sounds to rise up from within, the gibberish, and after 30 minutes of sounding this way to lie on the ground or a rock, listening for the universe to answer us. As Rajneesh often explained, we need to exhaust the mind in order to allow it to turn off, thus opening the door for true meditation to penetrate.

After lunch we continued with our afternoon meditation techniques, including *kirtan*, joyous singing, dancing, and music to celebrate the life force and to honor the teachings we'd received. The intention of our meditation, Rajneesh would say, is to allow that which separates us from the universe, the ego, to dissolve, becoming one with the moment. Bhagwan concluded each evening with another discourse.

I struggled with trying to quit smoking during my time in India. Threaded through my journal entries noting new awareness and peak experiences, I regularly mentioned this primary demon and how difficult I found it to quit. It seemed everyone smoked at that time, making it doubly hard, though I knew it was bad for me, and even unattractive. Smoking comforted me, not unlike suckling at the breast, and also settled my energy from the often, overwhelming inner shifts that came from meditating. A few years later in the Philippines, most of the healers that I worked with, or observed, chain-smoked—a cigarette the first thing they reached for after an intense healing session! Such examples helped me rationalize my addiction, but it remained a struggle for another ten years after my first trip to India.

At the end of the ten days of camp, I was stricken with severe dysentery. After a morning meditation I had to run into the woods to purge—the paradox of my painful gut coupled with the bliss of consciousness. I felt myself releasing "the shit" of the past along with the ever-hovering ego, including the rules and traditions that I'd swallowed while growing up. Now I could trust my inner compass.

I returned to Bombay for two more weeks faced with the dilemma of coming to a crossroad and wondering which path to take next, or more accurately, where my path would take me. I had heard that Rajneesh was asking disciples to help establish a farm in another area in India, and, unsure of what he would ask me to do, I again found myself anxious, in fear mode. If he asked me, would I go? I meditated each day on Chowpatty Beach, but clarity eluded me.

The final *darshan* occurred on the evening before I was to leave for New York. I had been to the huge outdoor Crawford Market in the center of Bombay, and while walking among the many vendors' stands overflowing with vegetable and animal alike, I spontaneously purchased five finches that called to me from their cages. The vendor put them into a large paper bag and punched holes in it. I left the market for the streets of Bombay with the intention of freeing the birds as I began to experience true freedom myself. Opening the bag, I looked up at the sky and thought, "now be free," and the birds flew up and away. Within seconds hawks dove down from the rooftops and attacked all of the birds, massacring them. I gasped, realizing that it is sheer illusion to believe any one of us can free another, much less ourselves. This experience told me I needed further guidance, and I vowed to take Bhagwan's words to heart that evening, even if it meant giving up my own vision.

As I later sat before him, his smile as radiant as ever, we gazed into each other's eyes for a long time before he spoke, "Yes, you will continue with your healing work, but, you must not go looking for it. It will come to you, very soon."

Rajneesh then listened intently as I spoke about my work, my desire to know more about psychic surgery in the Philippines, the healing direction of my life, and meditation. He stressed that meditation was part of healing, and that I must stay on my path, implying that the Philippines trip would come soon enough but not at that time. He suggested that I return to New York to "help people," to finish my training in the Alexander Technique, and to continue leading meditation techniques at the Rajneesh Center.

"Continue this, and a synthesis will happen. Your healing will become more inclusive and incorporate meditation within it. I will send you a message when it is time to either come back here or continue to the Philippines."

I left Bhagwan's apartment floating on air, my worst fears dissolving as I embraced the both/and of my teacher's message.

It's Hard To Treat Jesus

"Everything is a little bit of darkness, even the light."
—Antonio Porchia, from *Voices*

Upon my return from India, all the aspects of my outer life came together smoothly—my Alexander training, my practice progressively including more bodywork, and comfortably using my apartment as my office. Still, nagging questions kept haunting me inwardly: With the resulting bliss from meditation and affirmation of a loving teacher, was I avoiding my darker nature, my pain and insecurities? Was I short-circuiting my psychological and therefore spiritual path by pushing away my residual emotional pain? After all, Rajneesh encouraged both Western and Eastern approaches to cultivating wholeness.

Western psychology claims that such buried emotions perpetrate the root cause of all neurosis and psychosis, all anxiety and depression, creating a sense of ungrounded internal and therefore external reality.

The Buddhist perspective on the balance between confrontation and transcendence asserts that one need not confront all suppressed pain head on. Such endeavors would be endless, considering the Buddhist concept of reincarnation. If we succeed in shedding light on all of our pain, we would finish only to start again uncovering the pain of our past lives! Buddhism teaches bringing the laser light of awareness to our selves through meditation and to observe our behaviors or reactions without judgment. Buddhist psychology stresses that simply observing our neurotic patterns can "burn" and, therefore, purify them away.

I had experienced something like this through dynamic meditation, but felt strongly that I must return to therapy to explore my inner quandary and reveal whatever I might be avoiding. I needed the right therapist for such deep work, someone who wouldn't let me cleverly talk my way around the pain. Dr. John Pierrakos immediately came to mind, as I vividly recalled his Bio-energetic course at Esalen during my second summer there. I made an appointment to see him at his 57th Street office.

After greeting me he asked directly why I had come for therapy. I shared a few of my many insecurities: fear of public speaking, shyness when meeting new people, and fear of humiliation for starters. He looked me in the eye and said, "Those are just words. It's hard to treat Jesus! If you want to work with me you must let go of your spiritual persona!" And so, our descent began.

Bioenergetic therapy draws on many of the same principles as analytically oriented psychotherapeutic approaches, but foundationally stresses that most people store emotional issues and pain in their bodies as "muscular armoring." When confronting my own fears and anger in session, John instructed me to lie back on "the rack," a large padded stool, from which I could open my chest and solar plexus. He would push his fist into my solar plexus, encouraging me to express my feelings of anger and rage.

I often resisted this, telling him that, according to Alexander and Rolfing training that this method could injure the back, but he would have none of it, dismissing my concern with, "That's your body-worker ego, just let out your feelings!" I'd scream or rage, often getting nauseous and asking to rest for a moment. He proclaimed this my resistance and would send me to the bathroom to stick my finger down my throat and force myself to vomit.

After these sessions I'd leave much lighter, often with the awareness that neither my father nor my brother had accepted me for who I was. I'd initially feel that the Bioenergetic approach was helping me, but dread emerged as the next weekly session approached. It felt like torture, particularly reminding me of experiences with my older brother Butch.

My therapeutic work with John Pierrakos continued for nearly a year, until I realized that I no longer needed to confront the old pain. I had accepted it and stopped identifying with it. A full month passed before I could build the courage and commitment to tell John that I would be ending therapy. In the role of the critical father, nothing I did or said would win his approval.

Prepared for his usual response, "It's just your resistance," and dealing with "Daddy's" rejection, I arrived for my final session and blurted out, "I've pondered this deeply and have come to the realization that I don't need this anymore! I'm ending therapy!"

I braced myself and looked into his eyes. His face gradually began to soften, and a big broad smile came to his face. "I've been waiting for awhile for you to say that," and, with that, we came together in a long embrace, before I gathered my coat and left his office, feeling free at last.

Aikido

"Energy is the eternal delight...Energy is the only life."
—William Blake

I continued my dynamic meditations a few times each week at the Rajneesh Meditation Center and studied Aikido with Master Yamada Sensei at New York Aikikai in Chelsea.

Master Koichi Tohei's book, *Ki in Daily Life,* had accessibly introduced me to the principles of Aikido a couple of summers before when Master Tohei had been invited to teach a short course at the Psychology of Human Consciousness program at Stanford. He fully embodied the "soft power" of Aikido. True strength, I'd learned, came not only from force but also, more importantly, from yielding, a concept depicted aptly in my favorite Tarot card, Strength, that depicts a woman dressed in a white flowing robe, caressing a lion, the woman in total control of the beast. Such was the basic tenet of Aikido.

Master Tohei, the leading teacher of Aikido in Japan, trained with Morihei Ueshiba, the originator and "Great Teacher" of Aikido, but he'd expanded what he'd learned and taught not only the martial art but also how to use the "Ki" energy in life and spiritual practice. He stressed that Aikido helped its students unify mind and body so that they may attain the spiritual core of the practice.

Master Tohei showed a film of the grand master, Morihei Ueshiba, his teacher, actually practicing Aikido in his late eighties. A thin wisp of a bearded man, he walked slowly toward the mat, surrounded by eight burley Karate black belts. They bowed to each other in the traditional Japanese style, and, on signal, the eight men, all at once, attacked the old man. The "Great Teacher" seemed to dance in the center of the mat, as one by one the attackers flew to all corners of the mat, as if he sensed their energy before their physical body followed through and moved out of the way, gently using his hands to direct their forward attacks away from him, felling them to the floor. Observing the film in slow motion, the Master often did not physically touch his attackers, but "felt," their movements coming towards him, getting out of their way, as he moved their own energy against themselves.

After returning from my experience with Master Koichi Tohei at The Psychology of Consciousness program, I was eager to further my study and found the New York Aikikai, run by another student of Master Ueshiba's, Yamada Sensei. Both Tohei and Yamada held 8th Dan black belts, but that was where their similarity ended. Tohei trained in the martial art work with a focus on its spiritual aspects, Yamada strictly focused on Aikido form and mat work.

One evening in class while doing an exercise where we sat on our legs facing a partner, the goal being to throw our partner off balance while maintaining our own center, I got distracted and resisted my opponents push to the left, losing my center as he pushed to the right, knocking me down, my body falling over but my knees locking when I heard a loud "pop" followed by excruciating pain in my knee. I lay on the mat for some time, with no help offered, until a friend helped me get up. I hobbled out, never to return.

14

Touched by Rolling Thunder

"Handle even a single leaf of a green in such a way that it manifests the body of the Buddha."
—Eihei Dōgen and Kosho Uchiyama, from the *Zen Kitchen To Enlightenment: Refining Your Life*

"I like to think I'm doing a healing thing, a medicine thing, wherever I see people and shock the hell out of them with thunder and lightning, and see them start to wake up and start thinking in good ways. To see their eyes sparkle and start thinking about good things in this life is a healing. That's why I shock people. If I'm a little rough, it might be because I love people."
—Rolling Thunder from *Rolling Thunder Speaks,* edited by Carmen Sun Rising Pope, Rolling Thunder's wife

The pain and swelling worsened, and I tried to heal myself with Alexander, acupuncture, and osteopathic treatments, and, although slightly improved, the pain and swelling remained. I consulted a few orthopedic surgeons who both recommended surgery for what they diagnosed as a ruptured ligament and a torn meniscus. I learned that the meniscus does not have a dedicated blood supply and cannot, therefore, spontaneously heal itself. Determined, I continued my Alexander sessions and acupuncture but with only slow progress.

One evening while speaking to my girlfriend Rupa in Florida I enthusiastically shared that I'd been reading an inspiring book called *Rolling Thunder* by the journalist Doug Boyd, detailing his experiences with the Native American medicine man and wisdom-seeker of the same name. Rolling Thunder's message of togetherness and inclusiveness spoke to me deeply along with his commitment to rediscovering the healing powers of Mother Earth. I was also struck by the similarity between Rolling Thunder's vision of the human being as a microcosm of nature ("Every person is a model of life, so the true nature of a person is the nature of life.") and the Taoist philosophy in which human beings are regarded as exemplars of the natural world and encouraged to live in harmony with nature's immutable laws.

In one of those synchronistic moments that guide our individual destinies, Rupa excitedly shared that she'd heard that Rolling Thunder was scheduled to lead a conference very soon on an Indian reservation in Georgia. Hoping to learn more about Rolling Thunder's healing techniques, specifically in relation to my ailing knee, Rupa and I agreed to go together. I flew down to Miami, and we drove to the reservation in the deep woods of Georgia.

We arrived early for the conference and decided to walk along the river trail, to relax before our first meeting with Rolling Thunder, scheduled for 4 PM. Hobbling along at first, I noticed that as we walked my knee slowly began to calm down, and after only 15 minutes, I felt no pain at all, with a sudden urge to break into a run and jog for 10 minutes. All this and I hadn't even met the great medicine man yet!

I spent only four days with Rolling Thunder but the depth of his presence lives within me to this day. At the time of our first meeting, a group of 30 individuals came together and sat in silence at river's edge around a campfire. Rolling Thunder closed his eyes and after what seemed like an interminable ten minutes, he uncrossed his arms, looked up and said, "Looks like a storm's a coming!" We all looked up into the perfectly blue sky, watching in awe as the clouds began to gather, the temperature dropping, and the wind picking up. Soon thunder and lightning exploded across the now darkened sky and a torrential rain poured down all around us. Nearly half of the group left, probably to get rain gear, as Rolling Thunder looked up again and said, "Looks like the curiosity seekers have left," a smile taking over his face, as the clouds cleared and he began his talk.

He spoke eloquently and passionately about finding one's purpose in life. He went on to stress that, "The red people are the custodians of Mother Earth and our wisdom is essential now because the Mother is in a state of crisis. The other three colors—-the black, yellow, and white peoples—need to actively seek their visions and learn of their purpose so that we can all unite together to heal our many wounds and become whole once again." This reminded me of the Taoist proverb: "Find your center and you will be healed," the heart of which speaks too of connecting to one's spiritual power through seeking one's authentic purpose. Both philosophies emphasize a regenerative life process of dynamic healing, growth, and renewal—coming into balance.

Painting by Hank Grebe (mediaspin.com)

Rolling Thunder believed strongly in the valuable healing properties of herbs, the "helpers," he called them, like all living things have a "reason for being." These "helpers" he shared, "can heal (balance) the wounds of the body, mind, and spirit." His perspective certainly encouraged my further study of herbal medicine, as already inspired by my great grandmother, Esther, "the little doctor."

The following day we had individual meetings with Rolling Thunder and could ask more personal questions and seek his guidance. Rupa and I entered his cabin together. He looked first at Rupa, who resembles a Native American, and said that she had been a Native American in past lives, and that she would deeply relate with the coming days' teaching. "The Great Spirit will speak through you," he said, assuring her that they would meet again.

He turned to me and looked intensely into my eyes, reaching out to hold the mala beads that I wore with Rajneesh's picture on them.

"This carries powerful medicine," he said looking at the mala beads, "And you are to learn to use powerful medicine, but you must choose a teacher. We can both move you further along the trail, and, although at depth, we may say similar things, you must choose a path and stick with it, even though it ain't always smooth going!"

We gazed into each other's eyes for some time before he closed by inviting Rupa and me to work with him, if we felt drawn, affirming that we were both meant to bring healing to the people.

The pain in my knee gone, we left Rolling Thunder feeling acknowledged and more grounded on our spiritual paths. Though I felt called to one day study the medicinal use of herbs, it was Rolling Thunder's words in Doug Boyd's book, *Rolling Thunder,* that most stayed with me about working with medicinal vibrations: "I'll tell you a few things that you can take with you. You can start with this. You can take a glass of water and pray over it and make medicine out of it. A lot of times the Indians will be caught with no medicine and they want to cure a fever or something like that. They'll take a glass of water, pray over it in the morning when the sun's coming up. When the sun is rising in the morning, vibrations—what you would call vibrations in the earth, we call it Great Spirit's power—are strongest then and they're bringing forth new life. When the sun starts to rise, we make our prayer, and when you see the bottom of the sun, that's when it ends. Let the rays of the sun hit that water and you can make medicine out of it."

Over the years, I have experienced such healing through chanting and musical sound vibrations that reverberate with each chakra. I've also found that prayer and meditation can generate vibrational healing.

Rolling Thunder's most basic teaching has lingered long after that literal time with him, remaining an underlying commitment in my healing work:

"The most basic principle of all is that of not harming others, and that includes all people and all life and all things… Every being has the right to live his own life in his own way. Every being has an identity and a purpose. To live up to his purpose, every being has the power of self-control, and that's where spiritual power begins."

PART THREE
Around the World on a Healing Journey

"People heal with their minds (and hearts)...that's where the power is. Once you tap into it, you have joined up with a universal energy force. And with that power, nothing is impossible."

—Gerald Japolsky

15

A Surprise Call to the Philippines

"Our lives are often touched by chance, are they not? I call it magic, the crossing of our paths with the paths of others. How quickly, how completely, these magic meetings can turn us into directions we never dreamed of."

—Dee Brown, from *Creek Mary's Blood*

Not long after finishing my three years of Alexander Technique training and integrating it into my private practice, I began to have some clients who came purely for Alexander bodywork, particularly musicians, dancers, and budding actors. I also started experimenting at this time with healing and laying on of hands, particularly among my friends and fellow therapists. I found that, with full presence, my body could transmit electrical currents to those in need of healing. I would visualize a fibroid or tumor dissolving, the inflammation bathed in healing liquid, and consciously direct and transmit the love or surrounding positive energy through my hands and into my client. After a few surprisingly successful outcomes, even more people began coming for healings! My friend's fibroids seemed to disappear, and a fellow therapist's daughter had relief from longstanding asthma attacks.

My healing confidence grew and I soon became more trusting of my own intuition. I well remember a client, a male violinist for the New York Philharmonic. He told me about Florence Meschter, an amazing woman in her eighties, whom my client claimed was an incredible hand-reading analyst. He told me that when he held his palm out to her she could see things about his past and also shared what to look out for in the future. Though he sensed that she was psychic, Miss Meschter told him that such palm analysis was scientific—all clearly written in the hand and fingers, the craft being the ability to read the lines on the palm. When I called her to book a reading, she told me that she no longer took appointments with people who she did not know. Disappointed, I thanked her, but before we hung up, she said it had occurred to her that I might be interested in participating in a scientific hand-reading analysis class that she would very soon be teaching in a classroom at Carnegie Hall. We have one opening left she told me. I agreed to attend, and she instructed me to buy a text called *The Laws of Scientific Hand Reading* by William G. Benham, her mentor in the work, which she co-wrote. A few weeks after beginning the course, Ms. Meschter gave me a private reading. She held my hand in hers and essentially told me that she believed I could tell as much about a person as she could, by simply holding someone's hand in mine. I simply could not trust my intuition, without first exhaustively studying the process myself. "Learn what you can from me," she advised, "...and then try to forget it!" I stayed with the coursework for two years, and it surely did enhance my trust in my own intuitive healing skill. To this day I observe my clients' hands and use some of the simple skills I'd learned from Ms. Meschter to strengthen my diagnosis.

* * *

My social networks in New York also expanded at this time and my relationship with Rupa deepened. I considered settling down, perhaps upstate, or maybe starting a healing/meditation center in Santa Fe. After many years of seeking and wandering, the idea of living on more solid ground had its appeal, but such peaceful thoughts were not to last.

Having an apartment/office in the West Village, a sanctuary away from the chaotic streets of uptown, felt like heaven. One day I was relaxing after finishing my sessions, when the phone rang. The caller introduced himself as Lito Garcia. He had recently arrived from India, having spent some weeks with Bhagwan. He shared that he was preparing to set up a meditation center in Manila. Rajneesh had asked him to contact me, for our paths were to meet, and I could help Lito establish his center. He would introduce me to healers in the Philippines, some of whom he knew personally. I couldn't believe what I was hearing. Was this really happening?

Lito was a fireball— a slight, not very tall young man with mischievous eyes and a self-assured intensity. We smiled and bear-hugged with immediate connection. He was lit up with excitement about opening a meditation center, and my enthusiasm over the prospect of making real my psychic surgery premonitions fanned his flame! Impressed with my own well-stocked library, Lito wanted to create a library in the Philippines specifically with spiritual books but also books on psychology, healing, meditation, and other New Age subjects. Money did not appear to be an issue.

We enjoyed being in the city together, visiting Samuel Weiser's metaphysical bookstore, The Strand, and East-West Books. With Lito's carte blanche to create his library, I felt like a kid in a candy store even if the books we bought were to be shipped to the Philippines. I loved choosing them and buying a few for myself. To this day, I remain an unrecoverable bibliophile!

Before his departure, Lito invited me to stay with him at his home in Quezon City, just outside of Manila, for as long as I'd like and re-iterated that he would be most grateful for my help in opening his new center there. He encouraged me to bring nothing extra except a wetsuit. Lito was an expert scuba diver and would provide my tanks, regulator, and all the other paraphernalia that I'd need for what would become a lifetime passion for the meditative experience of scuba diving.

I immediately began planning for my trip. I had set aside money that my father had left me when he died and felt this would be a good use of it, deciding that I'd spend a year traveling the world in search of different healing modalities. But, the Philippines were first on the list. Many airlines sold "around the world" fares at that time, good for a full year, allowing travel on any airline as long as it was to occur in one general direction. I chose West to East, beginning in San Francisco, where I could first visit friends, then to Hawaii, Japan, the Philippines, Hong Kong, India, England, and back to New York.

Rupa and I spent time together in the weeks before my departure. I asked her to pick up a wetsuit for me from a sporting goods store on 42nd Street. Following the teachings of Rajneesh, we tended to wear the "colors of *sannyas*," that is, reds, oranges, and maroons. She bought me a red wetsuit. A few days before I left, we saw the film, "Jaws." As we were leaving the theater, still stunned, we stopped to read the poster outside. In huge, bold lettering, it warned: Things That Attract Shark Attacks and listed the smell of blood, too much movement, and the color **red**! We immediately exchanged the wetsuit for a blue one.

I knew that the theme of my around-the-world journey would be exploring the universality of healing. All healing rituals, no matter the originating culture, involve meeting the other in need with compassion and intentionally directing loving or healing energy toward that suffering other. In Hawaii they call the healing force "Huna," in China they call it "Chi," in Japan, it's "Ki," and in India, "Prana." All such indigenous healing rituals create a sacred container for such practice, a kind of sanctuary or protected space that honors the threshold from sickness to wellness, the in-between place where psychological and spiritual forces may emerge to promote healing. Such healing implies responsibility and accountability for mutual growth by both healer and healing recipient.

My First Encounter with Karmapa

One night while I was meditating at the Rajneesh Meditation Center in New York an old Indian man with a long, white beard and sparkling eyes that emanated both a subtle joy and a palpable serenity, introduced himself as Krishna Das. He had just arrived from India to help run the New York center. Since I went to the center regularly, Krishna Das and I became quite friendly. I guided him around New York, and he guided me to inner levity.

Krishna Das and some other friends involved in Tibetan Buddhism were very excited that Karmapa Rinpoche was due in America for the first time. The second most powerful Lama in Tibet, just below the Dalai Lama, Karmapa would be performing The Black Crown ceremony in New York for the first time in the West. Though the Dalai Lama rules all of Tibet, the practice of Tibetan Buddhism is of two schools: The Black Crown and The Yellow Crown. Karmapa Rinpoche headed the larger Black Crown School. Tibetan Buddhism asserts that if an individual witnesses this sacred rite they may attain enlightenment in that lifetime, requiring no further reincarnation.

I honored such ancient traditions but found the talk of such instantaneous enlightenment suspect. Krishna Das had met Karmapa in Dharmasala in the Himalayas a few years prior. He claimed that he and Rajneesh had both attained the highest states of consciousness and that simply being in Karmapa's presence had the power to transform. This was enough to convince me to attend.

The Black Crown ceremony was held at a large auditorium in midtown Manhattan, with over a thousand people in attendance. The ceremony lasted over an hour, as many monks chanted, clanged bells, and burned incense, creating an exotic yet meditative environment. My thoughts lifted above me and hovered above my head where I could watch them roll by like a slow train, a deep quiet permeating my heart. By the ceremony's conclusion, I had entered a state of *satori*, tasting the nectar of spiritual illumination. In reverie, I had become one with all that is, transported into a new realm of consciousness. This state, however, offered only a glimpse, as *samadhi*, a deeply meditative state of no-mind and sheer transcendence, becomes permanent only when one is truly enlightened.

Krishna Das shook me to wake me from my reverie, beckoning for me to stand in line with him for his Holiness Karmapa's blessing. Each person was invited to stand before him and look into his eyes. Karmapa was said to place his palm on the supplicant's third eye and put a string around his neck. People both laughed or cried after their blessing. Krishna Das stood in front of me in line, and when he and Karmapa looked into each other's eyes they began to laugh loudly, and, Karmapa got up from his chair and hugged Krishna Das. When it was my turn, Karmapa followed the typical procedure of activating my third eye. I felt totally calm and exhilarated by the experience. It would not be the last time I spent time with Karmapa.

Invitation to Hospitable Japan

That summer Rupa and I and a few other friends rented a cottage in upstate New York, near Phoenicia, where we could get away from the city on weekends and explore the Zen

Buddhist monasteries nearby. Rupa came up from Florida for the summer, intending to take prerequisite courses to prepare for the Alexander Technique training in the fall. We spent weekdays in the city and weekends upstate, having guests constantly, all therapists and teachers. We experimented with various meditations and also explored past-life regressions.

One weekend a friend of Rupa's, Steve Mindell, came upstate to visit. He lived full time in Japan, having moved there six years prior to teach English to employees of Japanese corporations. During his downtime, he had learned to play the shakuhashi, a traditional Japanese bamboo flute, and it had become his passion. He had become so proficient at it that he had left corporate teaching to become a shakuhashi instructor for Japanese students. How remarkable, I thought, a nice Jewish boy from Queens teaching the Japanese how to play their own instrument! After we got to know each other, Steve invited me to visit him in Kyoto and perhaps introduce me to some Japanese healers. I sensed that I would take him up on his offer in the not too distant future.

Just down the road from our cottage in Phoenicia, The Pathwork Center had opened, an educational and spiritual center based on Bioenergetics Therapy and stressing conscious living. I soon learned that John Pierrakos, my old therapist, and his wife Eva had founded The Pathwork Center based on John's therapeutic model and Eva's spiritual guidance. She had channeled teachings in higher consciousness. Though duly impressed, when asked if I would like to be further involved, I told them of my upcoming journey and that I had no idea where the road might lead.

Back in the city, I was caught in a whirlwind of activity: arranging to sublet my apartment, getting my vaccinations, and arranging visas for the Philippines and India, where I knew I would stay for more than only a few weeks.

Since my airline ticket took me westward, I decided to visit my friends in San Francisco and Berkeley for a few days before going on to Hawaii. I had hoped to find a healer in Oahu with whom to study indigenous healing systems, but it was not to be. Instead I visited a few friends in Hawaii, who I'd met a few years prior at the Humanistic Psychology conference, before leaving for Japan to truly begin my adventure.

Landing in Tokyo alone, with only Steve Mindell's address in Kyoto in my pocket, both frightened and exhilarated me. I found an inexpensive hotel, parked my backpack there, and walked the streets of this strange and lively city, both unfamiliar and familiar. Very few people spoke English, but all smiled and bowed as I passed them in the street.

I took the rocket train from Tokyo into Kyoto. The train whizzed along its tracks at more than 100 miles per hour. The farms and mountains in the distance looked like postcards of a foreign land, but the passing villages remained a blur. My reverie, open and accepting of whatever might come, faded when we neared Kyoto, my anxiety creeping in as I wondered if Steve would be home. And, how would I function without this culture's language?

When we pulled into Kyoto station, I walked to the exit, and got immediately into a taxi. The driver spoke no English, but he happily read Steve's address and recognized the neighborhood. I sat up in my seat, mesmerized, remembering that Kyoto was called The City of Ten Thousand Shrines. We stopped in what looked like an industrial area, with streets lined with large garage doors. The driver looked confused, so I pointed to the telephone number that Steve gave me for his landlord since he didn't have a phone. The driver kindly stopped at a phone booth and made the call, walking back to the taxi with a big smile before driving a couple more blocks to a corner, stopping, and beckoning me to wait for my friend at this corner. I paid him and watched the taxi disappear, leaving me alone. Within minutes Steve appeared walking toward me, indeed a sight for sore eyes. We embraced and walked to one of the garage doors. Steve opened it and then another metal door through which we entered paradise. Inside a vestibule we left our shoes and jackets before entering the main residence, tatami mat flooring throughout, furnished Zen-style: a beautiful wooden table with cushions around it on one side of the living area, colorful wall hangings, and simple furniture. Plus, at least 20 shakuhashi flutes lined the floor. Steve's bedroom was off the main living area through a sliding rice-paper door, his compact kitchen in an extended vestibule, and the bathroom, outside of the main residence along with the guestroom and a Zen garden with a small fishpond.

How ironic, I thought, that this jewel of a place lay behind a large metal door on a dreary street and how different from America and its emphasis on outer presentation!

Waterfall at Shinto shrine at dark

For a few days Steve helped orient me to Kyoto but even after I was on my own I felt alien as if I did not belong in this place. Steve admitted that although he spoke the language and taught Japanese students to play the shakuhashi, he too felt a bit like an outsider and probably always would. Eventually, he taught me how to play the shakuhashi, and I fell in love with the sounds it made, using it in meditation and carrying it with me later to India where I continued to meditatively play what Steve had taught me.

Often alone during the day, I would walk the streets and explore the temples and shrines. In the evening I met Steve for noodles or sushi, followed by my favorite place, the baths. Most Japanese houses had no showers or bathtubs, but bathing was traditionally a public event, and each neighborhood had its own bathhouses.

Upon entering, we would be given a plastic basket in which to put our street clothes, the men directed to the left and the women to the right of the reception area. The wall quite low, it would have been easy enough to look into the women's area but this was taboo.

We stopped first at a sauna to sweat away the day's impurities, next to the bath to wash with soap before we were clean enough to enter the hot baths. They reminded me of the hot baths at Esalen, except for the tap water instead of the natural mineral springs water. Departing this heavenly ritual, both of us felt like limp spaghetti.

Steve's landlords, a somewhat elderly couple, the Takahashis, invited us to dinner one evening, and Steve graciously translated for me. I told them of my journey's primary objective: to study healing across different cultures, and Mrs. Takahashi offered to introduce me to a well-known Japanese healer in the area who worked with "Ki" energy and attracted people from all over Japan. This wonderful evening with such a gracious hostess and her family left me filled with gratitude and wonder. What a true act of giving to a stranger with no expectation of reciprocity!

A few days later Mrs. Takahashi took me into Kyoto to introduce me to the Master she'd mentioned, first speaking with him in Japanese, then bowing and taking her leave. He did his best to tell me in English to observe him working and to look at the diagrams that he gestured towards contained in his books. I stayed for the afternoon and watched his form of shiatsu or acupressure, but the energy healing that he initiated when the patient had relaxed struck me as unique. He waved his hands over the patient's body and seemed to enter a trance-dance. During these "Ki" healings the energy in the room was palpable, but the language barrier made it difficult to fully understand his process. He apologized, wrote an address on a piece of paper, and directed me to a medical bookstore nearby where I could find these books translated into English. I purchased them and began studying the meridians (energy pathways).

At night in my room at Steve's home, I'd follow the flow of these energy pathways through the body and studied how they fed the organs. With its clearly Chinese influence, the ancient origin of this form of energy healing, I strongly connected with what I was learning and felt certain that my path would eventually guide me back to this modality.

The three weeks in Japan passed quickly. I traveled to various cities to visit shrines and holy sites and, to this day, I'm drawn to Japanese aesthetics; the rock gardens, water gardens, and Buddhist architecture and statues all stay with me. I suppose that my deep recognition with such varied cultures acknowledges my sense of universality of spirit and also the possibility of reincarnation.

The night before my departure for Tokyo to fly to the Philippines, the Takahashi family took Steve and me to a geisha house. I'd thought of geishas as performing sexual favors, but I learned that the role of the geisha is to offer total service, where the geisha anticipates one's every need. For the young geisha, this would likely include sexual favors. Our lovely, middle-aged hostess served us dinner, entertained us with traditional Japanese music, and performed a tea ceremony, a ritual that's intended to emphasize the unique, unrepeatable treasure of each moment. Our entire evening certainly lived up to that intention.

When we returned to Steve's later that evening, my new friends presented me with little gifts to wish me a safe journey, the most memorable being Steve's gift of one of his shakuhashis, making the evening a touching and memorable gateway to the next step on my journey.

The following evening I took the bullet train to Tokyo but arrived too late for public transportation. A bus driver drove me to a monorail stop still operating at 11pm., but when it reached the airport, all the doors locked, until the following morning, when my flight to the Philippines would depart. A security guard, who likely empathized with my predicament, allowed me into the baggage area where I slept the night on a bench.

Steve playing the shakuhashi

Arriving in the Philippines

Flying from Tokyo to the Philippines, high above the clouds, I reflected upon my destination, aware that the healing work of psychic surgery had initially called me to the Philippines and instigated my journey, now made possible by Lito's need and Rajneesh's encouragement. I intuited the intense experiences ahead of me and flying through the clouds, it occurred to me that I was like a cloud, floating about, carried by the wind, the winds of karma.

My connected web of experience echoed the truth of our interconnectedness as human beings. I was learning that we feel somehow connected to a thread, a thread that pulls and guides us toward our journey to wholeness, however I also realized we must confront the obstacles in our path, often the impact of past trauma in this life and in past lives. A story about karma I'd heard at a lecture in the States had long stayed with me, though I couldn't remember the man's name:

> *At his home in Maine, the storyteller would regularly jump into a nearby lake, swim out and back. But on one occasion he felt very exhilarated and swam much further than he'd expected to, realizing that he must still swim back to shore. As he approached the shore, he stopped to rest. His heavy arm-strokes had created waves, and while treading water he watched those waves move toward the shore, and come back, hitting him in his face. "My God," he thought, "that's karma!"*

Gazing out the window, suddenly my Black Bird appeared to fly directly toward 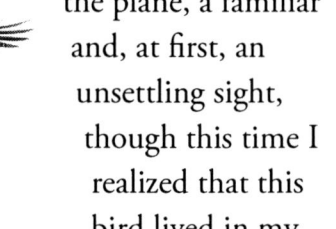 the plane, a familiar and, at first, an unsettling sight, though this time I realized that this bird lived in my imagination, there to remind me to remain present and grounded for the challenges ahead. As quickly as it had appeared, it disappeared under the sure scrutiny of my gaze.

Apprehensive after landing in Manila that Lito would actually meet me at the airport, I proceeded to customs, giving Lito's address as my temporary residence. Once through, I was thrilled to see his face, and we embraced with mutual joy.

In his car on the way to his home in Quezon City, he explained that the Philippines were under martial law and therefore we must abide by a strict curfew: after midnight all cars must be off the roads and everyone in their homes. Those in violation would be immediately arrested. Lito had arranged for a group of folks to join us at his home that evening for the official opening of his meditation center and asked me to lead them through a meditation.

Passing into a neighborhood that appeared upscale, all the homes stood behind walls with barbed wire or sharp glass fragments along their upper edges, preventing intruders from entering. An armed guard admitted us through Lito's gate. I'd never experienced such a militaristic environment, though Lito explained that a recent barrage of shootouts and other violent incidents had warranted the new government of Ferdinand Marcos to severely tighten security. Most people, he said, welcomed this change, feeling more secure and protected. In spite of this undercurrent of unrest, from the moment I arrived, I felt at home with the place and its people. In Japan I'd felt at home with its aesthetics and Zen-like spirituality and in the Philippines the warm, caring, often carefree people felt familiar. Perhaps it was my naiveté or a simple blind trust, but I sincerely trusted the Filipinos' goodness.

That evening about 20 people gathered at Lito's, and I introduced Rajneesh's dynamic meditation technique. Afterwards we socialized a bit over refreshments until near midnight, at the impending curfew,

Me in the middle, Lito to far right, celebrating the opening of Lito's meditation center

when everyone had to leave abruptly. We even had to drive some guests home to make certain they got in on time. At that hour driving on Manila roads looked and felt psychedelic with cars whizzing manically by in all directions. During my months in the Philippines, this ritual to make curfew became a kind of ambiguous exhilaration.

Lito had created a sanctuary in his home, a special room, strictly for quiet contemplation, with an altar and subdued lighting, and a large meditation area for the weekly meditations with a library and Rajneesh's taped discourses on loan or for sale.

Diving and Healing

A few days after arriving Lito took me with a couple of his friends on our first scuba diving expedition. Flying on his private plane to an island far from Manila, we were met at a small airport and jeeped to a village where he docked his boat. From there we headed toward coral reefs unknown to Western divers. My scuba diving lessons were simple and to the point. Lito showed me how to put on the equipment and how to breathe through the regulator. No buoyancy vests existed in those days; we wore only a wetsuit, a tank on our back with a regulator, and a weight belt. It felt seamless, even easy at the time, but looking back, I realize that we took enormous risks. On my first dive Lito accompanied me down to near 60 feet. As if immersed in another world, the surrounding beauty stunned me. My total immersion in water, moving through it like a fish myself, felt ironically grounding and naturally peaceful. The lush, colorful reefs and the myriad tropical fish, all curious, swirled around us as we explored, the fish coming up to our masks, as if to say, "who are you and what are you doing in our world?" Wondering if he could see the constant smile glowing behind my mask, Lito would look my way and give me an okay sign to which I'd respond with the same gesture.

After that first dive, Lito would leave me on my own and swim away with his spear gun to catch our dinner. I struggled with killing the fish that had only greeted me moments before, face to mask, but I surrendered to the circumstance, realizing that Lito's spearfishing was not only for sport but also for food. Although not a vegetarian until a year later in India, the idea of killing for sport repulsed me. Realizing that we must take the lives of either animals or plants to survive, I believe that taking *any* life should be prefaced with a prayer. In Carlos Castaneda's stories about his apprenticeship with Don Juan, the Yaqui sorcerer, he was taught that when the need to kill to survive arises, we must energetically connect to the other being and meditate on "in order to live I must take your life." Castaneda reminded his readers that this accountability allows human souls to progress following such necessary killing.

My primal fear of the deep had given way to only mild anxiety as Lito and the others went their own ways. I eagerly dove on my own for the first time, taking in the grandeur with my entire body. When I finally came back to the boat, the strong tide pulled me away, and I began to panic. I attempted to calm myself, trusting that Lito or someone would find me, but the current moved me farther and farther away from the boat. I decided

Lito with his underwater camera

to go back down, below the threatening current, and simply swim in the direction of the boat. Arriving at the side of the boat, I felt proud for making this astute decision and even better when Lito later laughed telling me that this was the first lesson taught to new scuba divers. I remembered this day years later when I secured my scuba-diving certification in Cozumel, Mexico in the late 1990s.

That night we camped out on an island with no roads or hint of Western civilization. We pitched our tents and started a fire. Gradually over the next hour the island natives congregated around us, squatting as they watched us intensely. Some remote out islands in the region still had tribal populations of native people that had never seen Westerners or any hint of technology. That night around the fire, watching the shooting stars stream across the heavens, the natives with us around the circle felt natural.

We cooked Lito's Mahi Mahi catch over the fire, and after dinner we shared stories of diving and healing as we watched the heavens, most of the natives presumably having returned to their village. Suddenly a huge star moved erratically in the sky, appearing bigger and bigger as it came closer and closer. We looked at each other around the circle to acknowledge that we were indeed seeing the same phenomenon. When the natives looked up toward the huge star, they suddenly ran off. The great "star" resembled a disc shape, hovering close and then quickly flying off. We believed we had witnessed a flying saucer, and our excitement kept us awake all night.

The next morning back at the boat Lito took us to another reef that he called Shark Alley. Having seen "Jaws" before leaving New York, I felt anxious but intent on facing my fear and diving to the reefs. We anchored about 80 feet above the reef when a boat with six native fishermen pulled close to us. Holding wooden, homemade spear guns, they waved, each tying a rock to his ankle, and jumped off their boat. Lito said that this was common practice among the natives. They began diving in early childhood, intentionally bursting their eardrums so they could quickly dive to 60 or 80 feet, staying at the bottom for up to five minutes before swimming to the surface with their catch. Lito explained that sharks, although very common in this region,

rarely attacked divers. If I was to see one, he advised me to remain calm and resolute, but, above all, not to swim away.

When I had my first shark encounter later that day, I felt strangely safe and relaxed in the presence of these majestic creatures. The horrifying images from "Jaws" evaporated as I admired the sheer grace of the royalty of the deep. This trip with Lito marked the beginning of my lifelong love of diving, but I have never been a hunter or fisherman and to this day the only thing I shoot underwater is my camera. Diving takes me closer to a meditative state than any other activity I know except my healing work. The quiet, the lack of radio, television and microwaves, and the total connection with the breath reminds me of Prana Yoga. Breath awareness not only preserves one's oxygen supply but also acts as a buoyancy tool. The diver must learn to use his breath consciously to adjust his depth by inflating his lungs to rise and expelling the air from his lungs to descend. The paradoxical beauty and danger create an immediacy that demands total immersion in the moment. Such presence in the undersea environment creates an awareness of Oneness with the living, breathing underwater life and can become a mystical experience.

Meditation is simply a state of oneness or nothingness, a space where the boundary between self and Other dissolves. Such a state need not only be sitting silently on a cushion watching the in and out flow of breath but can also come through the activity with which one authentically identifies whether through music, art, dance, plumbing, cooking, whatever the true communion may be. I have found my meditative state best through the study of healing, the art of photography, and the sheer pleasure and wonder of diving*.

Note: See fiveelementhealing.net which includes a video called "A Diving Meditation," admittedly amateurish, where I attempted to capture the meditative quality of a dive.

16

Psychic Surgery

"People tend to undervalue that which they believe to be impossible or unattainable…Beliefs that do not fit well into the existing ecology of the mind are more likely to be altered, rejected, suppressed, or forgotten."

—J. M. Balkin, from *Cultural Software: A Theory of Ideology*

"There are two ways to be fooled: one is to believe what isn't so, and the other is to refuse to believe what is so."

—Søren Kierkegaard

By the time we returned to Manila I was restless to move on to exploring the Philippines indigenous healing. Lito invited his friend, Prem, over that evening to share his experiences with many of these healers. We spoke about the healers in Quezon City and Baguio, a beautiful city in the mountains. Prem agreed to take me to meet David Elisalde, a well-known healer, the following morning.

We drove into a rather depressed section of town where we found a small house called The Black Nazarene Healing Center. At least 30 Filipinos filled the waiting room. Having little access to Western medicine, this was, no doubt to them, their doctor. I sat down in the waiting room and waited, hoping to be introduced to the healers. Almost immediately a man came out of the treatment room that I later learned was David Elisalde, his energy welcoming and matter of fact. He took me by the elbow and escorted me into an adjoining room (a dining room). Very directly he asked if I'd been to Baguio yet. Confusion flooded my thoughts, "how could he know?" He said he knew I wanted to visit Tony, but "I think you were meant to be *here*. Let's go into the treatment room, and you can watch. We'll talk later."

Looking back over my diary entries from that time I've attempted to make the following experiences plausible to the reader. I was carried by an energy that surpasses any high from drugs. The vibrations of a blissful trance-like state engulfed me during my experiences with psychic surgery, a state surely enhanced by my readiness to believe and to trust as well as the deep acknowledgment of being chosen!

For well over an hour I observed as David performed healings on one patient and then another, laying his hands over their bodies and entering a prayerful state, the energy palpably filling the room. With the third patient, a woman, David simultaneously placed his hands on her head and belly as she lay quietly on the table. Suddenly David used his hand like a knife and both of his hands disappeared up to his knuckles inside the woman's stomach, blood pouring forth. His assistant poured water over the wound, as he removed what looked like a tumor. He showed it to me before removing his hands from the woman's abdomen. The woman's face appeared ecstatic. She felt no pain, and no evidence of wound or scar marked where David had performed "psychic surgery." She smiled radiantly as she stepped down from the table, thanking him effusively and touching his feet with reverence, claiming she no longer felt pain in her belly.

After witnessing a few more "psychic surgery" procedures, David asked me to place my hands on his patients' heads while

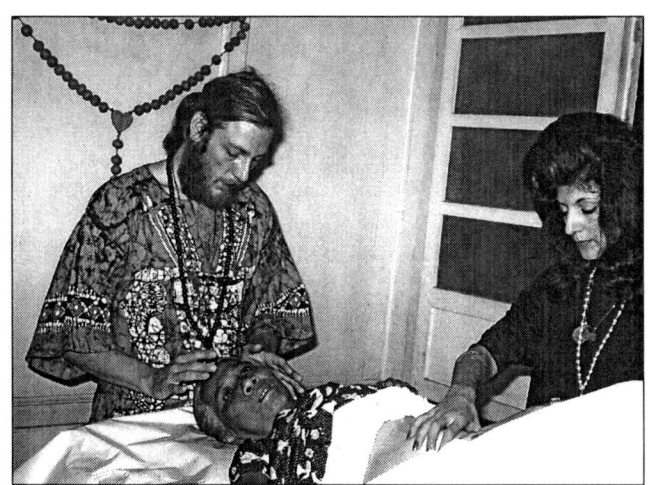

Assisting Helen Morgante, David Elisalde's wife

he worked on them, reminding me of my psychiatric aide days. How different the energy between ECT and psychic surgery! As I was holding an elderly woman's head, another woman walked into the treatment room. She and David made intense eye contact, and she took over the healings, casting me a welcome smile before she closed her eyes in meditation while resting her hands upon the woman's stomach. Suddenly she sliced at the patient's abdomen, her hand like a knife, and entered the woman's stomach. I later learned that this was Helen Morgante, David's wife and healing partner.

At the end of each psychic surgery procedure, the patient would sit up with a look of rapture upon his or her face before a member of David's family escorted one patient out and the next one in. It took some hours for the day's patients to empty the waiting room and, with only a few people remaining, David indicated that the rest needed only magnetic healing and that their assistant could manage those.

I'd noticed in the treatment room that Helen wore a large brass ring with a Pharaoh's head on her ring finger. I felt both a strong attraction to the ring and concern that it was unsanitary to wear during the procedures. Eager to get to know both of these healers and their stories, I accepted their invitation to share lunch. As we walked through the waiting room into the dining room, Helen and I looked intensely into each other's eyes for the first time and in unison, said, "Egypt!"

Helen declared, "We knew each other from a past life in Egypt. David was there too, and we've been waiting for you. Come in and meet the family," she said, "Perhaps we can put our pieces together."

David was already at the table alongside his brother and sister and a spread of various Philippine dishes of vegetables and chicken. We formally introduced ourselves, and I told them why I had come to the Philippines. Both David and Helen smiled knowingly and asked how I had been called there. I first mentioned the book by Harold Sherman, *Wonder Healers of the Philippines* that had repeatedly fallen off the shelf in Palo Alto and told them about the bookstore proprietor in Carmel. I also shared about the film I'd seen at Esalen of Tony Agpaoa performing "psychic surgery." Both Helen and David laughed.

"Tony is my cousin," David said, smiling. "He lives in Baguio City. His work has been suffering lately, but, if you'd like, we can visit him, I'd be happy to introduce you."

I reached into my bag and pulled out *Wonder Healers of the Philippines* and handed it to them. David mentioned that though the pictures in this book were in fact of Tony practicing psychic surgery that in a similar book the pictures identified as Tony were actually David.

"You must learn to accept these callings," Helen affirmed, "And, as we said before, we have been expecting you and are most welcome to be here. We will put you to work, but you must follow your heart."

I spent the rest of the day in their private quarters at The Black Nazarene Healing Center. We talked about religion and meditation, even the American Medical Association's (AMA's) opinion of spiritual healing, and finally about their lives.

David comes from a long paternal lineage of psychic healers. At that time, his father still practiced on another island in the village where David grew up. David's paternal grandfather, great grandfather, and great-great grandfather were all healers. Before Magellan took possession of the Philippines in 1521 for Spain and brought Catholicism to the archipelago, the tribal cultures had used many types of indigenous healing to free a victim's curse or negative thoughts, healing closely resembling psychic surgery. Though the Filipino society converted to Catholicism, its people held on to their tribal roots. They worshiped Jesus with the same respect that they revered their ancestral healing roots.

Helen Morgante had come from Australia, where she had performed intuitive healings without knowing what to call it, and developed a reputation as a healer. But, after some years of healing work, she became quite ill. With persistent low-grade fevers, she began to lose more and more weight, as if something was literally eating away at her. Neither doctors nor healers could determine what ailed her, and many thought she would die. On what she described as her "death bed," she had a vision that told her she must go to the Philippines, and that she would find healing there. She gathered the strength to make the journey and found David who, she claimed, healed her. Upon my return to Lito's at he end of that day, I felt I now had two families in the Philippines, Lito's and the Elisaldes. I told Lito about what I had observed and my excitement about working with David and Helen at their healing center, with the possibility now of developing as a healer myself.

Later, when alone, doubts began to haunt me. Had I been deluded, hypnotized, under a spell? All this because David and Helen had bolstered my ego? I stayed with my deeper truth, realizing I had to both follow where I was being lead and also diligently stay present and conscious while witnessing the healings. Only then could I determine whether I was being called or had become a victim of my inflated ego. I meditated on my uncertainty of this calling almost every night in Lito's sanctuary.

Working at the Black Nazarene Healing Center

During my first full week at the Elisaldes' Black Nazarene Healing Center, David and Helen gave me a bit more responsibility, allowing me to work with a few of my own patients. An elderly woman with advanced breast cancer came for treatment, her breast full of tumors. David explained that she needed magnetic healing on a regular basis; she was not a candidate for surgery, and I began to work with her. Over the course of a few weeks, the tumors visually shrank, and soon she appeared free of tumors, reporting that her energy was back to normal.

I learned that when Helen called on guidance for her healings, she saw a Greek Orthodox priest and showed me a painting of him, and I shared that I saw the same old man with a beard whom I imagined to be an old rabbi. When we compared notes, Helen and I realized that the priest and the rabbi looked identical. David shared that when he called for healing guidance, he saw Jesus. I felt strongly that we were vehicles for healing and could channel love and energy by calling on the image that evoked a sacred presence within.

During my time at the Black Nazarene I witnessed many "miracles," but it's the rapture on the patients' faces that stays with me to this day. Now as then each and every case of healing fills me with immeasurable gratitude and love for the spirit who works through us in mysterious ways.

I remember asking David and Helen whether healing was more often due to the psychic surgery rather than the magnetic and energetic healing. I wondered too about the spiritual aspect of the healing process. Both David and Helen were devout Catholics and called on their spiritual devotion when healing, but their response startled me, for both admitted that though the psychic surgery was not absolutely necessary for healing, such an experience imprinted the patient's psyche and body leaving a marked impression that could expedite healing. However, they shared, the healing effects could be just as dramatic without the blood or the patients' ability to observe the actual removal of a clot or tumor. I remained in awe, taking them at their word.

After three weeks of working at the Black Nazarene, David and Helen invited me to join them for All Soul's Day, November 1, for a full-day celebration at the cemetery. Considering me part of the family, they wanted me to meet the rest of their biological family coming in from other provinces to join the festivities. To the Filipino people as with many cultures, All Soul's Day celebrates the ancestral dead. Families visit the cemeteries early in the morning—taking along food, beer, and soft drinks—where they literally dance and sing on the graves of their loved ones. They believe that spirits never die, and each year on Old Soul's Day they expect their loved ones to visit from the beyond.

We took a Jeepney from the Elisaldes' house to the cemetery. (A Jeepney is a vehicle specific to the Philippines, a Jeep-like truck, with seating for 12 in the back, brightly painted and decorated.) Hundreds of people had gathered, already celebrating when we arrived. David made his way through the crowds, amid multiple hugs, to the graves of his mother and his first wife. David and others placed pictures on their loved ones' gravestones and took a few moments of silence to pray before bringing out the beer and sandwiches as they told jokes and laughed. I met David's father and another brother and a few of his uncles and aunts. As the day progressed people got a bit drunk and rowdy, but in a playful way. They referred to me throughout the day as family.

I learned that day that while Helen had fought for her life, David's wife had also fought for hers. She too had been struck with a strange illness, almost identical to Helen's, with fevers and wasting, and no one could heal her, not even David. David said he had repeatedly received the message that his wife was being called to the other side, and his efforts would never work. (I would have my own such humble experience in India with a young woman named Vipassana.) Finally, he had taken her to Western doctors, but to no avail, and after a few months she died. Only a few weeks later, Helen had come to him for healings. When she and David had shared their healing stories and mutual commitment to the spiritual call of their psychic healings, they had sensed they were meant to work together and perhaps open a healing center. It would be some years later that they decided to marry.

As the sun began to set on this All Soul's Day, we headed back home in a jubilant yet melancholy mood.

* * *

On weekends we would travel into rural areas to help people who had difficulty getting into Manila because they were either too sick or too poor. We accepted eggs or milk or vegetables as payment. I deeply respected the Elisaldes' commitment to their healing, their payment only secondary to God's work. They had a donation box at the healing center to which patients were asked only to donate what they could afford or felt applicable to their treatment.

I spent my days helping Lito with his meditation center and my healing work with the Elisaldes' at the Black Nazarene Center. I often felt I'd found two new families in the Philippines, two families where I truly belonged. However, while my experiences felt meaningful and self-nourishing, my rational mind continued looking for fault in my new work, as if it must make absolute sense rather than simply feel right. Western medicine would debunk psychic surgery years later. My experience felt real to all my senses. Daily I intently observed with my own eyes, as David or Helen reached his or her clean but unsanitized hand inside of peoples' bodies, and I experienced it too with my own hands. I heard the patients moan and cry before their treatments and witnessed their peace, even rapture afterwards. Still, doubt plagued me.

On a holiday celebrated across the Philippines we went to watch the parade flowing through Manila, and to my delight I observed the Western-style medical doctors and the indigenous Filipino healers walking side-by-side along the parade route, brothers and sisters in the healing profession. How wonderful, how healing, it would be if such a partnership could evolve in the States, the impressive technology of Western medicine working hand-in-hand with Eastern-influenced alternative and holistic healing modalities. Perhaps a bit ahead of its time,

I discussed and explored this vision in my 1995 book *In the House of the Moon: Reclaiming the Feminine Spirit of Healing* (retitled *Feminine Healing* as a paperback) with a plea for East and West to come together in the service of healing rather than propriety and greed. Nearly 20 years later, it is hopeful, at least, that alternative healing thrives in the West, though still not formally accepted and respected by the traditional professional medical community.

On my return from one of our weekend excursions, Lito informed me that we would be leaving the next day for another scuba diving trip to an even more remote island. I looked forward to the trip both for my love of diving as well as to embody all that had been happening and all that I was feeling. We stopped at his office on the way to his private plane, and while I waited for him to get his gear together, I remembered a teaching story where a sage guides Alexander the Great.

> *"Your kingdom is at stake. You say you are a king and have conquered most of the world; yet the more you conquer, the more you have to lose. I too am a king, and my kingdom is infinite. There is nothing you can take from me, and there is nothing left to lose."*

So says the sage to Alexander the Great. The more power you attain, the more diligently you must guard it. Reflecting on Lito's wealth, I realized that it is not the acquisition of possessions that is the problem, but the attachment and identification with those things we own. Though my family had built a successful business in the garment industry in New York, minor compared to Lito's family's fortune, the men in my family measured their success financially, giving them the allusion of power. Neither Lito nor I had any such allusions, rather seeking meaning through healing, reverence for all life, and conscious action.

Diving into the underwater world, held by the great ocean, in community with her creatures, calmed and soothed me and each dive opened my eyes to something wondrous that I carried with me to the surface. Nonetheless, when the time came, I was eager to return to the Black Nazarene and my healing practice with David and Helen. It dawned on me that the intense meditative concentration necessary while witnessing and then performing psychic surgery evoked a similar meditative quality as my diving, but the psychic surgery sparked with the element of fire while paradoxically my diving immersed me in the ever-flowing water.

Arriving back at the center, I found considerable commotion and what appeared to be an American television crew. Grinning, David greeted me and asked if I would explain psychic surgery to the producer. "We told them that you were the expert and could explain it better than we could," David cajoled.

The man in charge looked familiar and introduced himself as Sandy Baron from *AM, New York*, a popular radio talk show. I recognized him from having seen his face on television though he was now working in radio. We realized that we were both graduates of EST (Erhard Seminars Training) and shared our EST experiences in relation to psychic healing. He was spearheading a segment for his show on alternative healing, particularly psychic healing, and David and Helen had agreed to being filmed and interviewed.

I sat down with the crew and explained, admittedly in pseudo-scientific terms, the possible reasons for this phenomenon. I talked about the electromagnetic field of the human body, how the cells coalesce when their electrical charge magnetizes the cell wall causing them to adhere to one another.

"The pulse of life, the cellular pump," I heard myself say with authority, "is the dynamic interplay of sodium and potassium ions on the inside and outside of the cell wall. This dynamically causes positively and negatively charged particles to interact." Most of what appeared to be an impromptu explanation came from discussing such possibilities with a Russian physicist who had also witnessed psychic surgery. I went on to suggest that the electrical charge generated by the energy of the healer's hands changes the electrical potential of the cells. Rather than the cells meeting like magnets, this causes the cells to attract, thus changing the charge to a positive-positive field, where the cells repel or separate. This could explain why when the healer's hands are removed, the skin fuses and no scar can be detected. I told them I couldn't prove this theory but that my mind needed an explanation for what my hands seemed to feel. I acknowledged that officially at the Black Nazarene Center we shared our belief with our patients that divine energy takes over during these healings, and that we, as healers, simply allow the healing force to guide us.

As I concluded what I had to say, a few members of the crew volunteered for healings when the door suddenly opened and a couple from Australia came in. The man was in a wheelchair and had been paralyzed below the waist for the past several years. Medical science could not help him, and doctors had given him less than a year to live. They had come to the Philippines seeking healing.

Together we granted the television crew permission to film. We followed our usual practice: I moved to the man's head, placed my hands on his temples, and began to meditate, while David and Helen prayed. The camera rolled as David sliced his hand into the man's groin, separating muscle fibers and removing small fragments of tissue and bone. When he had finished on one side, he did the same on the other. While still on the table, Helen asked the man to move his legs, which he did, while his wife broke into tears. We helped him up, and asked if he could walk a few steps. He looked at us in awe and took ten steps on his own, his face aglow with delight and his wife beside herself with joy. The whole film crew applauded. I remember the distinct feeling of being where I belonged, being at home.

Encountering the Espiritista

A few weeks later, I heard about another healer in the Manila area named Alex Orbito, who also performed psychic surgery. I attended one of his healing sessions held in a church. When I arrived I asked two men standing outside where I might find him. "Come with us, and we will take you to him," the older man replied, introducing himself as Bishop Sison and the other man as Brother Carmello. "I trained Alex in the healing arts," Bishop Sison said. "We can train you as well." I told them I was there to only observe Alex Orbito work. Without further words, the two men guided me into the church.

Many people surrounded Alex, and others sat in pews waiting to be called for their healings. He looked up when we entered and acknowledged Bishop Sison,

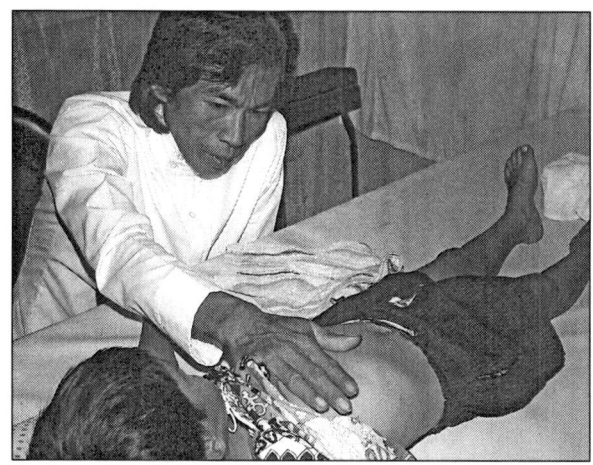

Brother Carmello, and me, smiled, and directed his full attention back to the person lying on the table. The two men encouraged me to watch closely and requested that I meet with them when I was ready.

Alex appeared to enter a trance state with each patient, his eyes rolling up in his head, his hands moving over the person's body. Suddenly his fingers would begin kneading the skin, usually on the abdomen, until one hand would disappear inside the belly, blood gushing forth. Like I'd seen David or Helen do many times now, he would extract a piece of tissue or bone fragment and remove his hands while an assistant poured water over the body and Alex's hands to wash away the blood. As I'd noticed repeatedly in sessions at the Black Nazarene Center, the patient would get up, radiant, thanking Alex profusely, before being gently escorted away to make space for the next patient.

After about 90 minutes of healings, Alex finished and came over to welcome me to the center. "So the Bishop has talked to you," he said matter of factly. "Welcome to the Espiritista. I know I'll be seeing you around." With that, he left, and I began to leave when I bumped into the Bishop and Brother Carmello again. I explained that I was already working with Helen and David and wanted to continue learning from them. The Bishop agreed not to press me further but suggested that I meet them on Sunday in two weeks in hope that I would change my mind.

I returned home in a fog. This group felt evangelical to me, exhibiting an overzealous Christianity that had repelled me in the past. I felt my loyalty deeply tested, and this awkward situation encouraged me to reflect upon my ego's quest for power. The energy in Alex Orbito's healing space had been rich and palpable, but it erupted disquiet in my heart. I meditated on this and realized that my encounters with the Espiritista lacked the energetic faith healing that I experienced at the Black Nazarene Center, and I also treasured my relationships with the Elisaldes.

The next morning I arrived early at the Black Nazarene Center to tell David and Helen about my experience, wanting to be transparent with my teachers who had become dear friends. They encouraged me to trust my heart. I sighed some relief as I prepared with them to leave for a healing day in the rural areas. We took off in David's brother's Jeep over rice paddies, into the mountains, stopping at various villages to perform healings along the way. As usual people welcomed and embraced us when we arrived and showered us with fresh eggs, vegetables,  and all the coins they could gather together to compensate us for their healings. Arriving back at Lito's late that night, my heart felt opened to the hilt, the spirit of healing as benediction. I felt proud to be part of David and Helen's team where healing was their gift to all who needed it, no matter rich or poor.

The following Saturday David, Helen, and I returned to the country to do healings in a province called Laguna, and especially to see a woman dying of cancer. After the healings we had lunch at David's brother's house in the village, sitting outdoors with, pigs, goats, chickens, and roosters, and dogs running amok, getting back late that night. On Sunday morning I returned to the Black Nazarene Center to work, and when we stepped out of the treatment room for lunch, our friend Prem, who'd gratefully introduced me to David and Helen, came running excitedly into the center. He had heard wind of a very powerful healer who was performing his healings in a church just outside of town, and wanted me to join him there. Prem and I left with Helen and David's blessing to see what this was all about.

When we reached the small church, and walked in, Brother Carmello was the amazing healer in question. My body tingled all over realizing that even though I had decided not to go further with the Espiritista work, here I was, in the church where I had agreed to meet Bishop Sison and Brother Carmello if I had decided to move forward. Brother Carmello called me to the front of the group where 40 or so Filipinos had gathered and asked me to sit in front of him. He entered a trance and began speaking in Tagalog, "The spirit wants to know how it can help Brother Jason." (Prem translated for me) "How can I help people more fully?" I asked. "You've already got the power; just learn to lose your mind," Brother Carmello channeled.

When the time came to begin the healings, Brother Carmello announced that I would be doing it! One by one people approached me, my body shaking as I laid my hand upon each patient. A man began to cry, claiming he was cured of a cataract. People reached out to touch me as my hands uncontrollably shook and vibrated.

After this synchronistically powerful experience, Bishop Sison repeatedly affirmed my healing power and nearly insisted that I accompany him to other provinces to perform healings. I refused. It was all too much, and I needed more time to process the intensity of what had been happening. I told him that I needed to honor my work with the Elisaldes, and that if I felt guided I would get back in touch with them.

Clearly impressed, Prem declared, "You really are a healer, Pare." (Pare is the Filipino word for "friend" or "brother," the abbreviation for "kumpadre.") Why didn't you go with them?" I told him that I realized great healing power had flowed through me that day, but I felt no connection to my heart. My ego pulled me back and forth and all I knew for sure was that I wanted to sleep. Prem drove me back to Lito's where I collapsed and slept until morning.

The next day I awakened with a strong urge to get to Black Nazarene early. When I reached the center, a small group of people had just arrived from Russia. David had already begun operating on an elderly man who was legally blind, when I entered the treatment room. He had pulled the man's eyeball up between his fingers and called me over, gesturing for me to hold up the man's eyelid so that he could release the pus. I followed David's instructions to the tee until he rested the eye again in its socket. Looking at the man's face I imagined how painful this must be, but he claimed he felt no pain, only deep peace. When David completed the healing, the man got up and looked at his wife, declaring, "I can see you! I can see you!!" Tears flowed all around, and again, I knew where I belonged, here in this place of heart.

Initiation into the Church of the Black Nazarene

After the blind man's healing and completing our day's work, I shared with David and Helen about my synchronistic experience upon meeting with Bishop Sison and Brother

Carmello the day before, and that I had performed an actual healing. Helen strongly expressed that she felt I was meant to join their healing team at the center, but the choice, she stressed, had to come from me. She and David agreed that they were willing and eager to give me more responsibility.

A few days later, David and Helen invited me out for dinner to discuss something important. They wanted to make me an official part of the Black Nazarene Healing Center, to ordain me as a minister so that I could perform healings in its name. They believed that Bishop Sison's invitation to join the Espiritista group was part of my initiation. Their invitation both touched me and boosted my confidence, and I had to make a choice.

The following week the annual Feast of the Black Nazarene took place, a processional celebration to honor a life-sized holy relic called the Black Nazarene. It depicts one of the Stations of

the Cross, Jesus carrying it on his shoulder on the way to Calvary. The Minor Basilica of the Black Nazarene, known as the Quiapo Church, is the statue's final resting place. David had named the center after this statue to which he often prayed for his patients.

Originally, the statue ostensibly portrayed a pure ivory Jesus, but was charred when aboard a ship during the Manila galleon expedition from Mexico, arriving in Manila from Acapulco in the first decade of the 1600s. An anonymous Mexican sculptor made The Black Nazarene, its name attributed to Nazareth, the place of Jesus's birth. The statue had survived unscathed, but its color had turned from white to black. Numerous scientific tests had proven that the black was not soot or ash, but an indiscernible process had created the permanent color change. People journey from far and wide to pray to this statue, and many miraculous cures have been attributed to it.

Once each year, the statue of the Black Nazarene is taken from the cathedral and pulled by huge, coarse ropes, some three inches thick, through the streets of Manila. My initiation began by taking part in this procession, attended by hundreds of thousands of Filipino men, women, and children across the Philippines who congregate in Quiapo, crowding the streets, singing and dancing. Pandemonium ensued as everyone tried to touch the moving statue with prayers for their loved ones. After touching or pulling the statue, numerous hands in the crowds lifted those blessed individuals, tossing them into the air. Others jumped from the statues and took their turns in the crowd.

Helen and David instructed me to push through the crowds, to take a position on one of the ropes, and to pull the statue. It seemed the most natural thing to do! People seemed to move out of the way to let me in, and, as I approached the rope, a man motioned for me to move in front of him, to grab the rope over my shoulder, and to pull with all of my strength. I became caught up in the fervor of the moment, and time stood still. After perhaps an hour, I realized that I had no idea where I was and, coming home to my body, felt an intense pain in my right shoulder. The rope had torn through my shirt and dug a deep, bloody wound. I passed the rope to another as if in relay and soon got lost in the crowd, endorphins apparently numbing my pain. I felt exhausted yet exhilarated by this experience, eventually finding a Jeepney going to Quezon City, knowing from there how to get back to Lito's house.

It was late at night by the time I arrived, and, when Lito saw my shoulder, he helped me wash the wound and dress it.

"Well, I guess you'll always have a reminder of your stay in my country!" Lito exclaimed, "Tomorrow we'll know if it needs stitches, but with curfew coming soon, let's get some sleep."

I slept soundly, and when I awoke the next morning, I went to the bathroom to look at my shoulder only to discover that it had totally healed, not the least mark of injury remained. When later in the day I shared this with Helen and David, both claimed to have had the same experience when they had pulled the statue. They congratulated me, and we hugged, the first part of my initiation behind me.

I realize today that such excitement as I experienced while pulling the rope through the streets in Quiapo would have released endorphins (endogenous morphine) that accounted for my numbness to pain, but the spontaneous healing? I was witnessing that every day at the time so it didn't seem out of the ordinary.

Having been in the Philippines for nearly three months, I had planned to meet Rupa in India soon, but knew that my work with David and Helen was unfinished. I wanted to go to India to spend a month with Rupa and come back to the Philippines but the costs were prohibitive. Rupa understood and postponed her trip to India for three months, when we agreed to meet there, however she did express her concern that I was perhaps bewitched and influenced by mind control. I understood her perspective, realizing I would question it if she had such experiences, but I trusted myself, felt grounded, sure that my study and participation with psychic surgery was much more profound and authentic than merely ego gratifying illusion.

Meanwhile, Helen began giving me lessons in "astral projection," assuming the subtle body, separate from the physical body, can travel outside of it. For example, within a meditative state two people can imagine a loved one and open to transmitting and receiving messages to one another. Each evening at 11:30 PM, either she would send an astral message to me, or I'd send one to her. The receiver was to open to a relaxed, receptive state, and the sender was to direct a message to the other. We wrote down what we thought we received or what we intended to send and the following morning we compared notes. We generated quite an "astral" dialogue, and within weeks we developed a keen sensitivity to each other's thoughts. One night I fell asleep before 11:30 and dreamed that I was on a large boat out at sea with many people onboard. In the dream, I felt pressure on my shoulder and turned to see Helen there laughing. It woke me up, and I wrote my impressions in my dream diary before going back to sleep. The next morning Helen chided that she hoped I wasn't upset with her for disturbing my dream. We enjoyed our connection and continued this practice for my remaining time in the Philippines.

Meeting Tony Agpaoa

Things had fallen into a nice rhythm: regularly working at the Black Nazarene Center, being given more and more responsibility for the magnetic healings as well as assisting with the psychic surgeries. Plus, I continued helping Lito lead meditations. He had a table built for me to offer Alexander sessions in his house so I could bolster my quickly dwindling resources!

The weekend following the rope pulling of the sacred statue for the Quiapo celebration, David and Helen took me to Baguio City, a mountainous resort, to visit some of their friends and to look up Tony Agpaoa whose work had drawn me to the Philippines in the first place.

The long bus trip from Manila to Baguio City gave me time to meditate and rest. When we arrived in the early evening and stepped off the bus, my lungs expanded, breathing in the sweet, crisp mountain air. The setting sun painted a palette of color across the sky against the mountainous background. David and Helen had arranged our lodging with their friends, and we hopped a Jeepney the few miles to their house.

The community of healers in Baguio is well known. Tony Agpaoa's center was located there at his Diplomat Hotel, but he was only one among many healers, including one of David's brothers who had formerly worked with Tony.

At dinner that evening David's brother complained that Tony had fired him, and suggested that Tony's self-importance may be interfering with his healing. He shared that The Amazing Randi, a professional debunker, ostensibly hired by the government, had observed Tony during a psychic surgery and debunked what he witnessed as deception. (The Australian government called in the same professional debunker years later when Helen and David journeyed to Australia to do healing in her homeland.)

David's brother feared that such publicity could be very disturbing to those who made healing pilgrimages to Baguio and could hit the economy hard if such a rumor spread. He wanted David to connect with Tony in an effort to determine how he felt about the poisoned publicity and what he planned to do about it. David arranged to have lunch the following day at Tony's place. The threat of "debunkers" stung. I loved these people and trusted their integrity even if their ancient healing practices may not pass the scrutiny of modern science. Could science measure the power of energy and faith?

We arrived at The Diplomat at the appointed time, but Tony was still in surgery. Tony invited us into the operating room to observe his final few operations for the morning. After the last patient left and I properly introduced myself, Tony gave me a tour of "the center." In the waiting room area, just outside the operating theater, colorful Biblical scenes and others from Tony's life were painted on the walls. One of the walls contained a viewing window so that family members or other permitted observers could watch Tony or his assistants at work. I remember thinking how egotistical it seemed to see Tony portrayed as a saint in these scenes. The healing environment in Manila was much less pretentious. Soon, Tony ushered me into the house where we met Helen, David, and Tony's wife and sat down to lunch.

We all relaxed over the good food and company, and, to my relief, the conversations stayed light and superficial. Even Tony relaxed and I caught a glimpse of the earnest Tony before his notoriety. He complained that his life had become very stressful, that everyone was watching him, waiting for him to make a mistake, and the constant pressure had taken its toll on him. He remembered much happier days when he'd run a center similar to the Black Nazarene when all that mattered was the healing.

After a brief pause, as if he too was absorbing what he had just told us, Tony turned directly to me and asked what had "called" me to the Philippines. I shared my passion, in general, for healing practices, mentioning how I had come upon *Wonder Healers of the Philippines,* wanting to journey to the Philippines ever since. He seemed most interested in my teaching Rajneesh's meditation techniques and asked me to stay for the summer and offer meditation classes at his Diplomat Hotel. He also offered to instruct me with healing. I thanked him but explained that I was happily working with Helen and David and planned to be in India by the summer.

As we bid goodbye, I realized that I had met Tony Agpaoa for the first and last time. Declining his invitation came naturally to me, as if on a guided path. Part of me mourned leaving Baguio, and I felt sadness for Tony's current plight, acknowledging his innate healing capabilities, but I felt grounded in my decision.

It struck me during this time that all the healers that I'd come in contact with smoked, myself included. It was uncanny that immediately after our healing sessions, we would go outside and light up our cigarettes! Reflecting upon this, it occurred to me how a healer must surrender to powerful energy channels in a healing room, opening their bodies to incredibly strong energetic currents between patient and healer. After a healing, my whole body would be buzzing with energy streaming through me. Perhaps we all smoked, I thought, to ground us, to pull the etheric energy back to earth. I sensed that other healers felt the same even though I had not heard them speak about it. (Today I regard smoking as toxic, but it remains a grounding gesture.)

The Initiation Stations of Mount Banahaw

A few weeks later David and Helen advised me that my final initiation would be a journey to Mount Banahaw, a holy mountain and active volcano in Luzon, where many Filipinos sought spiritual initiation. With David and Helen's blessing Lito joined me for this initiation, and we drove south for many hours to Quezon province, then followed dirt roads until Mount Banahaw soon

appeared in the distance surrounded by mist. The car struggled up the mountainous roads made of tiny stones and broken coconut shells. At last we parked and walked another mile to a hut, the guide's house, where we had dinner with our guide and two other initiates. He explained that we would depart at five in the morning for the two-day hike to the summit of the holy mountain, informing us that the previous week's typhoon had swept through and the clear skies suggested a good omen for our hike.

At sunrise, our guide awakened us for a small breakfast

and a cup of coffee. We learned that the base of Mount Banahaw is famous for its coffee beans. Lito and I had noticed that in the little villages that we had passed near the base of the mountain, coffee beans lay on blankets drying in the sun on the side of the road. We packed our backpacks with water, snacks, and a blanket.

Our guide led us up the mountain toward the summit and explained that we would pass certain "stations," that would determine if we could go further. I was most grateful to have Lito to translate for me. After about four or five hours of hiking, we reached the first "station," a waterfall. The guide instructed us to stand under the falls to dispel evil energy. He would then determine if we were cleansed well enough to move to the next "station." We stood directly under the falling water and had been told to pray or meditate. I felt cold at first, questioning what the hell I was doing there, but within moments my mind emptied, and a great peace came over me.

Our guide passed us through this station while explaining that during World War II the Japanese had invaded the Philippines and many soldiers had retreated to Mount Banahaw to hide from the American and Philippine forces, but the native people had no fear, for they wholeheartedly believed in the mountain's power to protect them and drive the Japanese army mad. Many years after the war, Japanese survivors were found insane, speaking gibberish. Our guide iterated that those who are not true to themselves could not withstand the energy of the holy mountain. This, he said, was why we must prove our worthiness to proceed toward the summit.

After a bite to eat and quenching our thirst we continued up the mountain until we reached the second "station," a labyrinth through the stones that we must crawl through, much like in a cave. Lito translated this station to mean "justice" or "enforcer of karmic debt." The guide iterated that if one is not true of spirit, the stones would close in on such an individual and crush him; only those true of spirit come out the other side.

His words frightened me, my mind screaming, "but I'm so much bigger than most Filipino men. How can I possibly fit through such tight passageways? Overriding myself, I squeezed in and began to crawl on my belly, my heart pounding in my chest, imagining as I inched along that the rocks were closing in on me. When the fear took hold, I would stop and calmly focus on my breath, relaxing further with each one. When I'd recovered my wits, I continued inching along. It took close to 45 minutes to crawl through the labyrinthine passages, the longest 45 minutes of my life, but when I emerged out the other side, Lito greeted me with a bear hug.

We camped underneath the rocks, the stars dazzling above us, bright in the sky. One hundred miles from the nearest electrical outlet, we experienced total darkness, illuminated only by the stars and half moon. When we awakened we ate fruit and drank plenty of water before continuing our climb to the top.

At another short break for water, I sat on a rock, feeling at peace within and with the world around me, the summit not far ahead, the sky blue with wispy clouds. Meditating on the beauty surrounding me, suddenly I saw a big black bird soaring through the sky, flying in my direction. "Is this real or a vision?" I asked myself, as the bird soared with wings outstretched, heading directly for me. I shook my head, blinked my eyes, and the bird was gone—another visitation from the Black Bird.

My heart

pounded as we continued up the mountain for the last mile or two, until we reached the summit. My awareness quickened as we stood amidst the stones where seven trees stood. With Lito's translation help I understood that, according to our guide, this stand of trees at the summit of Mount Banahaw represented "Surrender." Only the tree in the center stood upright, while the other six, bent by the continuous summit winds, leaned toward the one in the middle, resembling six seekers bowing down to their master. I wondered about its origin and its relation to Christ and his disciples as well as rituals existing before Christ's time. I also marveled at my experiences since arriving in the Philippines, especially my apprenticeship with the Elisaldes and my exposure to psychic surgery. "How could it all be real? I asked myself at the top of the mountain, my initiation near complete. "You saw it with your own eyes!" I answered. Admiring the stand of trees before me, the seekers before their master, an inner voice whispered, "Surrender!"

Snapped out of my reverie, I heard our guide speak, pointing to a plant Lito called "the plant of the heavenly father" or "the forever plant," that the guide said grew only on this holy mountain. Legend endowed it with healing energies, he told us, and, when picked and dried, it shriveled up into a small ball, but when placed in hot water, it expanded and turned dark green, looking just as it did when first picked. The guide stressed that the plant could be used over and over again, for it never lost its power. I took a few of these plants with me and used them sparingly for many years.

The hike down the mountain unfolded seamlessly. Too late to leave that evening, we slept the night in the guide's hut and traveled back to Manila the next morning.

We had a party at the Elisaldes' home in my honor where

they initiated me as a minister of the Black Nazarene Healing Center. They invited Lito and our friends from his meditation center as well as their friends and family. The initiation ceremony was subdued. David and Helen presented me with a certificate and also a ring with an eye in a pyramid, which all Black Nazarene healers wore. We then celebrated in the main house with food and beer.

That day I met a woman named Leena who I had briefly encountered at the center a few months before. An Australian acupuncturist and black belt in Kung Fu, she lived in Hong Kong, where she'd moved to further her Kung Fu studies near her master. Over time she'd developed an interest in acupuncture and Chinese herbal medicine and currently studied with a master in Hong Kong.

She had come to the Philippines for a week to work with David and Helen and to visit some friends. We felt a deep connection and spent every evening together for the remainder of her stay. Before leaving for Hong Kong, she invited me to visit her en route to India. Aware that my journey's focus was on learning all that I could about healing practices, I asked if her Chinese medicine and acupuncture teacher would consider allowing me to attend some of their sessions. She said she would ask him and write me his response promptly, knowing that I would be leaving the Philippines in a short month and must book the next leg of my journey. Within a week Leena's letter came with news that her teacher would allow me to observe and learn with him for a few weeks while I was in Hong Kong. We agreed that I would stay with her.

Shortly before leaving the Philippines, David and Helen invited me to meet an Australian friend, Peter Calarco, who would be sponsoring them in Australia and opening a healing center where they could work. Five years prior, he had been stricken with an inoperable, malignant brain tumor, and Western doctors had rendered him terminal. As a last resort he had come to the Philippines for healings with David and Helen and been cured. Back in Australia doctors found no trace of the brain tumor. After this miracle, Peter swore to devote his life to healing and opening an Australian Black Nazarene Healing Center. Now that I had been initiated as a full member of the Black Nazarene team, Peter wanted to meet me before he returned to Australia.

He was a dear man, humble and sweet. David and Helen had told him that I was on my way to India but he wanted to include me in any future plans for the healing center in Australia and offered to purchase my ticket from Bombay to Australia when the time was right. I thanked him profusely but told him that I could not make such a commitment at that moment. Part of me wanted to stay with my new family forever and drop all other intended plans. I had never felt so nourished, fully acknowledged for my gifts, for who I was, but I also felt I must continue to follow my quest.

Shortly before my departure, having shared a lot with David and Helen about Rajneesh and meditating with them both, we took photos to send to Bhagwan. He very soon responded with their *sannyas* names. This deepened our connection even more especially since we would soon part.

A flurry of activity marked my final two weeks in the Philippines. I was working at the healing center, leading groups, and facilitating meditations at the meditation center, while also running about Manila struggling through the bureaucratic red tape involved in getting an exit visa. At the end of such a long day with nothing but a handful of forms to show for it, David laughed and said, "You should know better than to do this by yourself. I know many people at the Bureau. I'll go with you tomorrow and get this taken care of." True to his word, the next day, within an hour, I had all my required paperwork signed, sealed, and delivered. David and I celebrated over a few beers but it was tinged with sadness, knowing I would be leaving so soon.

To my great surprise, just before I left, Helen gave me her Egyptian healing ring, the one I had noticed the very first day that I saw her work, "to keep our connection strong," she told me.

When our final goodbyes came at the airport, where all of those closest to me gathered, I felt great sadness and joy simultaneously, with such love. I felt sure we would work and practice together again and this was merely the closure of a chapter. My last memory of that day is of Helen, David, some of his family, Lito and some of our friends from the meditation center, all hugging and laughing as I entered the terminal for my flight to Hong Kong.

* * *

Flying to Hong Kong to meet Leena felt essentially inauthentic. No doubt the chance to better familiarize myself with Chinese medicine would offer me more knowledge and experience but I was most interested in pursuing the infatuation. Leena greeted me warmly at the Hong Kong airport and we took a bus to her neighborhood where she had a small apartment. We spoke with enthusiasm on the ride about our love for the Philippines, particularly about David and Helen and the possibility of creating a center in Australia which, being an Aussie, excited Leena immensely. When silence moved between us, she intuited my preoccupied thoughts of Rupa and what lay ahead for me in India, and the chemistry between us simply wasn't the same.

The next day Leena introduced me to Dr. Shen. He instructed us to go to a nearby Chinese medical store and to purchase specific acupuncture books in English. He also presented me with needles and an orange. With Leena translating, Dr. Shen told me to needle the orange for hours each day until it felt smooth and easy, displaying the correct finger positions as he demonstrated his needling technique.

Leena purchased some supplies that she needed and bought me the books that Dr. Shen had recommended, along with a standing acupuncture model, with all the points and meridians visible, and a battery-powered machine that, when attached to needles, provided both a point finder and a point stimulator. Back at her apartment she showed me how to operate the equipment and generously treated me for a bad cold that I was fighting.

When Leena was working or studying martial arts, I'd walk through Hong Kong, needling my orange, seeking out a few Buddhist temples while ambling along and also window shopping. Soon with Leena's translating help, I became Dr. Shen's gofer: I'd remove one patient's needles at the prescribed time while he worked on another patient in the next room. He would explain that when a patient is too hot, a cool-down treatment is necessary to extract toxic fire; when deficient in *chi*, and perhaps suffering from asthma, a patient needs lung and kidney support. Leena could not have been a more congenial and tolerant translator and I certainly learned valuable basic information about the underlying theories of traditional Chinese medicine. Dr. Shen, however, held no magic for me, no true healing energy like I'd experienced with Rolling Thunder or the Elisaldes. Though his instruction nourished a seed planted years earlier when working with Sidney Zerinsky in New York

City, I needed more time to move beyond my needle phobia and embrace the overarching benefits of acupuncture to the body's natural ability to heal, a seed that would mature much later when I earnestly began and completed my acupuncture training.

Before leaving Hong Kong, I received a letter from Rupa in India. She couldn't wait to see me, but her letter's primary purpose was to tell me of a gravely ill young woman at the ashram. Rupa had shared with people close to this woman of my encounters with psychic surgery in the Philippines giving them hope that perhaps I could heal her. Hearing this both excited and disturbed me.

17

Reflections on the Threshold

"They are playing a game. I see that they are playing a game. If I show them I see that they are playing a game, I break the rules and they punish me. Therefore I must play the game of not seeing I see the game."
—R. D. Laing from *Knots*

My experiences in the Philippines had a profound impact on me. I had witnessed multiple healings, experienced healings myself, apprenticed with healers across disciplines, and, perhaps, could call myself a healer. I had the experience, the commitment, and an ongoing desire to learn more about what called me.

My conscience, however, plagued me with ambivalence. Consciously, I knew that the ego could not rule a healing journey. Such was sacred. I'd read and become aware that the spiritual ego could present more of a problem than the material ego. For instance, people driven by money and the desire for power often reveal who they are through their arrogance, condescending talk, and attitude of entitlement. A spiritual ego, however, can present as a lack of ego, renouncing possessions, claiming no special healing power. If only posturing, such false modesty can become a form of spiritual materialism and manifest a superior, unconsciously destructive ego that reminds me of this teaching story:

> *One day a rabbi, in a frenzy of religious passion, rushed in before the ark, fell to his knees, and started beating his breast, crying, "I'm nobody! I'm nobody!"*
>
> *The cantor of the synagogue, impressed by this example of spiritual humility, joined the rabbi on his knees, "I'm nobody! I'm nobody!"*
>
> *The shamus (custodian), watching from the corner, couldn't restrain himself either. He joined the other two on his knees, calling out, "I'm nobody! I'm nobody!"*
>
> *At which point the rabbi, nudging the cantor with his elbow, pointed at the custodian and said, "Look who thinks he's nobody!"*
>
> —Stories from the Spirit, Stories from the Heart, edited by Christina Feldman and Jack Kornfield

Rupa's mention of my reputation as a healer and the expectations of my ability to heal this sick woman in India triggered my spiritual ego. I liked being called a healer. Thankfully I was conscious enough to realize it. It wasn't the first time I'd witnessed my spiritual pride emerge in a meditative state or when aware of my lack of attachments. These thoughts occupied me during the entire flight from Hong Kong to India.

I swung from conscious awareness to unconscious gloating over my experiences in the Philippines as "healer." Anxiety enveloped me. I had been humbly living my most profound learning in the Philippines: the difference between healing from power or healing by channeling love and acceptance, and I could not ignore this very split within myself.

* * *

"Everyone thinks that his things are not like all the things in the world. And that is why everyone keeps them."
—Antonio Porchia from *Voices*

The memory of All Soul's Day with the Elisalde family lingered: their total acceptance and simple joy and humility touched me deeply. All their family members accepted one another and I sensed no judgments like those I had experienced at my own family's gatherings. The Elisalde ancestors had mostly been healers for as long as anyone could remember, but also farmers and priests. Remembering the tone of their conversations one individual's service was no more respected than another's.

In comparison, it seemed the reverse was true in my family where respect is tied to material success and equals power. I thought back on my youth, how angry I could get over what I saw as superficial concerns. My family kept alive all of the traditions passed down from generations past—the Sephardic food every Friday night to bring in the Sabbath, the keeping of all Jewish holidays—yet I felt an absence of substance and deeper meaning. The rituals seemed empty to me and I could not relate to them. The Sephardic family heritage bonded them, gave them identity, and fostered their loyalty to each other, but I could not find my place in their bond.

A teaching story called The Guru's Cat comes to mind:

> When the guru sat down to worship each evening the ashram cat would get in the way and distract the worshippers. So he ordered that the cat be tied during evening worship.
>
> After the guru died, the cat continued to be tied during evening worship. And when the cat expired, another cat was brought to the ashram so that it could be duly tied during evening worship.

Centuries later learned treatises were written by the guru's scholarly disciples on the liturgical significance of tying up a cat while worship is performed.

—Anthony de Mello, from *The Song of the Bird*

When I remember my feelings as a boy and teenager, I feel the edge of another split, a magnified confusion between, on one hand, my repulsion for my family's inability to embody their words and traditions, and, on another, jealousy that they revered rituals that allowed them to feel that they belonged and felt connected. Years of intense and dedicated therapy helped me through my anger where I could learn to appreciate my family as they are, no better or worse than me. But it was their game I could not play.

My siblings and our extended family of Greek/Turkish Sephardic Jews all continued the businesses that their fathers and grandfathers had created for them. They believed that this afforded the younger generation a good living and also the glue to keep the clan together. I couldn't live up to these expectations. I had to acknowledge to myself that if I didn't play their game, I would be excluded from playing with them at all.

* * *

On the flight to India over a dark ocean, I realized that I had indeed changed. I thought of all the dear people who had come so deeply into my heart during the over six months in the Philippines, I had gained a new family based on understanding and acceptance as opposed to my family of origin, which as a whole, would never understand and accept the life I'd chosen. In their eyes I would forever be a failure. Tears welled up with the sadness of this awareness, how I had longed for their acceptance, how I would love to share with them some of what I'd learned, but their way was not mine. Thankfully both my mother and my sister had assured me that they appreciated my courage to seek a spiritual path, to find my own way, and, perhaps, I smiled, one day they would experience it for themselves.

Awed by the rituals I had experienced with the Elisaldes on All Soul's, I realized that our family had rituals too, perhaps not spiritual, but they reconnected us with our honorable heritage and invited us to acknowledge our gratitude to our ancestors for the life they gave us. I asked myself, "What have I received from my ancestors?" The gift I received from my father has become more visible to me in later life. I will always be grateful to him for teaching me to be responsible. He taught me through his example to be dedicated to supporting one's family. My mother gave me empathy, optimism, and a good sense of humor. And, of course, my grandmother and, particularly my great grandmother, gave me my healing roots. These women had not been particularly remembered or valued by the new leaders of the clan, but they live on within me.

With this relieved thought, the next caught me in an anxious grip thinking, "so much for not living up to my family's expectations, how could I possibly live up to the expectations of those waiting on my arrival in India, to *heal* the beloved girl?" My nerves braced with a familiar, old fear: if I identified with being a healer then I could fail, just as when growing up, if I identified with my family and their values, I could fail. The next thought released me like an outgoing wave. I realized that if I could stop identifying with failure, failure might have something to teach me. I heard an inner voice say, "I am that I am," a line from the Bible that's stayed with me throughout my life. God responded with these words when Moses approached the burning bush and asked Him under whose authority he must demand the freedom from the slaves' bondage in Egypt, "I am that I am," God said, "Tell them I am sent you."

I interpret "I am," as one's inner knowing, and connectedness to Being, not that I am this or I am that—a healer, a teacher, a carpenter, but rather "I am" because I exist. Reconnecting with this state of *being* rather than *doing*, my feelings of inadequacy dissolved. My summers at Esalen and years of practicing meditation had given me the tools to connect with the Oneness of Being, and flying toward my future I felt the practicality of this awareness. Smiling, I said to myself, "I have nothing to prove," as my ears popped on our descent into Bombay.

18

Vipassana

*"No matter how much power you have, you can't force healing.
All factors have to come together at the right place and time. Never do
anything out of ego or pushiness. What is needed most in healing work is
humility before the power of the Great Spirit."*

—Rolling Thunder from *Rolling Thunder Speaks*, edited by Carmen Sun Rising Pope,
Rolling Thunder's wife

Much more crowded than only a few years before and overflowing with chaos, I still felt remarkably at home in the Bombay Airport. I beamed, remembering how much I enjoyed playing the games of India: bargaining with everyone, the myriad of offers purveyed—from drugs to women. If they looked into my eyes, they would see that I too enjoyed their play. The familiar array of sounds and scents assaulted my senses—the pungent odor of incense and spices intermingled with the sour smell of human excrement. But Bombay was not my destination, rather Pune, a hill station, a six-hour taxi ride away.

After passing seamlessly through Customs, I made a beeline for the taxi stand, resisting the onslaught of the hackers, and found a taxi driver willing to take me the distance to Poona. He was happy to pick up a "big" fare and perked up even more when I told him I was on my way to Rajneesh Ashram.

"I know the *acharya* (teacher) and have visited him when he lived in Bombay. We miss him here, and also the cab fares!"

Rajneesh had a reputation as a spiritual renegade, for although he embraced many of the trappings of Hindu culture his fundamental message was that true religious experience could be attained through the structures of most any religion (prayer, meditation, sacred song, and so on). His discourses made clear that he believed no religion could claim exclusivity, in fact, that the concept of exclusivity became a detriment toward the experience of spirituality.

"My friends sometimes judge me," my driver went on, "but I would often attend his discourses. I do feel that he is an enlightened master."

He talked with me about how religions become deadened when the master dies and ritual replaces the uncertainty that living with a master ensures.

"If Jesus were alive today, the church would again crucify him!"

We continued our conversation or I should say I listened to every word he said as we began our ascent up the mountain. He had thrown a few rupees at the roadside temple as we began our climb, and when I asked him why, since I saw that all the passing cars and trucks were doing the same, the driver simply said, "you'll understand shortly," and soon I did.

The trucks on both sides of the road came ominously close to the edges of the road with sharp drops into the abyss below. The bullock-drawn wagons crept along, inching up, as cars and trucks passed them barely getting back in line without a head-on collision. I could hardly breathe, my heart in my stomach for what seemed like hours, until finally we reached the other side when once again all the cars and trucks threw rupees in the temple tray, thanking Rama and Krishna for safe passage. Once we were over the pass and my driver was quiet, my mind returned to what awaited me just a few hours ahead in Poona. My friend Mukta had helped to purchase the homes within which the ashram now functioned and, according to friends, a few hundred people were now working and living in this spiritual community, quite a leap from its humble beginnings in Bombay not so long ago. Many of the friends I'd made during my first visit to Bombay now lived at the new ashram. It would be wonderful to see them, I smiled to myself... and Rupa. I had allotted three months in Poona to recharge and to deepen my meditation practice, and then I wasn't sure—Australia, New York, Taos? I closed my eyes to bring the excited energy out of my head and into my belly, focusing on the *dantian* point, the center of the body's gravity, just below the navel, the body's inner energy pump.

My driver respected my need for silence and we drove peacefully through the streets of Poona, a deep calm within the taxi, despite the teeming life that filled the streets. We continued into a suburban area of old British-style homes coming to a stop in front of a large marble gate, the entrance to the Rajneesh Ashram. I paid the driver his fee, embraced him, and he drove off.

A few old friends standing at the gate recognized me and we ran toward each other and embraced. Tears overflowed and I felt home again, home being wherever we feel whole and complete. Wondering where Rupa was, I asked a friend who said she was in the ashram anxiously awaiting my arrival. Glancing through the gate, I heard a shriek of delight as Rupa ran toward me and I toward her into a massive embrace. Yes, home!

After many hugs and small talk Rupa took me to the flat that she had sublet for us, only a few blocks from the ashram. I looked forward to refreshing myself, taking a bath, but first we simply lay down together . . . and wept.

Soon after my bath, Rupa shared that we would be expected at the ashram and that people would be gathering in anticipation, hoping, praying that I could help their beloved Vipassana heal. (I learned that Vipassana means "insight into the true nature of reality.") The sick young woman, Rupa explained, was a Dutch devotee of Rajneesh who had been living at the ashram with her twin brother Viyogi. They were 24 years old. She had been having terrible headaches and dizziness and after a seizure had been rushed to the emergency room, where it was determined that she had a brain tumor. Doctors attempted surgery, but when they opened her skull, they quickly determined it was too late: the cancer had spread throughout her brain, and become inoperable. Vipassana now lay in hospital in a coma.

Though the images and smells awakened all of my senses as Rupa and I walked to the ashram later that evening, I felt a bit anxious about the expectations awaiting us. Multicolored saris created a sea of mutating color, titillating scents rose from sidewalk vendors selling bananas, *bidis* (small Indian cigarettes), *chana* (roasted chickpeas), and *pan* (herbal concoctions for chewing but not swallowing). The cooking aromas wafting too through the air mixed with a myriad of incense, from sweet to strong. Passing houses and flats, bullock carts and bicycles, goats and chickens, the sun began to set and the air became chilly as we approached the ashram. Gooseflesh emerged across my arms. A multitude of birds, every size and color, flitted and flew about before settling in for the night. Suddenly a hawk zeroed in on what I assumed was a rat, but it came straight toward me, so close I had to swerve to avoid contact. For a brief moment, I chuckled to myself, "my Black Bird has returned," but as I entered the ashram gates, my heart beat faster.

Pleading eyes looked through me as we approached. I arranged for Vipassana's friends and family to meet in her room at the ashram at eight PM that evening. Together, I stressed, we would do a healing ceremony for her. From both exhaustion and exhilaration, my body and mind soared with electricity—my travels, my welcome, and my daunting task at hand.

News had spread through the ashram that a new healer was coming (me!) and all of Vipassana's friends and relatives at the ashram gathered in her room, though she lay in the hospital. Entering the room many eyes latched upon mine, their gaze pleading, "Can you heal her?" "Will she be all right?" These aching faces of Vipassana's dearest friends and family, *sannyassins* wrapped in a sea of orange flowing robes, projected "healer" on to me. I introduced myself and hugged those whom I knew before explaining to the group of at least 40 people that our loving energy could support Vipassana's ability to heal her self. I shared that sending love and energy does not require the physical presence of those we are supporting, that Vipassana's energy permeated this space and we could connect to her from here.

I gestured for us to form a circle and join hands, and, for a few moments, to envision Vipassana—her voice, her laughter, her energy—and to allow her presence to penetrate each individual heart with the intention of our loving energy reaching into her.

To bring the vibrations to a higher octave, I invited the group to chant the sacred syllable "Om" with each exhale. Our voices rose in simultaneous harmony, intensifying the energy. When it had reached a crescendo, I asked the group to release their hands and to place them in front of them with palms up and to direct their love into Vipassana.

As I did the same, an intense, overwhelming pain filled my head, as if it would burst open. I had never felt such before and attempted to release the pain with my breath and again envision Vipassana, transmitting my thoughts of love and healing towards her. Again the intense pain in my head prevented me from communing with her.

As others completed their offering and slowly exited, exchanging hugs on the way out, I realized that I was drained. Thankfully her friends and family seemed content that they had contributed something toward Vipassana's healing, but I left with a deep sense of confusion and frustration.

Rupa and I walked back to our flat together. I expressed how I felt, and she attempted to console me, believing that those present had left content. This had never happened before. I'd performed multiple healings in the Philippines and even prior to my experiences with psychic surgery. I had also done many distant healings, but in neither case ever reacted with physical pain or discomfort. I was determined to go to the hospital the next day to give Vipassana a hands-on healing.

Happy to be back at the ashram and recommitted to my meditation practice, I woke up early, full of energy and enthusiasm. Rupa and I did our silent meditations together before leaving for the ashram and Bhagwan's daily discourse. Every morning we sat for two hours before Rajneesh and listened to his wise and insightful lectures on various subjects that included Hassidic stories, Zen parables, Sufi stories, and Christian mystical writings. His words were enlightening, but it was the silence between his words that struck me as more profound, for Bhagwan exuded an incredible aura of joy and serenity. As I left the lecture hall that morning, the ambiguous combination of elation and trepidation that I'd felt before the healing ceremony in Vipassana's room now returned as I imagined what awaited me at the hospital by Vipassana'a side. I left the ashram gates and took a rickshaw to the hospital.

Upon entering the small hospital by Indian standards but quite inadequate in Western context, people seemed to anticipate where I was going and simply pointed the way. In Vipassana's room a man with long black hair, who I soon learned was Vipassana's twin brother, Viyogi, repeatedly pushed down on a manual respirator that provided his sister's breathing. I introduced myself and shared what had happened the evening before. He had heard about the healing and knew who I was. Viyogi was grateful for whatever support I could provide. He began to explain about Vipassana's condition but I gestured that I understood and suggested that we go to her bedside. He nodded.

I stood by her side, the sounds of medical monitors beeping in the background and the hiss of air pumping into her lungs. I closed my eyes and entered my familiar healing trance. I directed my full attention to Vipassana, sending love and energy through my hands. As I felt the force move through my body and into hers, the same excruciating head pain ensued. I attempted to fight it and found myself forcing the energy through. A voice came to me loud and clear, "Leave me alone, I'm not going back, it hurts too much!"

"You can do it; you can fight it," I responded silently. Again I heard what I believed to be Vipassana's voice, "No, leave me alone." (We seemed to meet in the silence, outside of her body.) I trusted her message and left the room, breaking down as I sat on the floor just outside her door, before soon realizing that I got such a headache because I was attempting to heal a vacant body. She had already passed over and merely hovered somewhere in the room. Who did I think I was to make such a demand on this dear soul? I hugged Viyogi goodbye and slowly, more humbly, walked back to the ashram. (I imagine that David Elisalde felt a similar way when his wife was lost to him.) The experience left me shaken, and changed, for in all the years I'd been experimenting with healing and energy transfer, I'd never personally confronted this truth: it is not *my* will but *Thy* will be done.

Back at the ashram word had spread that Bhagwan would give a talk in honor of Vipassana that afternoon in his garden. People already streamed in, and I joined them. Rajneesh emerged and took his seat to begin his lecture:

"Go sit by the side of Vipassana—feel death. Don't feel sorry for her! If you feel sorry for her, you miss the whole point: you miss a great opportunity, a great door. Don't feel sorry for her: there is no need, she is perfectly beautiful. She is leaving this world with something gained inside… And that's beautiful when one is ready to die, because one is ready to die only when one has come to feel something beyond death, never before."

By reminding us, most in our twenties, that we thought we were too young to die, and that by identifying with her, refusing to let her go, we were missing a great opportunity. Rajneesh told us that Vipassana had already made her choice and that we must accept the gift that she has bestowed upon us all.

"Let her go, and you can receive her gift," he said, emphasizing that it was not our fear of her dying that had called us to save her, but the fear of our own death. "You must learn to surrender to the divine and let the light in," he added.

I understood this to mean that when someone is preparing to move beyond the body, a door opens to the divine. When someone tries to keep the dying in their body, the "healer" or beloved cannot receive the gift from the dying one, a glimpse of the beyond, and "insistence upon saving *her* is preventing *you* from receiving her gift." I felt as if Rajneesh was speaking directly to me in his discourse.

Tears fell everywhere.

As I walked back to the hospital I wondered how Viyogi would respond, what he would choose to do. When I reached her hospital room, many *sannyassins* (disciples) had already congregated to pay their last respects. Viyogi, knowing that no option remained, deflated the respiration bag for the last time— no struggle, only gurgling, and a deep exhalation. An explosion of light suddenly filled the room. It seemed to permeate all of us, and we shared a deep sense of benediction. She had indeed passed into the light and gifted us with a momentary glimpse of the beyond.

All were invited to participate in the funeral the following day, including the children who were not typically included in such rites. Vipassana's body was adorned with colorful flowers and carried through the streets of Poona, with a huge procession, singing and chanting all the way to the river and the funeral *ghats* (steps) to the riverbank. We were reminded that this was a celebration in her honor, and that to truly honor Vipassana's spirit one should act in accordance with what she would have wished. In her honor many sang her favorite songs and danced around her body en route to the water's edge, her body's final resting place, while others cried, grieving the loss of her physical body.

Indian culture believes death is a transitional period, a time to surrender one's attachment to the physical plane. The funeral pyre ensures detachment from the physical body for both the friends and relatives who witness it as well as for the deceased herself. It is especially difficult to bear when a young person dies, without time to prepare, to acknowledge that each of us will enter the unknown and return to spirit, the source of our being. The burning of the body also calls the spirit to free itself from the bonds of the physical body.

Her body was placed upon the *ghat*, with firewood piled all around her. Hundreds of people, mostly disciples dressed in saffron colors, began to dance around her, making circles and

singing joyously. As the energy continued to mount and more people, young and old, joined in the celebration, I saw a sea of orange and yellow colors merging into a moving, flowing form blurring around her body. A voice beckoned for the singing to cease for the moment as prayers were chanted, and Viyogi and his family ignited the wood and branches. The colors of the flames slowly grew into vibrant warm hues, blending with the flowing red, orange, and yellow robes of the dancers. Soon the singing accelerated again. Tears flew everywhere—tears of joy, tears of grief, tears of great release. As customarily reserved for the closest family member, the custodians of the burning *ghats*, who orchestrate the events at the funeral, asked Vipassana's twin brother to perform the final act of detachment—to crush the beloved's skull, both a practical and metaphysical gesture. Practically it releases the pressure accumulated from the excessive heat of the flames to prevent its bursting and send bone fragments flying. Metaphysically it represents the final detachment, the body a temporary home for the spirit. Tears streamed down Viyogi's face as he lifted the iron rod, hesitated for a moment, a look of deep reflection in his eyes, before crushing Vipassana's skull freeing her to move into her next incarnation.

This was the first time that many witnessed this final leaving of the world, and it left them profoundly moved. Slowly the music and dancing resumed as people slowly exited the funeral grounds. Walking back to our flat I knew that my healing approach would never be the same, deeply acknowledging that we are but conduits for a force that defies reason and awakens our humility.

As the Sufi saying so appropriately communicates, "Trust in God, but tether your camel first!"

I learned through the pain of Vipassana's passing that we can do what can be done to promote healing, but we must remain humble. I thought of Jesus during his final moment of doubt on the cross, "Father, Father, why hast thou forsaken me?" he asks, as if incredulous that after all his good work, why has God allowed such a travesty of justice to occur. Yet only moments later he intones, "Thy will be done. Into your hands I commend my spirit!" I interpret his first utterance as that of his dissipated ego before his unified transition into Oneness with God, with All That Is. Healing has become, for me, a sacred path toward this Oneness.

19

Stay Forever

"It is only with the heart that one can see clearly, for what is essential is hidden from the eyes."

—Antoine de Saint Exupéry, from *The Little Prince*

Back in the flat with my friends sharing our perspectives on Vipassana's death and the events of the past few days, I had no inkling that only the following evening I would confront my ego again, but on a different level. I had allotted three months in India as part of my around-the- world trip, having many fantasies about the steps beyond that, but committed to deepening my meditation while there, to recharge my energy for the next stage of my journey.

The following evening I was scheduled for *darshan*, a one-to-one meeting with the guru, in which one may ask whatever question one may have. I was thrilled to be face to face and one on one with Rajneesh again in this ashram setting. His Bombay apartment had been very intimate, but the large ashram held the same intensity. When I sat down before Bhagwan he placed his palm on my head, and I immediately felt the energy of our communion. We looked into each other's eyes in silence before he spoke, "Ramananda, I'm so glad you are back with me, you are home. Now stay forever!" Seized by both exhilaration and dread of the word, "forever," I had no words. Rajneesh gifted me with one of his robes and smiled warmly as I left stunned with elation and confusion.

Once back at the flat, I shared my experience to the envy of many friends but inside I felt panicked. How can he ask me to "stay forever?" Doesn't he know that I have other plans? Such questions dogged me as I suffered with dysentery and overwhelm during  the next few days. How could I stay forever? Such an invitation was considered the greatest compliment, an honor to be asked by the master to reside forever in his ashram community. I would have to give up everything, all of my dreams. I had planned to return to New York and to consider whether to reopen my practice or to move with my friend Ron from Esalen days to Taos, perhaps open a healing center. When visiting the Lama Foundation in New Mexico coming cross-country we'd fallen in love with the great blue sky, the expanse of land, the energy. We had stayed in touch all these years still nursing this dream. Helen and David Elisalde had also asked me to help them open a healing center with Peter Calarco in Australia while further developing my psychic surgery skills and teaching meditation. But here I was. I had decided to continue to acclimate to ashram life, with trust that the right decision would come to me.

A few days later one of the children's pet cats died, and the children wanted to have a send-off like Vipassana's. With the help of other adults, we performed a similar celebration. The children adorned the cat's body with flowers and created a small procession down to the river where we celebrated and cremated the beloved cat while the children sang and told stories of this pet's multiple lives around the ashram.

* * *

Over the month since Vipassana's passing, Rupa had been preparing to leave the ashram to resume her Alexander Technique training in the States. We both acknowledged our strong love for each other but the nature of our relationship had shifted, from passion to compassion, which somehow made parting even more difficult.

* * *

Not long after Rupa's departure Nishant and Samahdi moved in to share the flat, and Bhagwan begun to send people to me for healings. I had a treatment table made for me and reserved a room in the flat only for meditation and healing. My practice, a combination of healing work, Alexander Technique, and psychologically oriented bodywork, slowly filled.

My days had a wonderful sameness to them, a natural rhythm. I began each morning with silent meditation at our flat, arriving at the ashram by 7:30 AM, ready for the daily discourse at 8 AM. Breakfast followed the discourse and then I worked for a solid portion of each day. Offered at specific timeslots various meditations were open to all and ongoing throughout the day. Eastern meditations at the ashram followed precepts from Zen Buddhist traditions, Indian Vedic, and mantra meditations.

Dynamic meditation involved catharsis and deep breathing, and Nada Brahma meditation included chanting and utilizing energy for healing purposes.

Tai Chi was held at sunrise and sunset each day and other groups met based on primarily Western-oriented themes focusing on the release of repressed emotions, to free energy channels and to promote emotional and therefore spiritual freedom. I called the ashram, Esalen East, because it introduced many supportive and healing modalities for healing of all kinds. Rajneesh provided a spiritual anchor that went well beyond the Esalen Institute offerings by utilizing a myriad of Eastern meditation practices, creating a space for spirit to infuse the open spaces that emotional-release work created.

Having read *Cutting through Spiritual Materialism*, the profound book by the Tibetan Lama Chögyam Trungpa, I had begun thinking about giving up my dream of becoming a respected healer with my own healing center because such illusions felt inflated and born from ego. Trungpa describes meditation as a practice that takes us to the center of ourselves, to the essential spirit within, which never changes and can never be lifted from us. He teaches that those attached to the material world can humbly work through their attachments, but those caught by the sanctimony of having done so are susceptible to a much more insidious state: identification with one's lack of attachment. Thinking of those neophytes at the ashram who exuded a holier than thou attitude, I knew I did not want to be like them. The longer-term residents would say to one another, "Just give them some time, and that air will dissolve." After experiencing encounter and meditation groups designed to confront an individual's fears and self-imposed limitations, such arrogant attitudes began to dissipate as self-awareness deepened.

I was learning from Rajneesh that meditation intended to confront and diffuse one's ego. In Eastern spiritual practice, the ego keeps us separate from others and the divine energy that permeates all life. Rajneesh taught, however, that to try prematurely to drop the ego, before one has strengthened his or her essential connection to the divine energy, is like pulling an apple from the tree before it is ripe. It will be inedible; whereas when it becomes ripe it will fall naturally with no resistance. A pseudo-spiritual person is akin to the unripe apple pulled from the tree.

* * *

Although my heart felt full as my life became enmeshed with ashram life, waking up early and meditating, slowly walking to the ashram for discourse, working at the ashram on individuals sent to me for healings or bodywork/psychotherapy, and meeting people from all corners of the Earth, all seeking inner knowing, I remained unresolved about my future. Finally, I realized that I needed to make a decision and wrote Rajneesh a long letter spelling out all of my options with deep respect for his inviting benediction to "stay forever." I included all of the pros and cons of each option and sent it to Rajneesh, simultaneously booking an appointment for the following evening for *darshan*.

The next day I received a written response from Rajneesh that essentially advised me to do whatever I wanted to do! I realized upon reflection that either way I would feel rejected: if he told me to stay forever I'd be denied the fulfillment of a possible dream and if he told me to go that I would feel he did not want me. I was back where I'd started—only I could make this monumental decision, only I could truly parent myself.

A bit anxious before the following evening's *darshan*, having already been given his response, I mulled over what else to ask him, knowing I'd never left a *darshan* feeling quite as I had upon arriving.

Awaiting entry to Rajneesh's garden where he held *darshan*, knowing that a decision possibly impacting the rest of my life was on the table, I felt physically uneasy in anticipation. As I sat down before him, his usual radiant smile greeted me along with a mischievous look in his eyes. He began by saying, "So Ramananda, you have a question!" We both laughed, and I blurted out, "I really set you up this time; no matter what your response would have been, I could take it as a rejection. You sent me back into myself."

He smiled and responded. "The person you are looking at does not truly exist. I have ceased to exist as a separate entity from the All. When my ego dissolved, all that remains is a conduit. In your heart of hearts we are the same, and that is the only place I can truly be found. If you went back to New York or to Taos, but your heart was not truly there, even if we slept in the same bed, we could never commune. But, if you are where your heart is, then I will surround you like a climate and will always be there with you."

Tears welled up in my eyes, the resolution in front of me. My heart resided in India within this spiritual community. With this awareness, I spoke resoundingly, "Yes, I want to be here! This is where my heart is!"

"Good, welcome home! Now go back to New York and sort things out so that you can be here and part of the Buddhafield, for with enough people meditating, we can bring the energy to a higher level and create a space where meditation can descend upon you, upon us all."

A huge burden had been lifted. Having only a month left in India I decided it was time to play, to explore more of India and Nepal, for I knew that when I returned, I would be living and working at the ashram full time.

20

Karmapa and Kathmandu

"Great teachers are the realized ones. They are noble chiefs and leaders who have conquered all illusion... They have solved the riddle of paradox and duality. They can speak only the truth."

—Lynn Andrews, from *Jaguar Woman*

My dear friends Nishant and Samadhi joined me in my travels north to Delhi, Agra, and Nepal. Although we travelled together, we each needed our spiritual solitude, having all independently decided to move to the ashram and to commit to staying as long as we felt called, our whole life, if necessary, and now we must prepare ourselves. If we were to have an opportunity to explore India and Nepal, it had to be then, for we realized that once committed to ashram life, our future would be much less clear.

When our flight from Agra landed in Kathmandu, I felt the same déjà vu that I had experienced in India, Japan, and the Philippines. Similar to India but lighter of spirit and more playful, indeed a meeting of India and Tibet, many Tibetan refugees lived there.

Walking the streets of Kathmandu, a practical idea struck me! I adored Tibetan culture and its artifacts, particularly the *mala* (prayer) beads, Tibetan prayer boxes, and *thangkas* (Tibetan paintings and wall hangings). I would purchase such items that I felt were infused with spirit and sell them in the West—an excellent means to supporting myself in India!

During the first week I spent my days wandering through the streets, especially near the two Tibetan temples on either side of Kathmandu, and seeking out shops and individuals willing to sell paintings and old manuscripts. I very much enjoyed meeting the local people and deeply appreciated their warm invitations to join them in their homes for chai. The sellers of the ancient

Boudhanath Stupa, Kathmandu

artifacts seemed as moved as I felt over sharing their spiritual treasures, knowing without saying that they would enrich a welcome new home.

One day while roaming around the Bodhinath Stupa, a large Tibetan temple and residence, a monk approached me and asked what I was doing with the rolled up *thangkas* under my arm. He smiled and suggested that I have his holiness Karmapa bless them since he would be in town for the week. My heart raced, recalling my first meeting with Karmapa in New York some years prior.

The next day I learned that Karmapa was having an ordination ceremony at the Bodhinath Stupa, and I grabbed my wall hangings, tucked them under my arm, and hurried there. I asked a few monks where I might find him, and they pointed to the temple door, explained that the ceremony was in session. I waited in hope of encountering him when he exited the temple.

Waiting outside the door with some young Buddhist monks, only 10 to 13 years old, someone idly opened the exit door, and the young monks entered the temple, so I followed. The ceremony still in progress, the scent of incense permeated the space, and the sound of bells and chanting filled  the hall, but stopped abruptly. All eyes turned to us, with clear disapproval, as some older monks approached us to escort the boys and me out. We had crashed the party. My eyes searched the interior of the hall, amidst the disapproving stares, until I caught a glimpse of Karmapa, a huge grin on his face, the last thing I remember as the door closed behind us.

I waited outside, but after the ceremony, Karmapa was whisked away. Disappointed but somehow also elated, I stopped by a shop where I had purchased some items, and, over a cup of chai, the shopkeeper told me that the following day Karmapa would be performing the Black Crown ceremony at the other Stupa, Swayambhunath, on the outskirts of Kathmandu.

Nishant and Samahdi had to return to India to settle their affairs before their journey back to the States, but since I had a number of weeks left before my scheduled departure, I decided to stay for another few days in Kathmandu.

Again I left my room in the morning with five or so rolled up *thangkas* under my arm. Swayambhunath would be quite a hike and, with only a few days to enjoy Nepal, I intentionally tuned in to the vibrant culture's sounds and colors. Eastern religious shrines — Buddhist, Hindu—were everywhere, each covered with flowers and incense burning. Vegetable stalls, food stalls, stood one after another, and children looked up at me with mascaraed eyes of wonder. The vibrant colors of the clothing sung out in comparison to the purity of the whites in India. Faces of beggars and shopkeepers alike smiled and I thought about what Westerners were missing in their perpetual hurry and talking over and through each other. In

a Nepalese woman stonewriting

New York City people tended to look away, considering it aggressive to look someone in the eye, but in Nepal, gazing into a stranger's eyes is the norm, communicating to each other that we are not strangers but fellow seekers. I regularly had encounters with people whom I had never met where our palms naturally came together to say, "Namaste," meaning "the divine within me, bows to the divine within you." Such encounters and gestures of spontaneous connection relaxed and opened me, where the energy between us acknowledged each other with deep respect. I found this practice much more natural than the bow in Japan or the handshake in the West both of which can feel automatic and even distancing.

As I approached the many steps leading up to the Stupa, a

Swayambhunath Stupa

familiar combination of exhilaration and fear filled me. Many other seekers climbed the steps alongside me to attend the Black Crown ceremony, the entire area alive with a charged silence.

The ceremony was identical to the one I had attended in New York years before, but I was different, more available to the transmission of energy. At the end, we lined up to receive Karmapa's direct blessing, leaving the temple somehow transformed.

I observed an entourage leaving with Karmapa and walking across the plaza into the residence across from the temple. I waited and meditated outside, sitting on the balcony, watching the pilgrims arriving to see His Holiness. I delighted over the antics of the nearby monkeys who roamed freely around the

Stupa, and suddenly, with no warning, the Black Bird flew toward me. Startled from my reverie, I cautioned myself to be aware, not only of what was going on around me but within me as well. I had a strong premonition that I *must* meet Karmapa.  Just before the sun set I proceeded to enter the residence and asked a monk sitting at a desk at the foot of the stairs if I might quickly meet His Holiness to bless my *thangkas*. I would never ordinarily do such a thing and was not surprised when the monk who spoke broken English, told me that His Holiness was preparing for bed, and perhaps I could try tomorrow. I thanked him and walked back outside.

Overwhelmed with an urge to turn around and go back in, I followed my impulse. Nobody now at the desk, I proceeded up the stairs. When I reached the top, I met a man in his nightclothes and asked him if I might briefly see His Holiness. With this request, I felt an invisible pressure on my shoulder pushing me to my knees. Looking up at His Holiness in his nightclothes, I saw the same beaming smile as when we interrupted his ordination ceremony the day before. He placed his hand on my forehead and tranquility replaced my frenzy.

Led into a room with only Karmapa and his translator, I shared why I had come—an irrational desire to have my paintings blessed. He smiled and reached out to hold my *mala* beads before closing his eyes. My *mala* displayed a picture of Bhagwan Rajneesh. Releasing the beads, Karmapa told me that Rajneesh had been a Tibetan Lama in his past life and bringing meditation to the masses was important work. He told me to send his regards to Rajneesh and to share that he must take better care of his body, particularly his blood sugar. He then asked me from where I originated. I mentioned New York City, and he asked if I'd heard of Woodstock. I responded that I had often been there, and he informed me that a large Tibetan monastery was to be built in Woodstock, asking if I would come to visit. (In fact at that same meeting, he said that we would meet again there.) Mesmerized, I think I simply nodded in agreement. Finally, he placed his hand on each painting and again on my forehead before I was led out of the door.

Emerging into the courtyard, I walked toward the steps in the direction of my lodging. Suddenly I heard the translator call out. He wanted to tell me that His Holiness would like to see me again the next day. I thanked him profusely, walked blissfully down the stairs toward Kathmandu.

The next morning I woke up early and went out to walk the city streets to bask in the morning sun and dispel the chill. I grabbed a bite from one of the street stands, *chana*, a very warming chickpea dish cooked with Indian spices, and began my walk back to Swayambhunath. As I got closer, a fear gripped me. What does he want from me? I have a teacher. Will I have to choose? These and many more questions flooded me as I approached the stairs leading up to the Stupa. Suddenly I halted and turned to return to the village. To this day I wonder why Karmapa had invited me back.

The following day Karmapa left Kathmandu. I trekked to Pokhara with some people I knew to escape the city for pure country air. In this idyllic setting, sitting on the shores of a large pristine lake surrounded by the Himalayan mountains, I had time to meditate on all that had happened in Nepal before preparing to return to the ashram and readying for my journey back to the States.

A few days later I returned to Pune to prepare for what I imagined could be my last trip to New York. Before I'd left for Kathmandu, I'd been in touch with Helen and David Elisalde as well as Peter Calarco who was actively pursuing opening the healing center in Australia that he envisioned. They enthusiastically asked when I'd be able to join them, having run into many problems, the most serious being getting David a visa. Peter wanted to send me money for a ticket to Australia.

We all shared this vision of working together to create an Australian center for healing and meditation. I felt honored and elated about this possibility and assumed when I left the Philippines that this vision was indeed ordained. But my time in India had changed me. I indeed loved Helen and David, still wearing the Egyptian ring that Helen had given to me, a reminder of my deep connection to my Filipino mentors and dear friends. My heart was heavy with potentially disappointing them and rupturing our relationship. But my ego-driven image of becoming a world-renowned healer had all but dissolved after saturating myself with Rajneesh's teaching and becoming devoted to my ashram life. I wanted to truly know myself. My heart, my home, was now clearly in India.

When I shared this with them all, they accepted it, albeit with disappointment, but upon my return from Kathmandu, I found Peter Calarco waiting for me at the ashram, having flown in from Australia. He said he felt compelled to see for himself what had changed my mind and wanted to try in person to convince me to go back with him.

He showed me a picture of his wife on the steps of Lourdes. Superimposed on her white blouse over her heart (chest) area appeared a clear image of the face of a bearded man. With gooseflesh, I realized that it was indeed the face of

Rajneesh. For Peter, it was a sign that indeed I was meant to be with Rajneesh, and that perhaps he, David, and Helen would come to the ashram as well. He stayed for a few days, attended discourses, and before leaving gave me $300 to pay for my ticket to Australia or to use in any way that spirit guided me. Peter told me that he understood my choice and flew back to Helen and David in Australia. That was my last contact with my healer friends.

* * *

In India the bureaucratic red-tape necessary to get exit visas was extraordinarily difficult. I learned that many third world countries create blockages in their visa departments to collect extra funds, called *baksheesh*, to display power over others. I spent several days in Bombay gathering my paperwork, returning to Poona for a few final days at the ashram before many, "see you soons."

At the airport in Bombay, I noticed I was missing the Egyptian ring that Helen had given me when I left the Philippines. I had worn it the entire time in India. I searched everywhere, but to no avail. The flight from Bombay to London stopped in Cairo, where we exited the plane while it was cleaned. We were to wait in the lounge for a few hours. Once there, I happened to look down on the carpet, and there was the ring! It appeared in Egypt where Helen and I had determined long ago we had known each other in another life. Maybe we did. I knew for sure that my healing connection with Helen, with David, with the people and the land of the Philippines would stay with me across space and time. But, now my allegiance, my path was with Rajneesh, my healing work, and my family and purpose within the ashram community.

PART FOUR

Five Years of Ashram Life

"There is something magical about any intense, tightly knit group of people working together and playing together, feeling of being in the world while at the same time being apart from it."

—George Leonard and Michael Murphy, from The Life We Are Given

21
Returning "Home" to India

"There are a thousand ways to go home again."
—Rumi

"Humility is just as much the opposite of self-abasement as it is of self-exaltation. To be humble is not to make comparisons. Secure in its reality, the self is neither better nor worse, bigger nor smaller, than anything else in the universe. It is—is nothing, yet at the same time is one with everything."
—Dag Hammarskjold, from *Markings*

It took nearly a year to get things in order in New York to prepare to make a permanent move to India. Intending to build a solid foundation for what was to come, I had written frequently in my journal, noting peak experiences, reflecting on relationships, and learning to trust my decisions and choices.

But when I returned "home" to the Rajneesh Ashram in Pune, India, to "stay forever" it was time to let go, to learn to witness my ego, and become more aware of my attachments. I tried to no longer identify myself as a healer, a therapist, a teacher, or even a good lover, but rather to resolve to accept what life brought my way. In the ashram environment, enhanced by the expansive teaching of a master, I no longer relied on my journal to mirror my journey, turning instead to my self-awareness in keeping with Rajneesh's clear mirror and no-nonsense response to my reflections.

Simply Being

Having given up my cherished apartment in New York City's Greenwich Village and stored my extensive library of books and record albums at my mother's house, I arrived at the ashram with only a backpack of necessities, having given everything else to friends and charities. Though I had sacrificed my hard-won New York practice and taken the greatest leap of my life, I felt liberated, ready to begin anew. Where during previous sojourns, I had felt fear and anxiety, this time every cell of my body said "yes." My rational mind assured me that I had worked hard to earn my credentials and could restart my career elsewhere if my ashram experience did not work out.

Looking down into the clouds on the approach to Bombay, I felt a deep sense of peace and acceptance about what the universe had in store for me. I trusted the process. As the Sufi mantra states, "Trust in God, but tether your camel first!" I had tethered my camel by clarifying my decision with the Elisaldes and Peter Calarco the year before and by completing all of my unfinished business in New York. But, most importantly, I had followed my inner compass and was learning to truly trust myself.

I took a few friends with me to India, some to be introduced to Rajneesh for the first time, others who had followed his meditations in New York as well as listened to his discourses on audiotape. This time I was the senior traveller, advising them about what to do or not do upon our arrival, beginning with maneuvering our group through customs, warning them to expect an assault by hundreds of Indians offering them hotels, drugs, rides, and anything else a mind could conjure. We persevered through the multitudes to the official taxi stand, filled two cars, and negotiated a price for the five-hour ride to Pune. Slowly we snaked through the crowded Bombay streets. I observed my mates, eyes open wide, clearly awed by the sights and sounds, a myriad of scents and odors filling the air as we weaved through the streets, ever so slowly reaching the countryside, and up over the mountains toward Pune and the ashram.

The treacherous mountain pass had always made me anxious, but this time, lost in my thoughts I took little notice, until out  of nowhere, the Black Bird, flew toward the taxi's windshield, dissolving as quickly as its vision had appeared. Glancing into the backseat, my wide-eyed friends, held their breath as our driver maneuvered the sharp turns and edges with shear drops. They had not seen what I had.

I remembered a Sufi story about such a bird having to let go of its food in order to be free:

> *A blackbird found a large piece of food in the village and lit out into the sky with the food in its beak. A flock of his brothers chased after him and raucously attacked the food, pulling it from his beak. The blackbird finally let go of the last piece and the frenzied flock left him alone. The bird swooped and dived and thought, "I have lost the food but I have regained the peaceful sky."*
>
> —from *Stories of the Spirit, Stories of the Heart*,
> edited by Christina Feldman and Jack Kornfield

Could this most recent visitation be a signal that I was to let go of *my* security? "Now was the time," I told myself. I must trust!

A new elaborate wooden gate surrounded by a white marble frame surprised me upon our approach to the ashram, Shree Rajneesh Ashram, engraved above the arch. Many disciples sat on the wall or stood about having a smoke. As I got out of the car, a number of old friends ran over to welcome me home. We hugged, laughed, and cried at our reunion, as I introduced my friends to my fellow ashramites.

It was a lovely welcome but a simple one. I was given a small living space over a refinished garage called Francis House that housed Rajneesh's parents who were also his disciples. I would share the space on the converted roof with a man who would be my roommate for many years, Veresh. We shared a small squat toilet with another small room that was occupied by two female devotees. The showers were stone cold, but friends in another ashram room, lucky enough to have geysers (an appliance that heated the water as it gushed through), would allow us to occasionally indulge in their warmth.

In exchange for my room and board, I was to be part of the Groups and Therapy Department and would give individual lessons in the Alexander Technique as well as do healings. It sounded ideal, and it no doubt suited me, but all ashram workers were there for the same reason: to awaken to their full aliveness. As we were taught, we all respected each other equally—even those who cleaned toilets, perhaps especially those who cleaned toilets! I never lost sight of my good fortune.

Though Veresh and I arrived with few possessions we slowly made our crowded space into our little home, adding a kerosene burner for our morning coffee or tea and shelves to hold clothes. Looking back, throughout all of the years that we shared our small space, Veresh and I felt very content with never an argument between us.

As was the custom, I enlisted a local tailor to make me a few robes and some drawstring pants, all in ochre shades of orange, red, and maroon. A carpenter made me a wooden bedframe to hold a mattress and also a table to use for healing sessions and teaching The Alexander Technique.

Rajneesh and his disciples envisioned the ashram as a great experiment in the integration of Western therapeutic methods in combination with teaching many Eastern meditation practices. Rajneesh believed this would help free individuals of their psychic baggage to better elevate their consciousness. This felt familiar to me having experienced such teachings at Esalen, and the human potential movement had spawned many such personal growth centers in the U.S. and Europe. But, the ashram experiment was unique in that an enlightened master directed the teaching with the intention of moving individuals beyond the psychological and into the transcendental realm.

The concept of enlightenment or discipleship can be difficult to explain to the Western mind that views the traditional Eastern concept of surrender as a surrender of one's power or control to another person. In the East, surrender contains no element of competition, no power over another, as in patriarchal cultures, but it does posit the importance of a teacher. Surrender implies giving up the ego's wants and desires to the source of one's being, that is, surrender to existence itself. The teacher may be a true human master or any entity that an individual recognizes as actually mirroring or guiding him or her to an expanded awareness. An initiate must enter a process of dissolution, where one's awareness and experience unifies with the All. Only then can an initiate assist others in perceiving the same truth. Those of us drawn to live at the ashram found that Rajneesh's words and energy created a sure mirror into which we could come to see ourselves.

I clearly remember a *darshan* when Bhagwan explained to the actor Terence Stamp the significance of surrender in relation to living at the ashram—that being in spiritual community fosters a deep connection with the master, a necessary depth of involvement, for guidance, Bhagwan stressed, would not come from outside the ashram. I can still hear his words, "I need a passage to your heart." He further explained that being in the master's energy field enhances awareness and that each student can then observe the intensity generated from the master's presence. He instructed us all through his instruction to Terence—to attentively observe ourselves but not to take ourselves too seriously. "Such seriousness becomes a disease," Bhagwan would say, emphasizing that seriousness only exists in the past or the future, whereas living in the moment is always *leela*, that is, always playfulness.

Rajneesh gave Terence Stamp the name Veeten. He stayed at the ashram for many months before returning to the West to make movies. I remember Terence sharing with Bhagwan that he felt that making films for mass media betrayed his spiritual path. In response, Rajneesh gave him a task, asking him to do one movie for the public, followed by one for spirit.

The following year Terence performed as the arch-villain in a Superman film as well as played Gurdjieff in the film, *Meetings with Remarkable Men*, the story of Gurdjieff 's study with his teachers. A wonderful teaching story demonstrates the lesson Rajneesh shared with Terence (and therefore with us):

> *On a cold evening a monk, traveling the country, sought refuge in a monastery. Immediately recognized as a famous Zen monk, the abbot of the monastery brought a mattress and some tea and left the visitor in the shrine room to get a good night's sleep. In the middle of the night the abbot awakened to the smell of burning wood, and when he rushed into the temple he saw that the monk was burning some wooden statues of Buddha.*
>
> *"How dare you, you ingrate!! We give you refuge and you destroy our religious objects! LEAVE NOW!!"*
>
> *The following morning on his way to market, the abbot saw the monk sitting and meditating while facing a large rock.*
>
> *"What are you doing? You burned our Buddha statue and now you meditate to a stone!"*
>
> *The monk replied, "Last night, the Buddha within was cold; now he needs to commune."*
>
> —from *Stories of the Spirit, Stories of the Heart*,
> edited by Christina Feldman and Jack Kornfield

The people drawn to the Rajneesh Ashram were often people successful in the West but who remained unfulfilled—psychologists, psychiatrists, social workers, clergy of multiple disciplines—all committed to self-awareness and who resonated with Rajneesh's teachings. The ambivalence and self-doubt that had long plagued me dissolved. I had come home!

Though Rajneesh was not one to preach rigid precepts, he taught and stressed the essential importance of looking within. As Carl G. Jung had said, "...he who looks without, dreams, he who looks within, awakens." Bhagwan exemplified such a meditative life, believing strongly that the guide within required full freedom to come to wholeness and enlightenment. Like Jung, Rajneesh taught that only by going inward could we find ourselves. Though meditation was a primary practice of his teaching, he did not align with any particular religion or practice, believing that each of us is but a cell within a greater organism. He encouraged his devotees always to find true meditation through losing their egos and merging with it All. Whether cooking, art, music, or cleaning, all streams of work, he believed, could be attended to with meditative presence, as they all lead to the same ocean. A guru, he would say, merely points the way; it is our work as devotees to stay connected to the direction in which our teacher points. As recounted in Part Three at an early memorable *darshan* with Bhagwan, when determining whether to stay or depart the ashram for other explorations, he had stressed, "I don't live here, I live in your heart. You can only commune from there, not your head." In essence, he taught that only by sacrificing one's ego could such a communion occur. Rajneesh would often say, "Drop your individual ego, but not your compass!"

Compared, for instance to the great teacher, J. Krishnamurti, who had rejected his appointment as "avatar," early in his rise to fame, and who struck a quite serious tone, Rajneesh remained a bit of a trickster, at once relishing the attention he received, while declaring himself beyond the ego. A sparkle in his eye, he enjoyed, I think, like Rolling Thunder shocking his followers and the world to teach them the lessons he felt they must learn.

* * *

Ashram days began with Rajneesh's daily two-hour discourse, alternating months between English and Hindi, where ashramites listened with presence to his words while connecting to meditative states. Many of us felt that the Hindi discourses entered us more fluidly, as our intellects could not interfere. We could listen with our hearts rather than with our heads. As Rajneesh had often stated, "a problem arises because people come in search of knowledge, but a master cannot give you knowledge, he can only give you his wisdom, and wisdom only comes through the vehicle of love."

After the discourse and a short break for chai, we would go about our work. Initially, I saw clients in my room, offering sessions during the day, when my roommate worked. But, within only six months, the ashram expanded and purchased a few additional homes in the area, converting them into residences as well as group therapy spaces, meditation spaces, and individual healing rooms. I continued to keep my table in my living space but felt relieved to have a workspace separate from our small living area. The ashram booked all of my sessions and my clients paid in advance; therapists received slips each day upon arrival that clarified their sessions for the day. In addition to our room and board, we each also received a small stipend of spending money. After completing my sessions booked by the ashram office, I could also offer a few extra sessions to make more spending money, charging 100 rupees, about ten dollars.

As ashram life took me personally deeper into my own healing, my healing work with others also expanded. As I became more mindful, I was able to stress mindfulness as an essential tool for healing both mind and body.

251

22

The Alexander Technique and the Art of Meditation

"Change involves carrying out an activity against the habit of life."
—F. M. Alexander

When I was studying for my Alexander Technique certification, I came upon a short but deeply influential book called *Zen and the Art of Archery* by Eugen Herrigel, a German philosopher and professor. I realized that Herrigel's experience of creative flow, like Alexander's, directly spoke to my deepening awareness of the connection between deep healing bodywork and the spiritual path.

While teaching in Japan between 1924 and 1929 Eugen Herrigel sought a Zen teacher through D. T. Suzuki, a prolific author and professor who was instrumental in popularizing Zen in the West. The story goes that Suzuki informed him that one cannot simply study Zen but must choose an activity through which to *experience* Zen, thus Suzuki inspired him to find a Zen teacher. He then found Awa Kenzo. Herrigel chose traditional Japanese archery and his wife chose flower arranging, of course with different masters. Herrigel's book *Zen and the Art of Archery* intended to illustrate the Taoist principles of Zen Buddhism learned through his six years of study with Kenzo, a master of the art of archery, who Herrigel believed was a Zen master.

Herrigel experienced countless frustrations and discouragement during his study, finally finding a "knack," that he felt sure would please his teacher, but Kenzo walked away in disgust. Shattered, wanting only to please his master, Herrigel assiduously continued his practice. Kenzo occasionally watched him, saying, "The aim should be at your heart. Forget the target!" This struck me as directly related to the Alexander Technique, that is, forget the end result, the destination; *be* the means whereby.

Many months passed before one day Herrigel became one with the process, as he needed no bow, no target. The arrow left his bow as if by its own accord. He felt exhilarated and fully embraced when his master bowed to him. Herrigel had glimpsed what Alexander called "the creative principle," where we get out of our own way and let IT happen. IT has been called Oneness, Enlightenment, To Be One with All That Is. This state is quintessential ecstatic connection.

Note: It has recently come to my attention that Herrigel was allegedly associated with Nazi Germany. Despite my Jewish heritage, his influence helped stimulate my initial awareness of the relationship among creative process, physical embodiment, presence, and spirituality. It also suggests that one who has tasted the nectar (*satori*) may lose it again. Herrigel tasted enlightenment, but it was only a taste, for one must take such an experience *into* life, which is called *samadhi* or living *satori*, one's taste of enlightenment. Herrigel's story made me wonder if a master teacher like Rajneesh could fall from *his* state of grace.

Alexander at the Ashram: Meditation in Action

As introduced in Part Two, the Shakespearian actor, F. M. Alexander, finding no healing modality for a severe, career-threatening hoarseness, concluded that his symptoms must be caused by a habit or pattern of his own doing. To explore this, he turned toward meditation and mindful observation of his body's patterns of response. He learned to shift patterns that did not flow naturally through his body. Influenced no doubt by a Zen Buddhist approach, even earlier than Herrigel, Alexander discovered that energy naturally moves up through the human organism's spine, encouraging weightlessness when simultaneously aware of the need to be grounded. His groundbreaking explorations and findings became known as The Alexander Technique. It is important to recall this background in order to fully appreciate the following few pages.

As I found my stride in my work with the Alexander Technique at the ashram, its practice took on a new life. My previous standard healing sessions required no thought: a client entered my room and shared the problem—physical, emotional, or spiritual. We would meditate on it and then explore together whether a clear message presented through the symptom. The client would then lie on the table, and, as in the Philippines, I would get out of the way and allow the energy to flow through me as a conduit for healing.

But the Alexander work now went further. I carefully observed each student's habitual movement when sitting, standing, and so on, to guide him or her to first identify and then disperse habituated patterns. I also had to teach the student how to unlearn destructive physical patterns and to envision the free flow of natural energy through the body as surrender to divine intention. The spiritual focus of the ashram clearly influenced this new dimension of my Alexander work.

When I asked each student to share the difference between how their body had felt when they arrived and how they felt after our session, they invariably commented that sitting or standing now felt effortless! Often they would contract to the old habit, but having experienced the effortlessness of shifting awareness, they eventually learned to bring the old habits to consciousness. Through the felt memory in their body—and my hands—I could reconnect them back to neutral so they might fully re-member their ability to sit or stand naturally without habitual interference. This usually took a few sessions, but ultimately they opened to the joy of effortless movement.

Alexander learned and taught that human imbalance originates from our "doings." Health and healing must come by "undoing" patterns that interfere with total function. For example, when instructing a student on how to breathe more openly, allowing the breath to carry oxygen and energy into the body, such breathing releases CO_2 and toxins with each exhale. Alexander insisted that focusing on the breath actually instills more problems because the "doing" initiates the harmful patterns. He devised an alternative technique and called it "the whispered ahhh," where the exhalation (the non-doing aspect of breathing) included the whispered sound "ahhhhhh," upon exhalation, expelling air from the lung, and then consciously observing as the body breathed in the breath it needed. Again, the natural action is simply a matter of getting out of one's own way!

Rajneesh once said in a lecture, "...the more you breathe out, the more you breathe in. So if you want more life, breathe out more so that you create a vacuum inside, and more breath will flow in. You simply exhale as much as you can and your whole being will inhale. Love more, that is breathing out, and your body will gather energy from the whole cosmos. You create the vacuum, and the energy will come."

This story comes to mind:

> *Mulla Nasreddin was ill and went to the doctor's office. The doctor put him in a room, told him to undress completely, and she would return soon to examine him. A few minutes later she knocked on the door and pushed it open. She examined him and told him to go home and rest in bed for a few days.*
>
> *"Any questions?" she asked.*
>
> *"Only one," the Mulla said: "Why did you bother to knock?"*
>
> *The doctor answered, "Just an old habit!"*

Bhagwan explained that even in our gestures, old habits and patterns persist. Habits are easy to follow because they require no awareness. They have a life of their own. Awareness requires full attention to the moment and never comes from unconscious habits. Habits are necessary in life, but must be under conscious control or they can rule our lives.

In Zen Buddhism, as in most all spiritual traditions, the conscious focus is on the "here and now," the "eternal present," but the mind moves between the past and the future. The mind acts as a rehearsal to give us information that we can use to organize our thoughts, feelings, and actions for future implementation, therefore the mind is not suited for the here and now. However, the body lives in the moment, and the Alexander work teaches us to focus on and listen to the body, to systematically eliminate our programmed habits step-by-step, awareness-by-awareness, until we stop interfering with the energy that moves and enervates us, thus becoming truly in the flow of our existence.

Each night as I lay in bed at the ashram, the influence of my Alexander work took me into more deeply meditative space. One night I vivid dreamed that I was reading a book with total immersion. I read section after section, and thought to myself in the dream, "How interesting, a book called *The Alexander Technique and the Art of Meditation* has already been written!" When I turned it over to look at its cover, I saw to my surprise that I was the author! I woke up exhilarated, the vivid imagery clear in my mind. A few days later at a *darshan* meeting with Rajneesh I shared this dream, and he told me to write that book, and he would give me access to his library. I was thrilled! I suppose I have finally written that book— all in good time, only 40 years later.

* * *

A woman named Aneeta lived next door to us at the ashram and taught Sufi dancing as meditation as she had been taught by a Sufi master, Pir Vilayat Khan. She had also been a resident at Esalen. She came to visit the Rajneesh Ashram in Pune and stayed. Once each month, she would offer a three-day intensive, complete with whirling and abandon. After these intensives she would come to me with intense back pain that we would successfully address through massage and Alexander work. After four months of this pattern I asked her, "What do you think about when you teach Sufi dancing?" She thought for a moment and responded, "Well, as Pir Vilayat taught me, I think up from the center point and down into the earth from this same center point." This center point is known as *hara, dantian*, and many other words that connote the energy center of the body. It is located approximately midway between the pubis bone and the naval, at the second chakra, the sacral chakra, the center of the body's gravity and balance.

I drew a diagram of the spine for her to illustrate the *dantian* point as about six inches above the coccyx, also known as the tailbone, at the base of the spine. Again I inquired if she considered two forces of energy separating up and down from this point. She said, "yes," and I drew a horizontal line across the paper at this *dantian* point so that a portion of the vertical line representing the spine was *beneath* the horizontal line that I'd drawn across the *dantian*. I asked her to imagine that the torso was like a tree and that the horizontal line represented the earth. I pointed out that a part of the trunk is below the earth, but it doesn't oppose the rest of the trunk. The sun pulls up the entire tree, I noted; however, the roots, representing our human legs, act to root us to the earth. Using my hands, I swept up her body to express the direction of the body's energy, according to the Alexander Technique, to give her body a kinesiological or bodily felt experience. As she practiced this powerful mindful awareness, Aneeta never suffered back pain again following her three-day Sufi dance intensives.

Though I'd never considered myself remotely intimidating or judgmental, when I passed or encountered various ashramites who had worked with me in session—guards, carpenters, cooks, vegetable cutters, and room cleaners—they would self-consciously change their posture or sitting position. I never wanted to engender self-consciousness, only simple self-awareness.

I remember a *darshan* in particular when, after Rajneesh asked if I had any questions, I told him that when I was working with the Alexander Technique or in healing sessions with my clients that my thoughts would often totally disappear and be replaced by the same ecstasy and silence that I experienced in his presence. My healing work felt natural and totally meditative.

I told him that in session my ego seemed to disappear, as I felt guided to connect with and heal another's pain. It was as if I'd left my mind at the door upon entering my workspace, picking it up again, *or it me*, upon my departure. It was as if my mind waited for me—asking questions, casting doubt, preparing for the group that I was to lead, or wondering if someone I might have been attracted to would feel the same.

He laughed and told me that true meditation comes most easily through one's work, if one has found what the universe has in store for them.

"There is no need for any other meditation for you," he said. "And don't worry about your thoughts, there is nothing wrong in them. Just as the blood circulates in the body, thoughts circulate in the mind. The mechanism of the mind is to rehearse and plan; it is homework. When awareness becomes perfect then this work is not needed, and such homework stops automatically. So it is not a question of how to stop thinking, the more basic question is how to become more and more aware. Go deeper and you will create an environment through which your clients can feel the same. But don't blame the poor mind. It is its job to rehearse, to engage the past, and project to the future. Don't bother with the mind; simply learn to observe it as a watcher on the hill. In time the fire of your awareness will burn it out, and then what you experience in your work, you will experience in all you do."

— Bhagwan Shree Rajneesh, from *The Shadow of the Whip*

23

Sex to Super-consciousness

"Sex is just the beginning, not the end. But if you miss the beginning, you will miss the end also."

—Bhagwan Shree Rajneesh

I deeply appreciated the natural, effortless quality of Rajneesh and his teachings. I'd learned through experience that to return to wholeness, psychotherapy was essential to reclaiming discarded parts of ourselves. Deepening our spirituality felt like the next step, where from a place of wholeness we could transcend our egos, taste more expansive consciousness, and become truly enlightened. Living in a communal, spiritual place such as the ashram offered each resident an opportunity to become more conscious.

I came to believe that religion in its exclusivity actually cuts people off from each other and their real feelings. It preaches order and discipline but religious people often seemed detached, separate, from the sensorial world, living by "shoulds" and "should nots." Religions, including my own Jewish upbringing, seemed essentially controlling. My years in therapy and deepening my self-awareness through explorations at the Esalen Institute had guided me beyond the constrictive, traditional values imposed upon me by my parents, teachers, and rabbis, values that left me feeling bad about my natural feelings of anger, sadness, even joy, and certainly about my sexuality.

Prior to my therapeutic and educational focus on self-awareness, I felt shame when I became angry or sexually aroused. "Something must be wrong with me," I'd say to myself. I'd feel routinely humiliated when expressing such feelings and desire. Would the prophets of mystical traditions have taught that natural feelings and sensations are bad, punishable, if not in this realm, in hell? "If this is religion," I thought, "it's not for me."

It took me well into my twenties to begin to accept my intrinsic feelings and desires and longer to allow myself to experience a true sense of personal freedom. Though I'd always intuited that life held deep meaning, I considered myself an atheist. I believed that the imposition of religious rules blocked spirit rather than inspiring and encouraging followers to be true to themselves, to what moved them and brought them fully alive. At Esalen I became aware of esoteric religious groups that used age-old systems to foster attainment of wisdom or enlightenment. The Jewish mystics offered study of Kabbalah; the Essenes, the sect to which Jesus was purported to belong, carried his essential message; scholars considered Sufism to be the inner, mystical dimension of Islam; Zen Buddhism emphasizes the inner nature of the Buddha and how to live it in daily life, and theosophy seeks direct knowledge of the nature of divinity while anthroposophy, as founded by Rudolf Steiner, considers inner development as the root of divine experience. Such esoteric sects and philosophies honor the teachings of the masters—Jesus, Mohammed, Buddha, Moses—and often share a common message that encourages living such teachings rather than merely subscribing to the overarching principles of church, temple, or mosque as adamantly proclaimed by priests, rabbis, and mullahs.

This reminds me of the story "Bones To Test our Faith," that points to how we rationalize to fit reality into our preconceptions:

> *A Chinese scholar, who held the Bible to be literally true, was accosted by a scientist who said, "According to the Bible, the earth was created some 5,000 years ago, but we have discovered bones that point to life on earth a million years ago."*
>
> *Pat came the answer, "When God created earth 5000 years ago, he deliberately put those bones in to test our faith and to see if we would believe his Word rather than scientific evidence.*
>
> —Anthony de Mello, from *The Song of the Bird*

Seeking self-acceptance rather than acceptance from my Jewish tradition or my family has driven my spiritual journey and my healing. I didn't realize it fully during my ashram days, but clearly my seeking echoes a hero's quest, where I journeyed into the world in search of resonant knowledge to share one day. I learned who I was through *my own* resonant experiences. I found my soul and lost my ego over and over again, spiraling, not as progression, but as one soul's journey toward truth. No doubt I sought a father figure, again a resonant elder, who could guide me, but ultimately I learned to father myself.

* * *

Rajneesh's discourses spoke adamantly against organized religion. He reminded us that sex was totally natural, the first adult taste of the divine. When we orgasm, he would say, we experience the temporary transcendence of ego. We dissolve into a temporary but short-lived unity with existence. Sex, Rajneesh taught, is the lowest form of spiritual union, but it is a taste nonetheless.

A book published in 1973 called *From Sex to Super-consciousness* that collected Rajneesh's lectures in Bombay, translated from Hindi and intended for a mostly Hindu audience, prompted a threat on his life. Such bodily freedom pushed every button of the Indian community, for whom *Brahmacharya* (asceticism) is the goal. The following words were considered blasphemy:

> *"...Man cannot be separated from sex. Sex is the primary point: he is born of it. God has accepted the energy of sex as the starting point of creation. It is termed as sin which God himself does not consider sin. If God considers sex as sin there is no greater sinner than God in the world, in the universe. Have you ever thought that the blooming of a flower is an expression of passion, a sexual act? A peacock dances in full glory and a poet will sing a song on it. A saint will also be filled with joy. But they do not know that the dance is also an overt expression of passion, is also primarily a sexual act. To please whom does the peacock dance? The peacock is calling his beloved."*

> *"Because of this enmity, the opposition, the suppression, man is decayed from within. He could not be free from that which is the root of life, but because of the constant inner conflicts, his entire being has become neurotic. He is sick. This evident overflow of sexuality in mankind is due to so-called leaders and saints. They are to be blamed for it and until man frees himself from such teachers, preceptors, custodians, and their pseudo-sermons, the possibility of the emergence of love is nil."*

> — Bhagwan Shree Rajneesh, from *Sex to Super-consciousness*

Rajneesh emphasized that sex was spiritual practice at the lowest chakra (the *muladhara*), the energy center at the base of the spine, often referred to as the root chakra. According to ancient tantric texts, the chakras are meeting points of *prana*, that is, life force energy or *chi*, through which the *nadis* flow. I consider *nadis* to be energy channels similar to the acupuncture channels. As energy moves up the body through the solar plexus, the heart, the throat, and finally the crown of the head, spiritual experience can be transformed. Rajneesh stressed that as one progresses on the spiritual path, ecstasy of Oneness with all life becomes a totality, and sex can be left behind. This is not because sex is bad or wrong, but because the spiritual fulfillment from sexual orgasm is limited. Such teachings felt true for me, both intuitively and intellectually.

Though the ashram principles downplayed sex, neither elevating nor restricting its importance, many people came to the ashram in the first place with the delusion that ashram life invited open sexuality. After all, Rajneesh was known as the "sex guru," and it was incorrectly rumored that the ashram was the sight of great orgies. Those who came looking for such exciting adventures left disappointed, while those who understood Rajneesh's meaning in regard to sex felt open to it, if approached as a heartfelt and spiritual experience, but renounced the act in its more banal and permissive form.

It's true that often at night the ashram became a tantric playground. I still smile remembering my first night back in India in my new room trying unsuccessfully to calm my own arousal and get a good night's sleep while repeatedly interrupted by sounds of lovemaking coming through the walls. At that time, the ashram was in a rapid state of expansion, with small makeshift buildings and huts built daily, increasing the ashram population, but also decreasing any sense of privacy. All sounds carried. That first night, I felt some initial embarrassment but then broke into a laugh. "Here I am," I mused, "within a spiritual community, listening to others' orgasms!" It reminded me of how I felt growing up back in Brooklyn, never made to feel comfortable to expose my nakedness. And, in my early adulthood, I could only make love under the covers. Influenced by their conservative traditions, the Indian ashramites, I learned, felt especially squeamish about sex.

Another story comes to mind:

> *Two Buddhist monks were walking the countryside when they came upon a woman, crying on the side of a small river.*
>
> *"What is the problem?" asked the older monk.*
>
> *"I crossed the river this morning at low tide and got carried away picking herbs and flowers. Now I can't carry these back across the river."*
>
> *The older monk lifted her in his arms, carried her and her basket across the stream, and came back to continue on their journey.*
>
> *A few hours later, the younger monk looked askance at the older monk and said, "We have taken a vow of celibacy. We are not even supposed to look at a woman, yet alone touch one, but you carried her in your arms!"*
>
> *The older monk smiled and retorted, "I carried and left her two hours ago, but you are still carrying her!"*

In my earliest days at the ashram, I fell for a beautiful German woman named Vani, and we became involved. Our passionate connection intoxicated both of us, and we both felt intensely preoccupied with our sexual energy, sometimes losing ourselves in orgiastic bliss. We spent as much time together as possible, attending daily morning discourses side by side before turning to our ashram work, and then eagerly returning to each other's arms. We soon realized that we'd quickly become attached to both our sexual ecstasy and each other. Whenever an open moment or open space emerged, we would make love, bringing us ever closer to totally losing ourselves in the orgasmic tantric experience. Our obsession with each other soon turned to jealousy and possessiveness that ultimately created conflict. I had learned that the mind claims possession even of that which is meant to be fleeting, but we had lost our objectivity. I believed that the "eternal now" is a concept held sacred in all spiritual traditions: the notion, simply put, that when we try to grasp an experience, we lose it. At last we began to realize that our passion had become an obstacle on our journey to wholeness.

Word of our exploits had spread through the ashram, and, after our breakup, Rajneesh spoke in one of his discourses about the difference between passion and compassion, between the sun and the moon. He mentioned us by name, saying that when a relationship embodies passionate energy, it shines bright, just as the sun does, but if too intense and attached, like the sun it will burn out, leaving nothing but ash behind. He encouraged the entire audience to become more compassionate, more loving and gentle, to be more like the moon that reflects the sun, as it sheds its light in a more sustaining way, without possessiveness or jealousy. "Transform sex into the higher quality of love," he taught, by bringing the energy up from the sexual chakra to the heart chakra, where the dance can move it higher, to the third eye (the inner eye) and ultimately to the crown where the true spiritual orgasm occurs. Of course, over time the passionate energy often burns itself out, but gracefully nurturing our sexuality invites us to consciously transcend sexual climax to sheer prolonged ecstasy—slow, deep, and internal.

Never had I surrendered with such abandon to my passions and yet releasing Vani and our passionate relationship opened a door, connecting me to a seed within that craved nourishment, but gently so, rather than generating intense heat that can eventually erupt into a devastating flame.

* * *

The blissful, kinetic current at the ashram was unmistakable but ineffable. It was like no place I could have dreamed of being. I felt truly blessed to be an integral part of the community, devoted to Rajneesh, his words of wisdom washing over me each day, but knowing somehow that the real message rested in the gap between the words, the space created in the deep communion between master and disciples. People looked into each other's eyes with genuine compassion, acknowledging this energetic current alive between them, a current that drew us all together. Often upon meeting another, we would clasp our hands in the traditional greeting of India, and bow to each other saying, "Namaste," to acknowledge the divine within each other.

Bhagwan's lectures nourished the ashram itself as if a living organism throbbing with its vitality. Each month he gave two-hour talks, all seven days of the week, to set a mood, focusing on one spiritual path such as Sufism, Taoism, Zen Buddhism, or Hassidism as well as the mystical writings of Jesus, St. Francis, Heraclitus, or the Baul mystics, to name a few.

Having adored St. Francis as a child, in fact resonating with him throughout my life, I best remember the month that Rajneesh focused on him. When I was seven or eight years old, I found solace in a neighborhood churchyard in Brooklyn. It held a series of statuary of St. Francis with animals scampering and hovering all over and around him as well as scattered throughout the garden. I'd run and play with the figures, imagining the birds landing on my head and the deer and rabbits coming to me for conversation or perhaps advice. I loved St. Francis, but, when my father would find me there, he would drag me by the arm and pull me out of the churchyard, admonishing me to stay away from this place, saying harshly "You're Jewish," as if that response was enough!

I felt it no accident that my ashram room was located in Francis House. Sent out in the Crusades, from Assisi to battle the Muslims, considered infidels, on the battlefield, St. Francis saw the enemy as a good man, infused with the same divinity as his own. How could he kill such a kindred spirit? Having had an enlightening experience, living his Christ consciousness, he returned to Assisi, where he encountered only hostility for what the community deemed his cowardice. He had come from a wealthy family of cloth merchants (the men in my family too had made a good living as clothing merchants) but when Francis realized that their possessions were merely obstacles to the way of Christ, he boldly threw all the money and silk from his house into the streets. When his father realized what he had done, he disowned Francis, banishing him from the family home. Francis felt his soul guided him to build a house instead for Christ. As he labored building it, stone by stone, he begged for food to nourish his body so he could complete his task. In time people saw the light that he emanated, the same light, I imagine, that Christ emanated, and the kindred souls helped to build his church and spread the love.

Although Francis renounced the acquisition of possessions, modern mystics do not disdain owning things but rather caution against falling prey to identifying with and attaching to one's possessions. Francis saw each living thing as an object of God's love whether a person, a bird, a tree, or a rock. He referred to each living creature as sister or brother, as in Sister Moon and Brother Sun.

Like Francis I am and have always been a sensitive person aware of the aliveness of all life yet I have struggled with attachment, especially in relationship. In my five years at the ashram, a number of my relationships with women flowered, and in keeping with the community's emphasis on honesty and awareness, we directly confronted our uncomfortable feelings and obstacles, learning to recognize and compassionately accept each other's individual needs and capacities, moving on without immense strife and suffering. Old habitual patterns of jealousy and possessiveness, well stored in our body chemistry, would, of course, emerge, but our mission was to shine the torch of consciousness on such and resolve these reactions as soon as they emerged. Relationships, we were reminded, act as mirrors so that we can see ourselves more clearly, ultimately learning to be purposely at home with ourselves and our aloneness. As Rajneesh regularly reminded us, each of us is essentially alone. George Santayana had written, "Life is but a flight of the alone to the Alone."

While romantic or strictly sexual relationships at the ashram came together and broke apart fairly quickly, most of the ashramites wanted deep relationships and sought them out, choosing not to use *Tantra*, the yoga of sex, as an excuse to be promiscuous. Many ashramites alternatively chose a solitary, monastic discipline as their path. Rajneesh guided his devotees to listen deeply to and follow their hearts, their own, individual inner guidance.

I fell in love with Renu, a beautiful and compassionate young woman who I met in my second year at the ashram. Our sexual energy grew from playful experience to deep caring. We shared our passion for meditation, our love and devotion to learning from our teacher, in addition to our Tantric lovemaking. I became afraid of losing her and suppressed the depth of my feelings for a time because it triggered memories of my possessiveness in the past, which had not ended well. I did not want to repeat that behavior. As Renu and I became more intimate during the passing months, my fear dissipated until slowly but surely she began to pull away. She shared that she felt we had become too dependent upon each other— especially so in my case. She assured me that she loved me, but she also wanted to open our relationship sexually and cease the exclusivity. This news devastated me.

Having learned from Rajneesh's teaching and my own past experiences, I got over it sooner than expected, helping me to realize that I was healing an old wound where all too often in my relationships passion had precipitated possessiveness. Though sad about the split with Renu, my quick recovery from our break-up healed this essential old ego wound, and we remained close friends.

This memory brings a pivotal and humiliating awareness back that occurred during my first summer at Esalen. I had been dating Laury, a caring, intelligent, and beautiful artist, for close to three years. I could talk openly to her about everything and soon fell madly in love. When my feelings blossomed from casual to deep, I couldn't perform sexually. She gently understood, but in the end it was not the awkward sex but my possessiveness that drove her away.

After more than 40 years, we have recently reconnected. I am deeply grateful I've now had the opportunity to thank her for opening the gates of selfless love for me. A poem from my journals from that time illuminates this ecstatic feeling:

When love lives, all is alive, so Vibrant yet gentle
Heartsong fills the air
and misses no corner or crevice.
Every muscle, and beyond this every atom
screams of delight.
Be mine, not as a possession
But foreverly Now.

Finding My Soul Mate

After much reflection and a deepening self-awareness of my once insecure tendency to be possessive, during my last year at the ashram I met my best friend, companion, and wife of 35 years, Kadambari, at a Passover Seder that we celebrated at the ashram. When our eyes met, sparks ignited. We immediately felt as if we knew each other and united with a passionate hug. Many of the ashramites came from Jewish backgrounds from America, England, South Africa, and Europe, and to fulfill our tradition we would each year celebrate the Passover with a traditional Seder, bringing matzah and reading from the Haggadah the story of the freeing of Pharaoh's slaves in Egypt. We read the story metaphorically as freeing ourselves from our own self-imposed as well as societal and religious bondages. Kadambari and I had each come with another guest but felt certain that we would see each other again very soon.

One evening while on line for dinner before *darshan*, as guards had to arrive early to accompany Bhagwan, beautiful Kadambari, who was serving food, asked me for a date after *darshan*. We felt a strong attraction to each other, but having each recently ended other relationships, we proceeded very slowly without any commitments. Though we spent almost all of our time together after that, we held no expectations—decidedly different from my previous relationships—and, though we felt deep compassion for each other, our sexual life was not the central focus of our relationship. The natural growth of our love, its balance, continues to sustain our marriage to this very day.

We both thrived on the wonderful experiment of ashram life, a community dedicated to love and expansion of consciousness, as if returning to the garden but no longer fearful to eat the forbidden fruit. Rajneesh enjoyed referring to the Garden of Eden as the paradise that we were all born into. He would remind us that the animals too lived in paradise, but they felt no temptation to eat the luscious fruit of the Tree of Knowledge. We humans, he would say, were ordained to eat the forbidden fruit for knowledge created self-consciousness. When Adam and Eve realized that they were naked, exposed, and separate, duality emerged. Rajneesh taught that humanity's ultimate goal is to return to the garden, with awareness, with true knowledge of who we are, each of us, and it is this that distinguishes us from the animals.

This story told in Genesis expresses knowledge as sin. But as Jesus wisely taught, unless we become like little children— innocent, not knowing, we cannot return to the garden, cannot truly enter the kingdom of God. Rajneesh stressed the importance of developing the mind but also transcending knowledge to taste from the tree of true Being.

24

The Healers' Circle

*"He who works with his hands is a laborer. He who works with his
hands and his head is a craftsman. He who works with his hands, his
head, and his heart is an artist.*

—St. Francis of Assisi

The ashram attracted some of the best therapists in
the human potential movement from around the
world, particularly from the United States and England,
leading the U.S. residents, in particular, to refer to the ashram
as Esalen East.

When people arrived for their initial visit, they were
advised to participate in encounter or other psychologically-
oriented groups to break through defenses, to free up suppressed
emotions in body and soul, ideally releasing old belief systems or
resentments that obstructed the natural flow of one's existence.
This prepared them for Eastern meditation approaches, such as
Vipassana, a silent retreat where participants alternated between
sitting and walking meditations, and zazen, where participants
focused on conscious breath and chanting sacred sounds or
mantras while cultivating their sitting meditation.

The ashram encouraged guests as well as residents to participate in the wide variety of offered modalities that fostered self-awareness, specifically individual psychotherapy sessions, such as Gestalt therapy, primal therapies, and Bioenergetics as well as healing bodywork such as Rolfing, the Alexander Technique, acupuncture, shiatsu, massage, and other specific hands-on healing work.

After the morning discourse, the auditorium was used for various purposes, usually for one- hour slots, open to the public seven days a week. The ashram offered Sufi dancing; *nadabrahma* meditation, which focused on healing and sound vibrations, and Dynamic Meditation, the cathartic meditation that had initially drawn me to Rajneesh back in New York. The final meditation of the day ended by 6 PM to allow those few who would participate in evening *darshan* to have time for dinner.

As Alan Watts shares in his book *Psychotherapy East & West*: "...the psychotherapist must realize that his science, or art, is misnamed, for he is dealing with something far more extensive than a psyche and its private troubles.... Many psychotherapists have come to recognize that Eastern self-liberation methods can be essential to holistic healing. Eastern philosophy tends to believe that distress arises in people as it arises in cultures, what may be deemed *Maya*. This Hindu-Buddhist term refers not only to individuals' "illusion," but the illusion of the world's conception of a culture. The aim of this liberation is not the destruction of *Maya* but seeing distress for what it is, perhaps seeing through it. For when human beings no longer identify with the definition or label that others may have given them, they may at once open to the universality of their uniqueness—universal by virtue of the inseparability of a living organism from the cosmic whole."

I particularly appreciated that the ashram entrusted the process of a given therapist's treatment to the therapist's discretion based on the best healing approach for that client. In the West, we are under strict scrutiny in our private practices or facilitation groups and, in effect, must market our services to the public, giving talks and writing academic articles and books to substantiate our influence. Our private practices require time-consuming accounting of fees, invoicing, insurance claims, and taxes, all of which the ashram managed for us so that our work, devoted to bringing others to consciousness, came first. We collectively believed that all illness reflected blocks of energy flow, and practitioners used their specialty to free up those blocks in order to promote healing.

The ashram therapists bonded with open camaraderie, often discussing each other's cases and coming up with the best strategy for a client's well being. Though many of our clients were ashramites which made longer-term treatment and healing processes the most effective, we also treated visitors to the ashram from all over the world, particularly the States, all the European countries, Japan, South America, and often even from India. These folks usually stayed for only a few weeks or months, and it helped enhance their healing experience when we worked together to strategize their treatment plan during their stays and beyond.

All members of the ashram's therapeutic community were devoted to developing "observer" skills, the mindful practice of witnessing one's own ego. This encouraged us to use our intuition when providing guidance and lead practitioners to get out of their own way so spirit could lead their healing sessions. This philosophy held true for most everyone working in the ashram community as well as for artists who were working in various genres and mediums. Artists, perhaps more often than most, claim that when spirit moves them, their egos naturally yield, allowing the creative process to flow through them into their painting, sculpture, writing, scientific discovery, or, in our case, our healing sessions. We were not primarily artists but we well understood their meaning. We knew from experience the state of being "in the zone."

We wanted to be purely authentic and intended to eliminate as much inauthenticity as possible. For example, why ask friends or colleagues how they are if you're not truly interested? And, if such an inquiry felt genuine, listen with presence before responding. We were committed to accountability, honesty, and integrity, but most of us from the West had been conditioned to put on a happy face or retain a sense of appropriate politeness. At the ashram, the only approval we truly wanted was from our master, Rajneesh, and his discourses greatly influenced the general mood. When he spoke on Sufism, *Tantra* or the Baul mystics electric sparks flew, as these traditions honored ecstasy as a means to higher realms of consciousness. When he spoke on Zen, Christian mystics, or yoga, the energy turned inward toward a more meditative and contemplative way.

Ultimately it was less about the subject matter or the particular tradition that we learned about through the discourses and more about how the ashramites, in general, and, particularly in Bhagwan's presence, seemed all plugged into the same current with similar feelings—whether irritability, sadness, excitement, or joy—beyond our personal fluctuations.

* * *

I had known for sometime that I could let go of my ego and open to the healing spirit moving through me to my clients but what I offered did not always meet my clients' needs. When

I discussed this with my ashram colleagues, we agreed that it would be helpful to refer our people to other modalities, when better suited for them. We decided to create an ongoing support group and met each Monday in my living space. The group consisted of an acupuncturist from San Francisco, a chiropractor from New York, an internist from England, a Rolfer from California, a massage therapist from South Africa, and myself, trained in the Alexander Technique and psychotherapy with a deepening trust in spiritual healing.

Ashram Healers' Circle

The chiropractor taught the group for the first few months, guiding us in the basic tenets of chiropractic work: the workings of the spine and each vertebrae's association with which nerve, how to feel by touch and determine which vertebrae may be subluxated (twisted one way or the other), including some techniques for restoring its balance. A six- to eight-week series followed led next by the acupuncturist, the medical doctor, the Rolfer, and finally the Alexander Technique, until we all had a solid understanding of how each modality operated.

We circulated pertinent printed material for all group members, including diagrams, and after a year's time all of us felt much richer for the experiences. One modality never had propriety over another, as each therapist was first devoted to healing in the spirit of Rajneesh's teaching.

Birthing at the Ashram

An English friend provided gynecological services at the ashram medical center. An ardent believer in the Alexander work, he sent his pregnant patients in their last trimester to me to help them begin to open their pelvises. My friend shared that the hormones released during pregnancy actually make the ligaments around the pelvis act more like rubber bands than like tight clamps. And, I knew physiologically that the ligament known as the *pubis symphsis*, between the pelvic bones in front and the ligaments around the sacrum, have the capacity to stretch, allowing the pelvic floor to be exceptionally flexible. I worked both physically on the sacroiliac joints and intuitively to increase the pregnant womens' innate flexibility to their pelvic floor.

When a baby's head begins to bear down, a pregnant woman's typical reaction is to resist, sensing the head won't possibly fit through! This creates more tension, restricting the inherent flexibility during pregnancy, which often requires drugs for the mother to relax and more drugs to resume contractions, a vicious cycle—unnecessary stress for both mother and child.

We presided over at least 20 births during my five years at the ashram. It was my job in the birthing room to support the mother's breathing with gentle bodywork, reminding her to allow her pelvis to widen and adapt itself to the baby. I would also use acupuncture points to encourage both contractions and relaxation.

My first birthing experience lasted throughout the night. When the pushing finally began, dawn had broken. Exhausted, I told myself I doubted I'd sign on for more, and simultaneously as intense light filled the room and this new life emerged into the world, I realized I couldn't wait to attend the next birth.

At each succeeding birthing, the midwife would explain physiologically the exact state of the mother. She would allow me to palpate the cervix to sense the progress of dilation and also feel the baby's position through the mother's abdominal wall, advising that a health practitioner can always use such knowledge. I never did need that skill after leaving the ashram, but I realize that even all of these years later, I'd know what to do.

After ten or so homebirths, on occasion needing to administer acupuncture to turn a breeched baby, we encountered a breech that would not respond to the acupuncture stimulation of the acupoints. The midwife reached out to a clinic near Pune, and they arranged a room. Waiting for us when our taxi dropped us off at the entrance, the doctor, an Indian gynecologist/obstetrician, was also a disciple of Rajneesh. We were shown to the birthing room and instructed to prepare a warm bath, as the midwife, the physician, and myself entered the operating theater. Bright lights surrounded the table. We held the mother's hands, calming her down, as the doctor gave her a spinal epidural anesthetic. He explained that he would do the surgery but she would feel no pain. He would lay the baby on her breast before cutting the umbilical cord. After making an incision in her lower abdomen, he lowered the light, and cut the sack, taking the baby out and, as promised, laid the precious baby on her mother's breast for the bonding to begin. He soon cut the umbilical cord and gave the baby to the midwife to take to the next room where her first warm bath awaited her. He then turned the lights back up and stitched up the mother—a true Leboyer natural Cesarean birth!

A Brief Visit Back to the States

Two years or so after moving to the ashram I returned to the States to visit with my family and to share some Tibetan and Indian artifacts with a friend who I hoped could sell them for me. I needed to raise money to buy a motorcycle in India upon my return.

It was wonderful to see my mother and my older sister and her family who not only accepted and even respected me for following my own path, but also, I suspect, felt a kinship and similar call within themselves.

During my month in the States, I attended a pool party given by my elder brother Stanley and clearly stood out like a sore thumb. The ostentatious display of wealth got under my skin, prompting an acute awareness of my own material poverty. To them I would always be a failure because I did not make money. I briefly imagined staying in New York, setting up a lucrative practice, playing "guru," and accumulating enough wealth to prove myself to them. I knew this was nonsense, but the attitude coming from the majority of my family triggered an open wound, remembering deep-seated threads of disappointment often seen in my father's eyes, irritating remnants of my once insecure ego.

While these thoughts crisscrossed through my mind, an uncle, who I had very little relationship with, approached me and asked, "So you gotta go to India! We got everything here, what are you getting there that you can't get here?"

I looked him directly in the eye and said, "A wardrobe, I can choose what costume I'd like to wear."

My jab went right over his head, as he looked at me sideways and walked away.

Standing there thinking about what I'd said I realized how we wear costumes to reflect our identities (or to hide them). If we don't know who we are we tend to become preoccupied with our "costume," our show of wealth or position of power, professional or personal—doctor, lawyer, mother, father. I smiled to myself, ready to go home to India where I belonged.

This memory reminds me of those times that Rajneesh encouraged groups of us to attend J. Krishnamurti's teachings in Bombay wearing our orange clothes and beads. We would arrive early and sit on the front row where Krishnamurti could see us. I imagine Rajneesh thought this great trickster fun intended perhaps to get a rise out of his scholarly peer, for he knew that Krishnamurti detested "costumes," including the colors of sannyas.

I much appreciated Krishnamurti's wisdom and attended many of his lectures both in Bombay and in New York. Where Rajneesh's wisdom came from the heart with which I most resonated, Krishnamurti led from his intellect. In either case, surely both men had become enlightened, no matter what they wore.

25

Change in the Ashram Air

*"A hidden order in chaos is revealed by a new way of looking…
One thing that's clear is that chaos is feminine, and creation out of chaos
is the creation out of the womb, an all-containing potentiality emerging
out of darkness."*

—Rupert Sheldrake, from *Chaos, Creativity and Cosmic Consciousness*

Life back at the ashram was like living in an amplification chamber. Although the residents had a sense of purpose and an underlying commitment to the serenity of meditation, daily life could still feel like a rollercoaster, intense and unpredictable. Rajneesh, and, by osmosis, the ashram office staff, intentionally, at times, pulled the carpet out from under our feet, changing ashram rooms or job assignments without warning. Residents viewed these occurrences as tests to our centeredness! We tried to observe ourselves and to develop a "witnessing" consciousness, the ability to experience our emotional ups and downs while remaining aware that a part of ourselves remained detached from the drama. There was a profound shift in the air, as if the amplitude in a control room had slowly but surely been turned up higher.

When I returned to India in 1975 intending to live full-time at the ashram, there had been no more than 200 residents, but the numbers had now grown exponentially, as people came daily from all around the world, Rajneesh's teaching particularly attractive to the twenty-somethings of the 1960s and 1970s. The study of humanistic psychology had expanded, and students across the U. S. marched against the Vietnam War. It made no sense to our generation, and we began to rebel against the old rules, rules meant to keep us obedient and orderly. Our growing awareness told us that we had more human potential than we had been taught. The Beatles brought the teachings of Maharishi Mahesh Yogi to the West, and India became a symbol of an inward quest. The West, it seemed, relentlessly sought more possessions, more power, more control, but the East represented an alternative. Rajneesh resonated with those seeking a change, a bridge between unleashing our repressed potency by introducing us to Eastern practices of meditation. He became a magnet for these seekers, a celebrant of our intention to be whole, fully alive, in search of contentment through truth.

As more and more followers arrived, the ashram had no choice but to expand quickly. We needed much more housing, and more provisions to feed the visitors and ashramites alike. With the help of devotees who were also physicians from the U. S., England, and Germany, the ashram established a medical center. The ashram purchased more land from adjacent properties and built multiple bamboo huts. Ashram accommodations were at a premium, and a food pass was worth pure gold.

Enterprises sprung up overnight, and an auditorium was built to hold up to 6,000 strong for Rajneesh's discourses and to gather for meditations during the day. The old lecture hall

behind Rajneesh's residence was now used only in the evenings
for the intimate, one-on-one *darshan* experiences. Gardens and
flowers blossomed and bloomed in abundance as love found
many ways to manifest.

The ashram opened a restaurant and a cafeteria in addition
to the residents' dining area. A boutique sold fine, handcrafted
jewelry made on the premises, often with spiritual designs;
clothing in yellow, saffron, orange, reds, and purples, also
ashram-made; cassettes of Rajneesh's lectures, and a sheer
multitude of books as all of Rajneesh's discourses, which were
recorded and transcribed into book form. The ashram had
a pottery studio, made fine musical instruments, and had a
publishing division for editing, layout, and design. It was a
joyous zoo, for, as Rajneesh had so often proclaimed, he was not
interested in his disciples becoming buddhas, but rather "Zorba
the Buddha," meditators who celebrated life itself.

With the facilities bursting at the seams and the expense
of running such a large operation, the ashram administrators
constantly needed to raise funds. A seamless operation was one
thing but keeping Rajneesh safe from harm was most important.
This prompted some individuals to vie for more powerful and
prestigious jobs, such as ashram office positions and assistants to
Laxmi, Rajneesh's private assistant.

With all the commotion of rapid expansion a split
arose between inner and outer circles. Ashram residents were
at a disadvantage as those closest to Rajneesh took power.
Joy remained in the outer circles where those of us with no
inclination toward power over others continued our respective
work with love, leaving the bureaucratic endeavors to those who
seemed to thrive on them.

I most appreciated the simplicity of ashram life and my therapeutic work and attempted, as did many of my colleagues, to keep a distinct distance between the bureaucracy of the commune and the routine of our daily lives. I was most fortunate to live near Rajneesh's home with rare need to make decisions for anyone but myself.

The Darshan Guard

Rajneesh provoked a strong reaction from his audiences, often attacking their alignment with fixed belief systems, organized religion, or political parties. As he once declared in Bombay, "All my statements are addressed to someone; each of my statements has its proper address." He relished pressing buttons to wake people from their lethargic tunnel vision, but such triggers angered millions of people worldwide, and some wanted nothing better than to avenge his insults to their Gods.

A Scottish osteopath named Shiva became Rajneesh's primary protector. He looked perpetually fierce, sitting by his master's side, eyes peeled for any sign of attackers. Shiva claimed he learned karate and aikido after his assignment as Bhagwan's bodyguard.

When credible threats on his life reached the ashram, Bhagwan named ten people to assist Shiva as bodyguards, his "darshan guards," me among them, a, tall, thin pacifist; an English doctor, even slighter than me, and eight others. It was curious as to why he chose any of us, as none among us had any proper experience as bodyguards. He knew, however, that we were diligently loyal to him, never missing his discourses; we were competent, and always scrupulously reliable in our work. Rumor had it that everyone in the outer circle was envious, for we ten became part of Rajneesh's inner circle, most evenings

very near Bhagwan at *darshan* and flanking him protectively
at morning discourses. All members of the Darshan Guard felt
honored that Rajneesh had selected them to protect him.

When Shiva initially met with us he looked toward heaven
asking how he could convert this motley crew into a protective
force. I imagine he said to himself, "My God, this is what he
sends me?" but he painstakingly began to train us.

The Darshan Guards met with Shiva on the rooftop of the
main house where he diligently attempted to teach us martial
arts. We met every morning at dawn for our training in karate,
judo, and aikido, the martial arts that Shiva had learned himself,
and he tried his best to pass all he knew on to us. At first it
appeared hopeless, but with our combined commitment we
increased our awareness and martial art abilities and came to
stand at the ready. When visitors with additional martial art
expertise came to the ashram, Shiva would enlist them to teach
us their skills as well.

* * *

Though Rajneesh surely appreciated beauty, he held no
attachment to material possessions and spoke boldly about the
spiritual demise of the Western people for whom acquisition
of objects of comfort was more important than true spiritual
devotion. He tickled his naysayers' noses in the sand asking
devotees to bring him watches— Rolex, Cartier—and Mont
Blanc pens, only to give them away to others. The press as well
as the Indian community endlessly criticized Rajneesh over his
Rolls Royce, asking why a so-called spiritual" master would
possess such an ostentatious vehicle. They assumed he used his
followers' donations for selfish purposes. Many of us knew such
antics were staged dramas, ploys to make a stark point about
the emptiness of materialism. He never rode in his fancy car

except from his residence to the lecture hall, a mere few hundred feet apart. Besides that daily jaunt to the auditorium, he hardly ever left his quarters. But the Indian newspapers and magazine articles abounded and reached America and Europe complete with photos of the "sex" guru wearing a Rolex in his Roll Royce!

The Indian government wanted to stop him at all cost. They banned the ashram from receiving building permits or purchasing property and sent government officials to review the ashram's financial activities. They stopped awarding visas to foreigners who listed the Rajneesh Ashram in Pune as a destination on their forms. Counter to this, many of Rajneesh's American and German followers married people from England, Ireland, Scotland, Canada, and Australia where no visas were necessary at that time.

The practice of acting as Bhagwan's bodyguard offered me a challenging and rewarding meditation. Before that time I would typically close my eyes during discourses and allow the energy to carry me where it would, but with this crucial responsibility I had to remain alert and aware of each and every movement around our master, on guard for individuals with knives or guns or willing to harm Rajneesh with their bare hands. With much newly cultivated discipline, I learned to stay open to Bhagwan's words and energy field while remaining diligently alert—a meditative practice that stays with me to this day.

Even when not on duty, the Darshan Guards always sat in close proximity to Rajneesh at lectures and *darshan*, a privilege envied by both inner and outer circles. After six months of this job in addition to my therapeutic work, I felt as if a faucet had been turned on as a continual, ineffable energy unceasingly flowed through me. As if turned up an octave, my work became both more focused and more intense, with incredible results, where clients often had cathartic responses to my treatments.

Sometimes, however, the flow came too fast, building pressure and intense energy that I couldn't relax at night, finding myself buzzing, my cells pulsating, rather than sleeping soundly. After a month or so of this intense energy, as if my body had no choice but to adapt to it, I developed an exceptionally high fever. Having had both malaria and dengue fever (known as "break-bone" fever) over the years I'd been at the ashram, I had intimate experience of the joint pain associated with these mosquito-borne diseases, and knew unequivocally that such fever felt much different than my current state. Waves of emotion moved through me and felt released through my copious sweat. This lasted for over a week, but the ashram doctors could find nothing obviously wrong with me. Many knowledgeable visitors came to visit me during my week of fever, but with no other symptoms, we interpreted my condition as a deep emotional and physical cleansing. My defensive, protective valve had blown off.

When the fever finally broke, I felt relieved of pressure, but exhausted, as if I'd been on a perpetual LSD trip, the same intensity with even some visions or hallucinations. Though I'd taken no drugs or had alcohol for five years and no longer felt any draw to chemicals, natural or otherwise, I constantly felt high, but still somehow performed my bodyguard work each morning and my therapeutic duties in the afternoons. I assumed that I must be purging whatever trauma and toxins had been stored in my cells and tried to be patient, but each morning upon waking I hoped the intense energy would subside. Finally, after two full weeks, without explanation, I felt refreshed, renewed, and again relaxed, but something inside me had changed.

The fever had broken, leaving me with a profound sense of well-being peppered with a subtle sense of doubt. I tried to push the doubt aside but found myself thinking about Rajneesh's message that one can only truly attain the meditation of sitting on a mountaintop if he can take it also to the marketplace. Buddha's words also came to me:

> *"It is proper to doubt. Do not be led by Holy Scriptures or by mere logic or inference, nor by appearances or the authority of religious teachers. When you realize that something is unwholesome and bad for you, give it up. And when you realize that something is wholesome and good for you, do it."*
>
> —from *The Enlightened Mind,* edited by Stephen Mitchell

I've reflected often over the years on the origin of that fever, believing it had in fact burned away toxins and perhaps even trauma. But, after reading Krishnamurti's biography, where it states that he attributed his lifelong propensity for headaches to improperly cleansed energy channels, I wondered if my fever was due to a similar energy blockage. Krishnamurti spent many years opening his energy channels, until one day a flood of energy brought him to enlightenment. I dare say I have worked long and hard to clear these channels, but enlightenment? Not yet.

26

A Finger Pointing to the Moon

> *A seeker said to Buddha, "I do not ask for words, I do not ask for silence."*
>
> *Buddha sat quietly.*
>
> *The seeker said admiringly, "The compassion of the World-Honored One has opened the clouds of my illusion and enabled me to enter the path." Making his salutations, he departed.*
>
> *Ananda (Buddha's chief disciple) then asked Buddha, "What was it that this stranger realized that he so praised you?"*
>
> *The World-Honored One replied, "A high class horse moves even at the shadow of the whip!"*
>
> —Bhagwan Shree Rajneesh, from *The Shadow of the Whip*

In the spiritual community that G.I. Gurdjieff led in France, an old man lived there who was the personification of difficulty—irritable, messy, fighting with everyone, and unwilling to clean up or help at all. No one got along with him. Finally, after many frustrating months of trying to stay with the group, the old man left for Paris. Gurdjieff followed him and tried to convince him to return, but it had been too hard, and the man said no. At last Gurdjieff offered the man a very big monthly stipend if he returned. How could he refuse? When he returned everyone was aghast, and on hearing that he was being paid (while they were being charged a lot to be there), the community was up in arms. Gurdjieff called them together and after hearing their complaints laughed and explained: "This man is like yeast for bread." He said, "Without him here you would never really learn about anger, irritability, patience, and compassion. That is why you pay me, and why I hire him.

——from *Stories of the Spirit, Stories of the Heart*,
edited by Christina Feldman and Jack Kornfield)

My ashram life continued to nourish, sustain, and inspire me, but the aggressive disdain for Rajneesh in the Indian community, including crowds gathering and turmoil ensuing outside the ashram gates, created increasingly bad press from around the world. An air of suspicion and anxiety began to pervade the ashram community with rumors flying that the ashram may even have to move its location. The hovering turbulence reflected the eternal truths carried in the wind of Rajneesh's wise words and yet his outward choices left us at times mystified as the ashram began to radically change.

Rajneesh had chosen another Indian woman named Sheela to replace Laxmi as his personal assistant and put Sheela in charge of the imminent ashram move. I'd met Sheela in New York and observed her in India, noticing the clear difference between Laxmi 's deep devotion to Rajneesh and her commitment to meditation, her eyes forever radiating love, while Sheela seemed shifty, inauthentic, and even perhaps untrustworthy. I assumed that her restless, often obstreperous manner would become bored with mundane administrative duties and that she'd move on to more stimulating endeavors.

I now wonder if choosing Sheela foreshadowed Rajneesh's intention to self-destruct.

Sheela had married a Jewish man from New York and spent many years living in the States. A flamboyant but affected woman, she clearly stood in awe of Bhagwan, but she had no meditative proclivity and, to my mind, seemed unconscious and insensitive. Her wealthy parents had known Rajneesh since his days as a professor, and I assumed he must also have a financial reason for entrusting her with such high-level responsibility.

I vividly remember when Rajneesh sent her to me for a healing. She'd arrived punctually but declared that she had no idea why she was there. I invited her to lie on the table and to relax with her eyes closed. She refused to close her eyes and laid tensely on the table while I attempted to channel love into her. She asked repeatedly, "Is it over yet?" When she finally left the room, I realized that I was drained of energy and grappled with why such a person would be given such power at the ashram, though Rajneesh insisted that Laxmi was technically still in charge.

Breaking My Back

With all the impending unrest inside and outside the ashram walls, with only my room for solitude, I began to feel claustrophobic and on my half day off each week, I took motorcycle rides into the countryside, most often to a beautiful lake about an hour outside of Pune. Riding through the small villages, feeling the wind on my face, relaxed me. I shared the narrow back roads with bullock carts, goats, chickens, bicycles, rickshaws, trucks, and driving on the British left side of the road was always an adventure. My girlfriend Kadambari often rode with me on back and having our own space refreshed us. I became much less obsessive about attending lectures and mornings when I was off bodyguard duty I'd allow myself to relax in bed with my girlfriend and a cup of coffee or chai. This semi-detachment reconnected me with my inner voice, and I'd imagine life outside the commune, what it might be like to have my own life again, but just as quickly as such a notion arose, I'd put it away, unable to truly imagine being separate from the integral ashram community to which I belonged.

After my experience with the most recent fever and its intense aftermath, I had surely realized that I must bring whatever I'd learned in India into the world but I wasn't sure when or how. The ashram community respected my healing work and many of my clients referred to me as "magic hands'" when I'd pass them. If I returned to the States, the men in my family would no doubt marginalize my work. I could imagine them saying, "So what's a healer or meditator really do? And, what do you have to show for it?" This memory brings a joke to mind:

> Two men bump into each other in the street, knowing each other from attending their sons' baseball games and events at school.
>
> "Hi Joe, it's been ten years since our kids graduated; what's your son up to?"
>
> "Hi Pete, well, he's okay, but can't find himself. He goes from one job to another, drinks and parties, but hopefully he'll find his way. How's your boy?'
>
> "He too seems to be lost and searching, but he's found meditation and some spiritual thing. At least he's doing something!"

One ordinary day, feeling exhausted after discourse and a full day of Alexander work, I felt a bit achy and decided go for a ride. I headed out on my cycle to indulge in a yummy mango pulp with cream, planning to get back in time for *darshan*. My back felt unusually sore. After my bout with dengue fever, I'd learned to listen better to my joints and back when they alerted me to slow down, to take it easy. When putting my motorcycle on its stand, my back severely spasmed. Hoping that a good night's sleep would resolve the problem, I missed *darshan* that evening, but morning came and the spasm had worsened. I could barely get out of bed.

My friends kindly came to my room to massage and Rolf me and after three days I felt much better but not well enough to get back to work. Word came from the office that if I was to miss any more work I must go to the medical center for professional advice. I found this ludicrous since *I* was the person people were sent to for back problems, but I didn't make waves.

I saw a German doctor at the medical center who I did not know and who seemed to know very little about back issues. He advised me that I should do traction for a few days. I told him that I'd learned that traction was the wrong treatment for lumbar (lower-back) issues and that, even if rarely an appropriate treatment, such a patient should not walk immediately following traction for it left the ligaments overstretched and prone to injury.

Word of my refusal to follow the doctor's treatment reached Sheela, by then well in charge of administrative affairs. She sent a firm message that I was to drop my body worker's ego and follow the given medical advice, implying that if I further resisted, my role as darshan guard would be in jeopardy. Again, not wanting to rock the boat, I conceded and followed orders against my better judgment.

I had always followed my own path, but also preferred to keep the peace. Like my mother, I tried to be diplomatic and find ways to do what I wanted to do, never intending to hurt another's feelings. When I considered, for example, saying "no," I would experience great discomfort, causing me to sometimes disregard my inner knowing. The decision to stand up for oneself or another when it will create conflict must, in my opinion, be worth the emotional effort. Standing one's ground is preferable but when and how requires conscious discernment. The Serenity Prayer speaks directly to such a moment of decision:

God grant me the serenity to accept the things I cannot change, the courage to change the things I can, and the wisdom to know the difference.

I've learned to take the time to turn within for inner guidance but in this circumstance I did not take that time to listen to and to trust my inner wisdom.

Walking very slowly back to my room after the first traction treatment, I heard a sudden and loud pop accompanied by a ripping pain in my lower back and down my left leg. I knew that I had ruptured a disc, for the exact reason I had refused treatment in the first place. I failed to acknowledge "the shadow of the whip," needing, I suppose, to feel the full sting.

As I lay in bed, in pain, I realized, remembering a rabbinical story, that I had not paid attention to and honored my inner knowing:

In the last century, a tourist from the States was visiting the famous Polish rabbi, Hafez Hayyim. He was astonished to find that the rabbi's home was only a simple room filled with books, the only furniture a table and a bench.

"Rabbi, where is your furniture?" asked the tourist.

"Where's yours?" replied Hafez.

"Mine? But I'm only visiting here."

"So am I," said the rabbi.

—Anthony de Mello, from *The Song of the Bird*

During the following month at the ashram, healer after healer came to my room to work on me, but I knew I needed surgery. When suggested that I undergo the operation in India, I respectfully declined and arranged to get back to the States. I had called my mother to inform her, and she had set up an appointment with a neurologist who had recently performed back surgery on my brother at New York University Medical Center. Kadambari agreed to join me and to stay with me during the surgery. She not only helped me through it but also never left.

It took a broken back to make the painful and difficult decision to move on, to take my practice into private life back in the States, to share all that I had learned about healing and consciousness. As I had in the Philippines with a real family that knew and understood me, I had to leave my ashram family and begin again. This ending felt abrupt and sad. I had revealed myself in India as I never could in the West, and the love among all ashramites ran deep.

I understood and embraced the concept of surrendering the ego and surrendering had never been more on my heart and in my mind. I believed, as Rajneesh taught, that we have an inner compass, a barometer that tells us what intuitively feels right or wrong. Surrender does not intend us to sacrifice this inner compass, but our ego, and that boundary can indeed seem blurred. Ashram life had taught me that our work is to allow spirit to live through us that we may commune with the source of our being. Only then might we truly awake and fully incarnate.

Living Meditation

I remember a story about the Indian master Ramakrishna:

His head disciple had been with him for over ten years, but one day while Ramakrishna was talking to his disciples, this man asked a question.

"I've been with you for many years and at times feel close to surrender, my trust immense, yet you often talk about reincarnation and karma, and, since I don't believe in these concepts, it interferes with my surrender. What should I do?'

Ramakrishna responded by explaining that he should be grateful for not believing in reincarnation; it would be worse if he did believe in it.

"Either you know it, or you don't, drop belief and BE!" he proclaimed.

Back in the States, healing from back surgery, I felt a bit lost, so far removed from my friends and colleagues in India, but at heart, I had moved on. I had to start over, or at least pick up where I'd left off in New York, knowing that my path would clearly be an extension of my past, but how, where, to begin again?

My mother joyously welcomed Kadambari and me back into her world, but the other connections with my biological family remained predictably detached. My sister-in-law shared some wise advice with the two of us saying it didn't matter how many diplomas we had on our walls, "they'll never truly accept you without money." In my heart I had already come to grips with this awareness, but my mother so wanted us to fit in. I can hear her saying, "I know who you are and I am very proud of you, no matter how the others behave, but please stay connected with your family." It felt right to keep family bonds in good stead, and we continued to attend weddings, Bar Mitzvahs, and funerals, but the dye was cast. Only my dear mother along with Aunt Sulica and my own sister Estelle and her family respected my path, and that was more than enough for me. Estelle and her daughter Andi had visited me in India and followed a spiritual path similar to my own.

I began to pull the pieces of my new life back in New York together: to re-establish my practice and to secure a much-needed income. We lived with my mother temporarily and with her perfected role as Jewish mother, she catered to our every want. As wonderful as she was, my old fears of dependency re-emerged. I realized that my meditation had been undisturbed at the ashram, and our current situation challenged the depth of my meditative work.

With the help of my brother, Butch, we found a small apartment in Manhattan to sublet at a low rent for a few months. My back was slowly but surely healing, and Kadambari and I both needed this privacy to meditate and envision our way forward. By word of mouth, I secured a few clients using a portable table in our apartment. We trusted that our next steps would be revealed, though the inspiration that I had been used to was slow to manifest.

Veresh, my old roommate at the ashram, called to tell me that I should stay put as the ashram was moving, but I informed him that we had no intention to return. The ashram inner circle had arranged to purchase a large home in New Jersey, which was to be a temporary holding area until they could find land, in the States, on which to build a new commune.

Strangely I had no desire to be a part of it. I had surrendered my ashram life, and my heart continued to be open and appreciative for all that I had received there, but I knew I no longer belonged within the ashram community.

* * *

We knew a number of people who were (or had been) Rajneesh's devotees who had relocated to the metro area from India. My therapist and body-worker friends, who had lost their reliable source of income, and were in great need of community, supported the idea that Kadambari and I launch a healing center on Long Island. We temporarily rented a house with my niece Andi and planned to offer support groups and private sessions in bodywork or psychotherapy as well as a training program in what we called "Rajneesh Bodywork," a perfect interim solution to our way forward. It never felt perfect but our idea blossomed with so many of our fellow ashramites seeking new opportunities. Our vision stayed on course for ten months and we developed a solid client base, earning a manageable income as we stayed true to our inner compass and our meditation.

Kadambari and I had grown much closer while transitioning from our ashram life to life back in the States. We loved each other and, although neither of us felt the need for marriage, it felt right, and also gave my mother a celebration that she could help us arrange! It was a joyous affair and an odd delight to share this day with both my biological family and its many elders *and* with our friends, many dressed in ashram orange, as we all danced and celebrated life.

During this time my dear friend Ninad, also called. (I had been training him to teach the Alexander Technique and healing work while at the ashram.) He was busy getting things in order to leave India for good. He told me of the thousands of people stranded in India with no money or means to return to their homes, and that everyone was selling all of their possessions. He asked what to do with the few things I had left behind, including my motorcycle. I asked him to please sell my things and to give the proceeds to those folks who needed it in order to return to their homes. My heart ached for my community, but the tide had turned. Even when word got out that Rajneesh was temporarily in New Jersey, Kadambari and I felt no need to visit there.

Shortly after this, Sheela and her crew purchased land in Oregon on which they intended to build their new ashram. Within weeks they had built temporary housing and moved Rajneesh and the inner circle there, putting word out that workers would be needed to create the roads and build all the facilities.

* * *

A few months later, not long after getting our healing center up and running on Long Island, we received a phone call from Laxmi. She had been asked to leave the ranch in Oregon,

 having lost all position and power, and wondered if she and Deeksha could stay with us on Long Island for a short while. Deeksha had run all the kitchens at the ashram. I loved Laxmi and, of course, wanted to help, if I could, but I also was eager to hear the inside scoop from such an intimate disciple.

She arrived at our door, her smile exuding the same radiance that I'd remembered. When I asked her how she felt about the changes taking place, particularly about Sheela's influence, she looked at me openly, her big smile growing even wider, and simply said,

"Laxmi (she never referred to herself as I or me, only by the name Rajneesh had given her) is very happy! Only he has the vision, and he lives in my heart! Laxmi continues the dance; he is here!"

Word had gotten back to the new regime in Oregon that two individuals who had been asked to leave the ranch were staying with us. Sheela actually called us asking us not to welcome them, calling them "negative." We refused to follow her wishes and told her that such a request was not in harmony with Rajneesh's teachings. I continued to believe that Rajneesh was intent upon destroying the entire artifice and any hint of his ashram representing a religion of any kind.

Much later, attempting to square my own experiences of five years in India with the demise of this community, Laxmi's words rang true to me. Only she could say so simply what I had to grapple with for a very long time. The essence of my spiritual journey with Bhagwan, what meant most about it, was my inner awakening and expansion of meditative space evoked by his energy and his teachings.

The ashram politics, with the change of control from Laxmi to Sheela, remained non-essential background noise—power games by greedy people—and I successfully avoided being impacted by it. But the community had begun to resemble a religion or cult with a system of rewards and punishments. Why did Bhagwan allow this? Was he showing us that the only truth was inside ourselves? Laxmi said it clearly and simply, "He lives in my heart."

Rumors became more and more rampant in the U.S. media, the tabloids publishing vindictive articles about the "Rolls Royce guru," "the sex guru," and his Rajneeshees, who they called members of a religious cult. I did my best to detach from this gossip and to focus my energy on my professional life, but this disconnect between the master I cherished and the politics and media frenzy about him turned my stomach, despite the fact that my memories and open heart to his message remained intact.

* * *

We continued Bhagwan's meditations and listened on occasion to his old lectures, but, essentially, we remained detached from the upsetting ashram developments and its destructive energy. As the ranch in Oregon began to implode and people dispersed, Rajneesh was arrested while attempting to leave the country and actually spent a few days in prison, where I was told he had the sheriff and guards enraptured, his escorts to the airport sharing hugs before his expulsion from America.

A story comes to mind:

A big, tough samurai once went to see a little monk.

"Monk," he said, in a voice accustomed to instant obedience, "Teach me about heaven and hell!"

The monk looked up at this mighty warrior and replied with utter disdain,

"Teach you about heaven and hell! I couldn't teach you about anything. You're dirty. You smell. Your blade is rusty. You're a disgrace, an embarrassment to the samurai class. Get out of my sight. I can't stand you."

The samurai was furious. He shook, got all red in the face, was speechless with rage. He pulled out his sword and raised it above him, preparing to slay the monk.

"That's hell," said the monk softly.

The samurai was overwhelmed at the compassion and surrender of this little man who had offered his life to give this teaching— to show him hell! He slowly put down his sword,

filled with gratitude, and suddenly peaceful.
"And that's heaven!" the monk said softly.

—from *Experiencing Spirituality* by Ernest Kurtz and Katherine Ketcham

My Master's Essence Will Never Leave Me

To rekindle the intense experiences of living for five years in an Indian ashram, I recently saturated myself in Rajneesh words, in print and on tape, and spoke with friends familiar with his teachings. I realized that even when things there were falling into chaos, there was nowhere in the world I would have preferred to be.

It's uncomfortable to remember that final year, 1979, at the ashram and the following few years back in the States. I felt such ambivalence. As Rajneesh was not speaking during those years, all information came via Sheela from the ranch in Oregon, often stating that these were his words. To this day I don't know the real truth for certain. I have many friends who felt Rajneesh betrayed them, and others who took the shock as a momentous wake-up call. *I* still believe he knew what was happening and, in fact, orchestrated it, taking full responsibility for the actions of the ranch and its administrators. I knew Rajneesh, wholeheartedly trusted his intentions, his words, his teaching, but many of his devotees in public life betrayed his memory. I shudder at the stories that clouded Bhagwan's reputation and by association all those devoted to him. It's difficult to openly share about this phase of my healing journey, my ego preferring to be perceived as pure, in itself a telling revelation.

I can hear Rajneesh's words clearly, "Don't make a religion out of me! I am simply a finger pointing toward a greater reality, but I am merely a finger. Don't be attached to the finger or you will miss where it is guiding you."

He repeated over and over again in his discourses that his words were but guides, reality, he insisted, could only be experienced, never understood. When a disciple once asked him why he spoke for so many hours each day, if words could never express enlightenment, he would tell a story about a disciple of Buddha who asked the same question, to which Buddha replied, "So why does the bird sing?" All spiritual teachers from Christ to Mohammed to Mahavira and Lao Tzu have overflowed with words sharing their wisdom through metaphor, through teaching stories.

Rajneesh taught that all organized religions are dead, based on traditions and practices that keep people asleep in comfort and safety with their belief systems in place. A true spiritual teacher, he would say, believes in the ever-changing unpredictability of life, encouraging his disciples to live in the eternal now. He often referred to a common Zen proverb, "If you meet Buddha on the road, kill him!" meaning it is not the outer Buddha, but the Buddha within that we must seek.

The Indian community and the powerful press took his words literally rather than spiritually when he stated:

"Many times I speak against Mohammed or Mahavir or Buddha. This creates a problem. I am speaking deeply about them, and yet at the same time, I am speaking against them as well. Whenever I seem to be speaking against them, it appears to be so only because the listener is giving importance to the lamp. But for me, when I am revealing something very deep, the emphasis is on the light. So whenever I appear to be speaking against, it is because the emphasis is on the lamp and not the light."

—Bhagwan Shree Rajneesh, from *Dimensions Beyond the Known*

In spite of what happened to Rajneesh and his devotees, my heart will be forever grateful to have known and learned from my master. He continued to teach and lecture for a few more years after his deportment, but purposely, I think, destroyed his dreaded concern that a religion would be made of his words. Back at his residence in India, he died peacefully in 1990, at the age of 58, five years after leaving America.

I knew many quite influential and well-known therapists, physicians, and theologians from my years at the ashram. Many of them have since written books on psychology, spirituality, and philosophy, and, though often exceptionally worthwhile, their bios do not reveal the name of the ashram where they lived in India, concerned I suppose of being associated with Rajneesh's fall from grace. It is not for me to judge the teacher by the events his work has provoked in the world, but by the transformation his work has inspired in my own heart and soul.

While writing about my five ashram years, a dear friend, Bodhichitta (Andrew Ferber, M.D.) gave me cassettes of Rajneesh's discourses that had been recorded after Rajneesh had left Oregon, while living temporarily in Uruguay. I hear the identically calm, meditative voice, imparting the same universal wisdom that had drawn millions to him. When speaking of the dissolution of the Oregon ranch neither his word nor his voice held a trace of anger. I imagine he would say that the Tao does not blame. It takes full responsibility for each moment and for its consequences. This affirmation reminded me of the banner that Bhagwan hung over his chair when he personally led meditation camps in Rajasthan, India. It read: "I am not here to teach, but to awaken."

I am a finger pointing to the moon. I can do nothing else, but look to where I am pointing and not at myself.

PART FIVE

Living an Integrative Reality

"The purpose of life is a life of purpose."

—George Bernard Shaw

27

Beginning Again

"I said to my soul, be still and wait without hope, for hope would be hope for the wrong thing; wait without love, for love would be love of the wrong thing; there is yet faith, but the faith and the love are all in the waiting. Wait without thought, for you are not ready for thought: So the darkness shall be the light, and the stillness the dancing."

—T.S. Eliot from *Four Quartets*

Despite ten months of building a loyal clientele in our mini healing center on Long Island, Kadambari and I both felt ready to move to a more vibrant, resonant community. Our many friends in Woodstock, New York, encouraged us to join them in the beautiful Hudson Valley where artists gathered and spiritual energy flourished. Remembering many years before when Karmapa had invited me to visit him there, I felt a strong affirmation of synchronicity.

One memorable weekend sealed our fate. We were visiting our friend Samvid at his home in Woodstock on Mead Mountain Road, a mere short walk from the Tibetan monastery that Karmapa Rinpoche had long ago suggested that I visit. That very weekend, Samvid received a phone call from the monastery inviting all of the neighbors on his road to meet with Karmapa who wanted to meet them! Samvid mentioned that he had guests and asked if we could accompany him. The monastery representative warmly agreed and soon we found ourselves walking down the mountain and into the gates of the monastery. A huge structure belonging in Nepal or Tibet rather than upstate New York, I felt I'd time traveled back to Nepal.

Tibetan monks and their families clearly lived in the few homes immediately surrounding the large temple as an abundance of multi-colored prayer-flags hung from the trees and over the doors and windows of the dwellings. Upon our arrival, we were graciously escorted into a reception room within the temple where Karmapa sat on a cushion facing the small gathering of neighbors. Speaking through a translator, his laughter and gentle banter reminded me of the day when I'd long ago interrupted the ordination ceremony in Kathmandu. His same mischievous smile greeted me as we entered. He leisurely munched on grapes while inviting his guests to address any concerns that they may have about the "intrusion" of such a large monastery in close proximity to their homes. With typical Woodstock *laissezz-faire* the neighbors welcomed their new "friends" and expressed excitement about having a place to meditate just next door!

Sadly, that same day we learned that in spite of his radiant appearance Karmapa had been diagnosed with cancer, and his grape diet was to support his cleansing. I could not be sure whether he remembered me or not, but it didn't matter, for again I felt at home. In my mind and heart, he had called me to visit, and I had come. We bowed to him; he blessed us both, and, as we departed the chamber, we synergistically knew we had decided to relocate to the area. Shortly after our visit, Karmapa left his body on November 5, 1981.

With a gift from my wife's parents, we soon put a small down payment on a house in Woodstock, completed our Long Island lease, and shortly after moved to our new Hudson Valley home. I immediately opened my practice, offering my unique combination of bodywork, psychotherapy, and energy healing, but found it difficult to define my healing services. Was it psychotherapy, bodywork, or simply healing? I needed a container, a vessel, in which to integrate my work offerings and knew something was missing. When clients would recommend my services, they told me that they struggled to describe their experience. I referred to my healing services, as just that, and encouraged them to do the same—emphasizing its benefits, I suggested, might interest others. At the ashram a wide array of eclectic healing modalities had been accepted and understood, and, although my bodywork was called the Alexander Technique, fellow ashramites had realized that the work could include emotive psychotherapy, deep bodywork, or lighter touch Alexander Technique as well as intense vibrational healing. In Woodstock people seemed to accept the term "healer," but I knew I needed to synthesize my knowledge and find the missing link not only in my practice but also within myself. I trusted my sense of connection with this new place now called home, but I also felt discomfort over the lack of integrated clarity about how to create a container for what to call my work. Meditating as patiently as I could, I waited for guidance.

* * *

While at a garage sale to gather furnishings for our new home, I spotted a Chinese cabinet, painted in brilliant reds and black that would make the perfect centerpiece for my healing room where it remains to this day. It reminded me of when I was seven or eight years old with my parents buying something at an antique store. As I looked around that shop, enamored with the myriad of objects in all shapes and colors and the musty smell of old things, my eyes fell on a Chinese cabinet with many small drawers, each one with different Chinese characters etched in gold. I had to have it and told my parents so in no uncertain terms. They laughed. The cabinet that I'd wanted as a child was indeed a Chinese herbal cabinet, each drawer to be filled with a different herb, and much like the small one in my Hudson Valley office today.

When I saw the cabinet at the garage sale, I remembered sitting and reading on the cliffs at Esalen overlooking the sweeping Big Sur coastline. In those days I had only just been exposed to the precepts of Taoism in the *Tao Te Ching* and they had moved me profoundly. I had immersed myself in the ancient wisdom of the *Neijing, The Yellow Emperor's Classic of Medicine*, one of the most important Taoist texts and the supreme authority of Chinese medicine. Attributed to the great Huang Di, the Yellow Emperor, who reigned during the third millennium BCE, the *Neijing* was believed to be nearly 5,000 years old and yet offered timeless wisdom.

One of my favorite passages in *The Yellow Emperor's Classic of Medicine* appears on the very first page when Huang Di asks his minister and guide, Qi Bo, why people in the days of old enjoyed longer, happier lives. Does the world change from one generation to the next, he'd asked, or have people forgotten how to live in harmony with the enduring laws of nature? Qi Bo gently answered the young emperor's questions, speaking at length about the dramatic changes in lifestyle and philosophy that have contributed to the then present predicament of chronic disease, premature aging, and a general state of disharmony, which linger to this very day.

"In the past," Qi Bo observed, "people practiced the Tao, the Way of Life...." He explained that the principle of balance, of yin and yang, had once been understood, and the laws of change as well: that health was dynamic and connected each individual to the world of change within and without.

Traditional Chinese medicine offers a system for living that encapsulates both thinking and being and states its principles both lyrically and with profound pragmatism. This wisdom, in which sages and scholars had devoted their lives to understanding and describing the vital, life-giving connections between the universe, the earth, and the human being, had existed for nearly 5,000 years, and I wholeheartedly embraced it.

During that first year in Woodstock, my ever-growing appreciation for the balanced wisdom of Chinese medicine met my long-standing yearning for a healing practice that matched my philosophy of life. I realized that I must integrate Chinese medicine, and specifically acupuncture, into my practice.

Sid Zerinsky had offered to train me in acupuncture back in the early 1970s in New York, but my fear of needles and my over-commitment elsewhere had made such dedicated study impossible at the time. I'd also briefly studied acupuncture with Master Shen in Hong Kong, even purchasing needles and books as well as acupuncture plastic models of a man and a woman with all of the points inscribed (they remain in one of my offices today) but I had not been ready for formal study. Even in India, I'd been exposed to the acupuncture pressure points with the many ashram acupuncturists in our healing circle, but only now could I commit to the missing ingredient, Chinese medicine, and pursue it post haste through the study of acupuncture now available in the West.

28

The Unifying Metaphor

"A healer does not really heal; a healer can only present a mirror."
—Lynn V. Andrews, from **Healers on Healing**

In Gestalt therapy I'd learned about the essential importance of closure, and my pull toward studying Chinese medicine now carried the impetus to integrate it into my practice. It epitomized the necessary unifying metaphor to bring the work that I was already doing into a cohesive whole by intrinsically bringing mind, body, and spirit into a single system of healing, one that had been practiced and respected for thousands of years. This calling also nourished my yearning for wholeness.

Champa (Carol), a dear friend from the ashram, had also moved back to New York and wanted to attend acupuncture school, so we decided to do it together. After much research, as no schools existed in New York State at that time which allowed needle insertion by anyone other than an M.D., we found an excellent school in Stamford, Connecticut. It offered a program geared to working people, and was only 30 minutes from New York City and 90 minutes from Woodstock. It required a few evenings each week and a number of weekends, but the schedule made it possible to maintain a job while attending school. The Tri-State Institute for Traditional Chinese Acupuncture offered a three-year program with the same cumulative hours as a full-time, three-year program, plus a diploma in Acupuncture and the ability to sit for the National Boards exam, accepted for certification in many states, though not in New York at that time.

I had always enjoyed studying but my deepening awareness of Chinese medicine's wisdom spoke to me as nothing before, as though I was actively synthesizing my psychotherapeutic knowledge, my connection to bodywork, and my faith in the power of vibrational (energetic) healing. We learned hundreds of acupuncture points and how to locate them anatomically as well as how to apply them to open channels of energy. While studying the points I realized that I could not only sense the hot spot where my client needed healing but also my finger was literally pulled toward it.

I remembered how right it felt when I played with my first toy doctor kit at the age of five. I also recalled my palm-reading experience with Florence Meschter, who had assured me that I could intuitively read palms; nonetheless, I needed to take the course to satisfy the student in me. I felt the same earnest desire in response to acupuncture. I devoured the texts, voraciously highlighting all of the acupoint instruction, and yet if I closed my eyes and placed my hand in a given area, the acupoint pulled my finger to it like a magnet. Still, study I did.

In addition to learning the multitude of acupressure points during the first year of acupuncture school, we also studied their meridians (the energetic pathways on which the points acted as access points) and the organs or functions associated with each energy channel. It all made sense to me as my psychological, physical, and spiritual spheres of work now coalesced as if part of my being. During previous hands-on healings I had often stimulated many of these points, but acupuncture affirmed my intuition with a solid foundation of learning.

Acupuncture gave me the long-awaited unifying healing metaphor for synthesizing all of the healing modalities that I had absorbed, weaving a rich web where mind, body, and spirit united. My growing knowledge enriched my healing toolkit with acupressure, needles, burning moxa (dry mugwort) over the acupoints, and cupping. (Back in Brooklyn, my grandmother had used her version of cupping when a member of the family became ill. She called the glass cups, bankes!)

The Power of Stories

"The shortest distance between a human being and the truth is a story."

—Anthony de Mello, from *The Song of the Bird*

I came to believe that the powerful essence of Chinese medicine had the potential to reconnect us with our stories. Our life experiences, our stories, carry the larger picture that reveals our soul's journey. The key is to be aware of it. Each of us is essentially whole, and our symptoms create opportunities to reclaim our wholeness. This truth plays a central role in all indigenous healing systems, having survived the test of time, each grounded in its culture of origin, believing stagnation or blockage to be at the root of all "dis-ease."

Wholeness seeks balance. All indigenous systems, including traditional Chinese medicine, Indian Ayurveda, Greek Hippocratic medicine, Roman Galenic medicine, Native American medicine, shamanic healing, and, even to some degree, "modern" Western medicine, work to balance energy and promote alignment with our natural, energetic flow.

As Dr. J. R. Worsley stated in *Is Acupuncture for You?*: "The doctor of acupuncture must strive to see his patient not as he is at the time of examination but as he would be if he were whole and perfect in body, mind and spirit, with every possibility of his unique being realized. The personality of a person when ill will not necessarily be true to his own real nature, and may indeed be very different. The work of the doctor of traditional Chinese acupuncture is to help this sick person become renewed, revitalized, and brought to the fullness of his potential."

At the heart of a living metaphor is a story, perhaps a relatable cosmic mythology, but that which is universal is also individually personal. As the cosmos is a living organism so too is the earth, nature itself, and in turn, each living creature. When nature lives in harmony, the life force flows and flourishes. Teaching stories have the power to reconnect individuals to particular issues that have disconnected them from their root energy, what the Chinese call rootedness in the Tao. Though ineffable in words, the Tao reflects resonance where the All is contained in the Each as the Each is contained in the All.

Chinese medicine offers a metaphoric bridge to experience our individual issues, physical or emotional, as somehow universal. Acupoint names such as Heavenly Palace, the Gate of Hope, the Great Mountain Stream, and Walks Three Miles create images that offer us a visual means of healing as we awaken to a greater field of true connection with the source of our being. Each of the Five Elements (or Five Transformative Powers) also offers us a lens through which to experience our place in the greater living whole.

Sharing our stories and naming the images within them give our physical ailments context, where we can engage the cause behind the symptom. Listening carefully also to classic teaching stories may also help us realize that we have become attached to an old, unresolved story of wounding. Such awareness sheds light on stuck patterns and has the capacity to shift blocked energy. The teaching stories threaded throughout this book speak to this intended purpose.

* * *

My fascination with Chinese medicine first arose as a young man at Esalen immersed in the Chinese classics. Reading the Tao and other ancient texts reminded me that everything changes—day mutates into night, night into day. I began to notice this yin and yang in all phases of life and could associate the elements to the natural flow between them as well as to the spring of the first light, the summer of mid-day, the autumn of the waning light, and the winter of the deep night's stillness. I imagined the perfect image of the element Earth as that ephemeral window of twilight, where all is in perfect balance. "This is the truth," I thought to myself.

There were very few books on traditional Chinese medicine when I began my study in the 1960s and those that did exist tended to be dry and unappealing. Dr. J. R. Worsley's books, however, and the theories he shared felt whole, containing the emotional and spiritual qualities that moved me. It was Dr. Worsley who brought five-element acupuncture to the West based on the belief that "in most cases the cause of physical, mental, and spiritual distress resides within rather than in external circumstances."

The Basics of Chinese Medicine

This section is intended to simply introduce the layperson to the theory and metaphors of Chinese medicine. To understand the progressive unfolding of my work, it is necessary to be familiar with its container.

The Tao

Taoist philosophy forms the philosophical heart and soul of traditional Chinese medicine, most eloquently described in the *I Ching* (Book of Changes) and the *Tao Te Ching* by Lao Tzu. The concept of *Tao* is consistent with the Native American concept of the sacred hoop, for it is imagined as an invisible web of interconnections that support life, infusing all of nature with balance and harmony. In the *Tao Te Ching*, Lao Tzu states:

There was something formless and perfect
before the universe was born.
It is serene. Empty.
Solitary. Unchanging.
Infinite. Eternally present.
It is the mother of the universe.
For lack of a better name,
I call it the Tao.
It flows through all things,
inside and outside, and returns
to the origin of all things.

Yin and Yang

Where Tao expresses unity—oneness, the source, the essential nature of the universe—two primordial powers, *yin and yang*, emerge out of this unity and alternate in the continual process of change between increase and decrease, expansion and contraction, fullness and emptiness. Yin and yang are not opposites or contradictions, for Taoist philosophy teaches that everything in life literally and figuratively contains its opposite. Over time, each half is transformed into the other in a continual cycle of change. "The secret of Tao in this world of the mutable," according to the *I Ching*, "is to keep the changes in motion in such a manner that no stasis occurs and an unbroken coherence is maintained."

Throughout Chinese thought and medicine, the concept of yin and yang establishes a fundamental principle that expresses the dance between universal and personal, day and night, light and dark, outside and inside, masculine and feminine. All reality consists of both/and rather than either/or. When the complementary powers of yin and yang flow and interact in harmony, balance emerges, honoring the Tao. When the yin and yang dynamic is unequal, and therefore out of balance, conflict ensues, rather than complement. The Chinese imagine the yin and yang as ever-changing aspects of a unified whole. This suggests that life lived within a changing universe requires a continual rebalancing from within to align with the ineffable Tao, the All That Is.

As Fritjof Capra posits in his groundbreaking book, *The Turning Point*, "this correlative and dynamic way of thinking is basic to the conceptual system of Chinese medicine. The healthy individual and the healthy society are integral parts of a great patterned order, and illness is a disharmony at the individual or social level."

The Western mindset all too often takes an either/or view of reality and dismisses the eternal, vital, flowing dynamic of the yin and yang, instead perpetuating a hierarchical principle that wields power over people, creatures, and natural resources. The

Tao lauds both the divine, creative energy of the yang and the equally essential yielding, receptive way of the yin. The Chinese would insist that the yielding, receptive way of the yin offers the greatest source of wisdom for human beings. In our turbulent and divisive world, where "power over" often carries the order of the day, we could all benefit by strengthening our yin and moving toward the balance of constrained action and intuitive waiting, each imbued with true presence.

Qi (Chi)

The nature of *chi*, or energy, embodies the yin-yang dynamic. Yin carries the negatively charged molecule and yang, the positively charged, and their interactive, interdependent play produces electricity, the vibrational energy in Chinese medicine. Chi manifests the life force in nature and energizes all life, moving through both the cosmos and each of its humble creatures. As long as the energy flows, health and well-being thrive. When the chi is obstructed or blocked, dis-ease follows. Imagine a mountain stream, flowing clear. We are taught to only drink from a stream if the water is flowing; if a stagnant pool forms, we know such water has been blocked and will attract pathogens. Moving water perpetually changes, and pathogens require stagnation to grow.

Chi does not take concrete physical form but emanates a force field as when we "feel" others' energy and even that of places. The Chinese consider the earth a living organism with a unique force field permeated with energy channels that perpetually change and move through its surface. We call places at which the deeper energies come closest to the surface, the acupoints of the earth, such as vortexes of energy where ancient (and modern) people often create sanctuaries and shrines. These places are often called vortex points, but I always think of them as acupoints to the earth's core of vital chi. The human body too echoes such underground channels, similar to blood vessels and nerves but invisible to the naked eye. These pathways or conduits of energy carry chi through the body, and their currents have the capacity to nourish all the human organs as well as the emotions. The points along these channels that vibrate close to the body's surface are the acupoints that, with needles or pressure, provide access to a body's energy and can affect the flow of that energy through a particular channel.

When we begin to understand chi as the reservoir of energy that it can be, a regenerative but depletable resource, we learn to accept life as totally unpredictable and ever-changing, an adaptive process where our ability to sustain balance influences not only our overall health but also the quality of the life force that lives through us.

Each living creature is essentially a microcosm of the earth and as such acts as unique "cells" in the greater body electric. Promoting healthy bodies can actually help to restore our own health and the health of our planet. When we align with what brings us alive, what moves us, we align with the essence of who we are and this contributes to health on earth and perhaps even throughout the cosmos. As Rolling Thunder once taught, each race, much like each of the four directions, is essential to the whole. Red people, black people, yellow people, and white people are all just that, human beings. But, each race, just as each direction, carries a unique function while remaining always part of the whole.

29

The Five Elements & Their Seasons Support a Balanced Life

"When the Five Phase (element) theory was fused with the yin/yang cycles, the result was an elaborate system in which every aspect of the universe was described as a well-defined part of a dynamically patterned whole."

—Fritjof Capra, from *The Turning Point*

More informative and less experiential than my story's narrative, this chapter offers a look at my knowledge of the Five Elements, what I have coined the Five Transformative Powers, that establish the very root of my practice.

Traditional Chinese medicine follows the fundamental cyclical flow of nature itself. The seasonal turn of the year flows through us and we flow through it, each associated with an element of energy, of chi, the life force. Having integrated my own study of traditional Chinese medicine into both my professional practice and my own life, enriching both immeasurably, my hope is to share some of Chinese

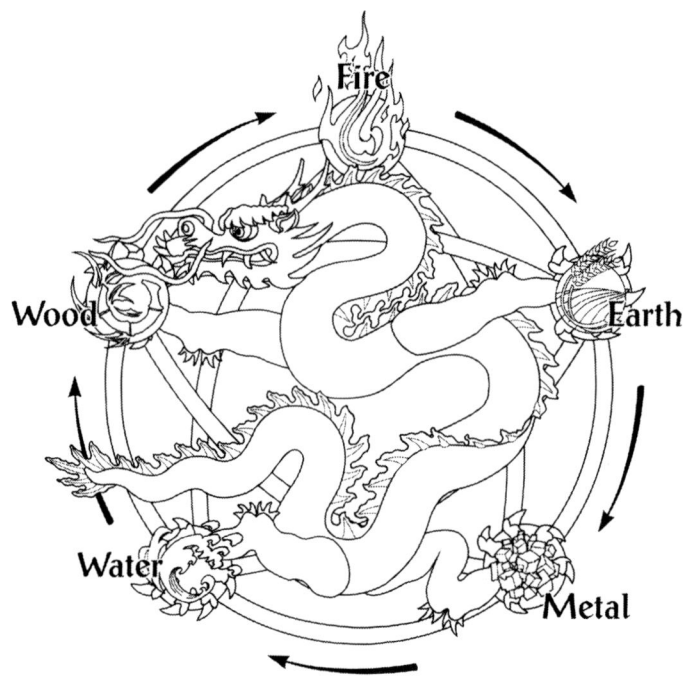

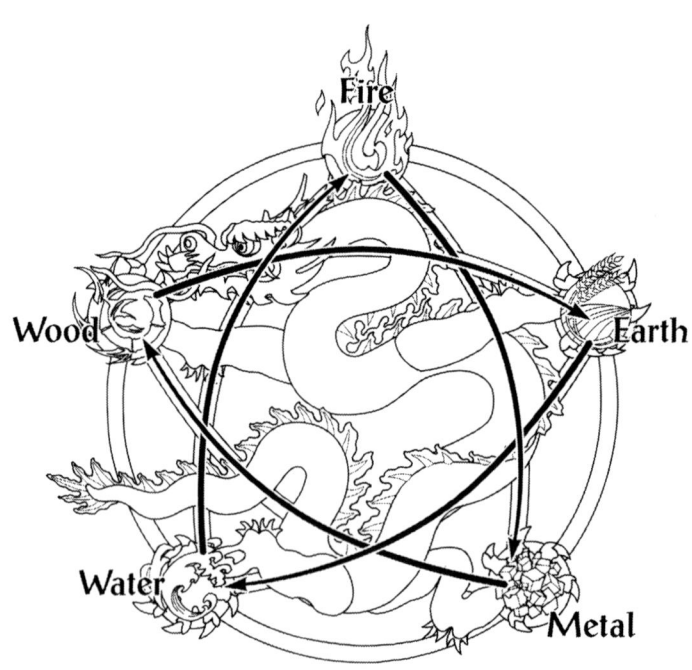

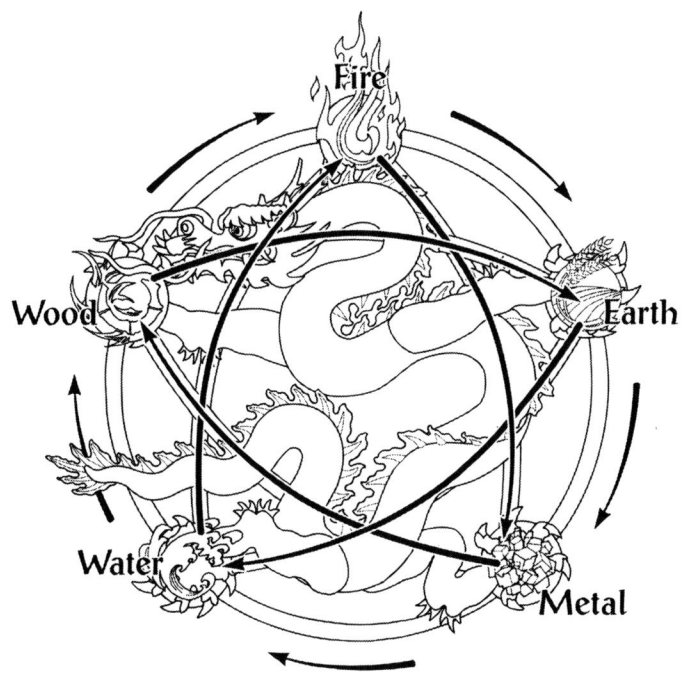

on facing page: Generation Cycle, top left; Control Cycle, bottom left;
Control Cycle & Generation Cycle combined, above

medicine's wealth of knowledge to inspire alignment with this natural flow of seasonal and elemental energy that supports a balanced life, physically, emotionally, and spiritually. All of us can relate to and potentially share affinities to one or more of the five elements.

Rolling Thunder taught that the human race has four directions and four colors of skin, and the Chinese believed that humanity consists of different types of individuals with varying constitutions. Both agree that when an individual is alignment with who they truly are, as microcosm, they actually nourish the Earth, as macrocosm, to function as an integrated whole.

Identifying the elements with which you have an affinity can help you better balance your health and well-being.

For more in-depth study, refer to my book, *Chinese Medicine for Maximum Immunity*.

The Five Elements (or Five Transformative Powers)

Thousands of years ago Chinese physicians developed a system that was an essentially practical, yet metaphorically inclusive, system of healing that they called *Wu Hsing*, or the Five Element System. This system inherently pulls us toward our unique healing journey. It teaches us that who we are, why we behave as we do, and why we have proclivities towards certain diseases, both physical and emotional, reflect our imbalances. They believed that these five elemental energies—Wood, Fire, Earth, Metal, and Water—guide the physical, emotional, and spiritual existence of all human life, as they do the cycles of growth and change in the external, natural world. Each element acts as a mirror that reflects back to us the energy with which we resonate in a given moment. An excess or deficiency in any one of these basic forces immediately and powerfully affect our physical health and emotional well-being. When we align with the system of the Five Transformative Powers and learn to connect to and flow with the external currents that directly affect us—the seasons, the weather, emotions, and spiritual experiences—we can balance ourselves in relation with such currents and gain optimal health. Beyond the lyrical yet practical beauty of this Taoist approach to living lies a unique simplicity.

Each of the Five Transformative Powers carries a unique nature and spirit, and every human being has a constitutional affinity to one or more of them. My affinity with this system offered me a framework that provided a foundation for both integrating the heart of my healing practice and for living a harmonious life.

Working in concert to ensure harmony and balance, the two interwoven cycles of Chinese medicine, the Generation Cycle (the Sheng) and the Control Cycle (the Ke), together represent the interdependence and interconnectedness of the Five Transformative Powers.

The Generation Cycle, also known as the Mother/Child cycle, illustrates the relationship of nourishment and support of one to another. Just as the seasons transition seamlessly from one to the next, each element generates the next element. Considered the mother or generator of Earth, when Fire cools, its ash creates matter. This matter deep in the Earth becomes Metal. Metal's enriching qualities make Water. Water nourishes and sustains Wood. Wood gives birth to Fire and the circle of life eternally begins again. The Control Cycle establishes boundaries and therefore balance. Water controls Fire by quenching it. Fire restrains Metal by melting it, allowing it to shape and mold. Metal inhibits Wood by cutting it. Wood restrains Earth by rooting it in place. Earth controls Water by absorbing it and containing it. Each element or transformative power also is associated with an emotion. And in keeping with the Tao, each element is also associated with a yin organ and a yang organ.

Yang organs tend to be conduit organs, more superficial than yin organs, which are essential to life. Each yin organ opens to a different sense organ: Wood opens to the eyes; Fire opens to the tongue; Earth opens to the mouth, Metal to the nose, and Water to the Ears, both figuratively and physically.

See the Appendix at the back of the book for a more detailed description of personally relating to the five elements and their associated seasons.

30

The Holographic Imprint

"Because everything in the cosmos is made out of the seamless holographic fabric of the implicate order, he (Bohm) believes it is as meaningless to view the universe as composed of 'parts,' as it is to view the different geysers in a fountain as separate from the water out of which they flow. An electron is not an 'elementary particle.' It is just a name given to a certain aspect of the holomovement. Dividing reality up into parts and then naming those parts is always arbitrary, a product of convention, because subatomic particles, and everything else in the universe, are no more separate from one another than different patterns in an ornate carpet."

—Michael Talbot, from *The Holographic Universe*

Back in the summer of 1973 when attending the Psychology of Consciousness program at Stanford University I visited the Museum of Fine Arts in Golden Gate Park with my friend Becky. We discovered an entire section at the museum called The Sensorium, which offered a kinesthetic awakening of the senses. At the exhibit called the Tactile Gallery, we were instructed to leave all loose clothing and items, such as wallets, in a safe box at the entrance, as we prepared to begin a labyrinthine journey in absolute darkness, where participants walked, crawled, or climbed, moving forward only by touch.

Some of us only wearing our underwear, we moved deeper into the labyrinth, touching velvet, silk, plastic, rough muslin, and everything in between. At times when the enclosures grew tight we literally squeezed through the narrow passages on our hands and knees. As we neared the end of the roughly 15-minute experience, we pushed through rubbery walls that felt distinctly like a birth canal, arriving into an open, resting space with very soft lighting.

I shared this thrilling sensory experience with my colleagues back at Stanford and we booked the Tactile Gallery for private use one Sunday morning and thoroughly enjoyed the experience—completely naked!

* * *

My senses all awake, I stopped short when we approached an actual hologram, the first I'd ever seen, of an apple resting on a table. I clearly registered the laser light and a few mirrors, but nonetheless the apple appeared, in all its detail, to be physically there. The docent suggested that we circumambulate the apple slowly, noticing its clarity and visibility from every angle, yet when invited to touch it, the apple was *not* there, only its holographic imprint. Whereas today we are familiar with holograms, when we saw this apple, holographic technology had only existed for about ten years. That day was the first time I heard the expression, "pattern of interference," the essential nature of a holographic imprint, I immediately associated it with what I'd long sensed about each individual's relation to the whole universe.

Such "interference" is akin to patterns in water, for example, when ripples occur after a pebble is thrown into a smooth pool. If more than one pebble hits the water simultaneously, the ripples intersect forming wavelike patterns that could be recorded onto a metal plate in order to holographically imprint an object, such as the apple in the museum. A laser steam of light is then beamed onto the object through mirrors and subsequently recorded, leaving patterns of interference on the plate similar to the process of making a photographic negative. When the laser is reflected off the plate, the three dimensional image is reproduced, thus the image of the apple. In contrast to a photographic negative, if the "interference" negative is cut in half, the laser will still create the complete image, even though it will be somewhat less clear. Remarkably, if the plate breaks into a thousand pieces, each tiny fragment will still contain the whole image though with less and less clarity.

This foundational premise—that each part contains the whole image and each image contains every part—has grounded both my spiritual journey and my evolving work as a healing practitioner. Great physicists and researchers alike believe that our very universe is a hologram, and that each of us is but a microcosm of its whole. Many diagnostic and treatment modalities within Chinese medicine follow this same principle. My years of acupuncture training and experience, particularly my attention to the pressure points and the pulses, tell me unequivocally that each part of the human body contains the story of the whole body, if we learn how to read it.

The Micro-Systems of Acupuncture

The micro-systems of acupuncture intend to diagnose the whole individual by reading the part, such as the tongue, the pulse, and the ear, in addition to reading the traditional acupressure points along the meridian system channels to determine how each isolated sensitivity reveals the level of function (or dysfunction) for a given organ.

In 1957, the French neurologist Paul Nogier elaborated on the ear as a diagnostic tool, noting that an inverted fetus mirrors the ear. He mapped patient symptoms and complaints to acupressure points to treat specific dysfunctions in the body. For thousands of years Chinese medicine has drawn the inner shape of the ear as an inverted fetus, where a certain area represents an individual organ. The ear also contains emotional points, where tenderness at a specific point can reflect a blockage in a given organ. The tongue and the pulse are two primary micro-systems I'll discuss below.

Exquisite pain upon contact with a given acupressure point can, for example, indicate blocked energy. This guides the experienced practitioner to explore the underlying causes of such sensitivities and provides essential information for determining a treatment strategy.

Other holographic systems can also read the body's general condition, such as, palmistry, the study of the shape and lines of the hands; reflexology, the study of the foot and ankle as reflection of the whole body; iridology, the study of the iris of the eye, and phrenology, the shape of the skull. Looking back to my acupuncture training days, I realize that many of us were familiar with diagnostic skills from this wide variety of modalities. We all used them independently to diagnose our clients' symptoms and complaints, and, more often than not, we came to very similar diagnoses. To this day, like most holistic healing practitioners, I call forward all of my knowledge, including my intuition, to enhance my diagnosis. But, most often, I turn first to the tongue and then to the pulse to explore in depth.

The Three Pillars of Chinese Diagnostics

1. **Listening to the client with presence** is first and foremost the most important Chinese diagnostic pillar. A client's story reveals much about the condition of his or her body, mind, and spirit. Most people are well aware of their issues and have lived with them, if not learned from them. The practitioner's best diagnostic tool is to encourage a client to trust her intuition and tell her story.

2. **Reading the pulses** is the second pillar of Chinese diagnostics. Used for thousands of years to diagnose energy flow throughout the entire body, reading the pulses gives the healing practitioner diagnostic information about each organ system of the body. It requires an acute sensitivity as well as a keen presence with and attunement to the individual. Strengthening this sensitive acuity can take years of practice.

   Reading the pulses involves much more than simply taking a pulse rate. This complex, artful practice requires learning how to palpate the many pulses on the wrist. (See page 283 for more on this from Dr. Leon Hammer.)

3. **Carefully inspecting the tongue** provides the third pillar of Chinese diagnostics.

A friend who had recently trained at the Chinese Medical College in Beijing once told me about the tongue museum that she'd visited, which is filled with wax replicas of tongues and photographs of the same tongue extended. Chinese characters explain how to read each tongue, describing in detail the meaning of its color, texture, and coating. The geography of the tongue, which associates specific locations with an organ, also provides diagnostic information.

The Five Element School

The primary training program at Tri-State Institute for Traditional Chinese Acupuncture offered traditional acupuncture as taught in China, including Taoist principles, but included other approaches to acupuncture as well. The program purported to teach both the concept of treating a symptom and addressing its cause but actually never created a cohesive curriculum for how to truly assess underlying imbalances and therefore the root causes of symptoms. Exemplified by our required white lab coats, the procedures felt downright clinical at times, as if mimicking the Western medical model. This ran radically contrary in my mind to the original practice of Chinese medicine some 5,000 years ago, its enduring focus on one's internal nature as a healing source, relatively unchanged. I therefore prefer the term "complementary" medicine when working with both Western- and Eastern-influenced healing modalities.

At Esalen in the 1960s I met many individuals who had trained at The College for Traditional Chinese Acupuncture in England with Professor J. R. Worsley. His work encompassed the gestalt, the whole mind/body/spirit approach to healing. At Esalen and in succeeding years my like-minded colleagues called Worsley's model The Five Element School. I appreciated learning all that would have been taught in China, but the emotional and spiritual influences behind the symptoms directly spoke to me.

I was one of four graduates at Tri-State chosen to participate in training at the Five Element School in Columbia, Maryland, called the Traditional Acupuncture Institute (TAI). They created a special program to introduce their holistic model to practitioners of traditional schools. We were taught diagnostic and treatment skills while also being introduced to and exploring the five-element approach.

A group of ten of us from around the country gathered and agreed to meet for our training each season for a full week. The first week was devoted mostly to basic classroom instruction that established a solid foundation for the Five Element School's approach to the art of Chinese medicine. Although the entire staff of the Traditional Acupuncture Institute were instructors, its founders, Bob Duggan and Dianne Connelly, led the teaching. Most of the faculty had trained in England with Dr. Worsley. Their procedure for diagnosing a patient intrigued us— how they palpated the pulse and performed preliminary treatments to clear the surface of aggressive energy to prepare the core for treatment. The instruction inspired all ten of us, many of whom were at the top of their fields. Dr. Leon Hammer, who would become my dear friend and pulse-taking mentor, was one of them.

With each seasonal gathering at TAI, we celebrated with our new friends and teachers, experiencing through meditation and intentional exercises to become one with each season as we lived it. We became aware too of how a season lived within us, while focusing on processes for determining each participant's elemental affinity.

I deeply appreciated the spiritual tone ingrained in this work. A teacher would first needle an acupoint and share the name of that point with the client, such as "Allow Tears," enabling him or her to visualize its function with the intention of connecting the client to the point of tension or even dis-ease. I follow this naming practice to this day to verbalize the essence of each acupoint that can lead to the spot in need of healing. Connecting with the spirit of the blockage or obstacle by naming it brings awareness to both as living entities in need of healing.

After learning the basic level skills of acupuncture, we were each assigned to shadow various TAI practitioners and to ask questions. I particularly enjoyed and benefited from this sharing, for we had the opportunity to learn from some of the most well-respected acupuncturists in the country whose systems focused on treating the core energetic imbalances, with the natural assumption that after resolving an imbalance, a symptom or symptoms would disappear.

Noticeable and satisfying, after showing us how they treated their patients, our TAI teachers would ask how we, the more symptomatically trained healers, would help to resolve physical issues, like frozen shoulder, knee pain, or headaches! Knowing that their philosophy believed that treating the core imbalance would resolve the symptom, this request both humored and satisfied me. Their request gave us an opportunity to balance the two approaches, one addressing the symptom, the other more holistic, treating the cause, where learning both would certainly strengthen our tools when helping a client's pain and discomfort.

My acupuncture training has not only given me a valuable tool for guiding my clients to recognize themselves as integral parts of an ever-changing whole, but it also has deepened my spiritual awareness of my life's work while opening a deeper connection to myself.

Learning from Dr. Leon Hammer, the Master of Pulse-Reading

"At last he takes her hand, raising it in both of his own. Now he bends over the bed in a kind of crouching stance, his head drawn down into the collar of his robe. His eyes are closed as he feels for her pulse. In

*a moment he has found the spot, and for the next half-hour he remains
thus, suspended above the patient like some exotic golden bird with folded
wings, holding the pulse of the woman beneath his fingers, cradling her
hand in his. All the power of the man seems to have been drawn down
into this one purpose. It is palpation of the pulse raised to the state of
ritual. From the foot of the bed, where I stand, it is as though he and
the patient have entered a special place of isolation, of apartness, about
which a vacancy hovers, and across which no violation is possible. After
a moment the woman rests back upon her pillow. From time to time she
raises her head to look at the strange figure above her, then sinks back
once more. I can see their hands joined in correspondence that is exclusive,
intimate, his fingertips receiving the voice of her sick body through the
rhythm and throb she offers at her wrist. All at once I am envious—not of
him, not of Yeshi Dhonden for his gift of beauty and holiness, but of her.
I want to be held like that, touched so, received. And I know that I, who
have palpated a hundred thousand pulses, have not felt a single one."*

—Richard Selzer, when describing his meeting with Yeshe Dhonden, personal physician to the
Dalai Lama, from *Stories of the Spirit, Stories of the Heart*

Inspired by Dr. Leon Hammer's knowledge of the
pulse, I stayed in touch with him after the conclusion of the
TAI training. Together with a few other acupuncturists, we
persuaded him to teach us his uniquely sensitive method of
pulse-taking, about which he was writing a book. He had
apprenticed with a Chinese expert diagnostician and herbalist,
Dr. John H. F. Shen, for more than seven years, spending at
least two to three days each week with him. Over the years he
had witnessed Dr. Shen practice his pulse-reading method with
thousands of patients. His method gathered information on the
functioning of every organ system of the body but he focused
equally on reading how an individual processed emotional
conflicts, and was even able to clarify at which age certain
traumatic events may have created stagnation in the body.

Chinese reading of pulses goes far beyond the Western
means of checking the heart rate. By touching into different

positions on the wrist, a sensitive practitioner can isolate the pulse-read on different organs and their functions. By touching gently into each individual pulse one can discern different pulse levels—physical, emotional, and spiritual. The basic fundamentals can be easily taught to students, but developing true sensitivity takes years and years of practice, preferably with a great teacher such as Dr. Hammer.

I gathered a dozen people for a two-weekend introductory pulse-work workshop. When Dr. Hammer took our pulses he could tell us, for example, at what age we had lost a parent or experienced some other shock. The depth of information that he read in the pulse at times felt like a psychic reading yet he claimed that all the information lived in the pulse, if one would take the time to learn to read it. The workshops gave me a solid basis for further study of the subtleties of pulse-taking, but his invitation to apprentice with him at his practice in Saratoga Springs, New York, gave me the opportunity of a lifetime.

Every Tuesday became Dr. Hammer day. I would drive up from Woodstock to Saratoga Springs, spend the day seeing patients with him, taking pulses and discussing the intricacies of each patient's situation. He was forever patient, caring, generous of spirit, with an extraordinary intelligence, all this, with

Me and Leon during early fall in 2015, just before this book went to press

humility—the father I'd always wished for. We would endlessly laugh and brainstorm together.

His background in psychology and his work with Fritz Perls, Erich Fromm, and Al Lowen, provided us with a common vocabulary, particularly bringing a psychological perspective to traditional Chinese medicine. I studied with Leon regularly for nearly two years, until the birth of my son. In fact, just after we had conceived our son, Leon was visiting Woodstock and took my wife's pulses, only three weeks pregnant. He confirmed that indeed she was pregnant, and she was carrying a boy.

Dr. Hammer gave me much more than an essential skill to enhance my practice, he gave me his loving affirmation, and this nourishment opened wider a window within that allowed me to see more clearly into my clients' conditions.

A beautiful book, *Fourth Uncle in the Mountain* by Quang Van Nguyen, a Vietnamese practitioner of Chinese medicine, with the help of Marjorie Pivar, documents the young Quang's apprenticeship with his father, an esteemed healer and doctor of Chinese medicine. While learning to understand the pulses he writes:

> *"My father began, 'By reading the pulses we can tell how well the internal organs are working.'*
>
> *I looked questioningly at him.*
>
> *He continued, 'Like the heart, the stomach, the liver, the kidneys, and so on, we can feel if the organs are weak or congested or inflamed, or if they are working just fine.'… 'So' my father continued, 'once we have an idea about what is going on inside the body, we can make medicine to help the body to function better.'*
>
> *I put all my concentration in my fingers, but I could not tell. He told me that it wasn't enough to know if the pulses*

were high or deep or even. There were such other qualities as floating, slippery, rough, surging, tight, string-like, hollow, soggy, scattered, hidden and knotted.'

The following two passages from Dr. Hammer's book *Dragon Rises, Red Bird Flies: Psychology, Energy & Chinese Medicine* epitomizes his own philosophy:

"Chinese medicine has been for me the fulfillment of a search for a congenial system of healing that embodies the inseparability of body and mind, spirit and matter, nature and man, philosophy and reality. It is a personal, subtle, gentle, yet highly technical medical system, which allows me to be close to essence—the life force—both my own and that of others."

"The reasons for using it, teaching it, and discussing it are twofold. First, it works. Second, it is a masterpiece of harmony, intricacy, and movement, which never ceases to engage me, and intrigue me. It surrounds me like nature, or a great work of art. I am consumed and renewed at one time."

—Dr. Leon Hammer, *Dragon Rises, Red Bird Flies*

For over 25 years now I have used pulse diagnosis with every client, both before each session to clarify the current state and after each session to ascertain the effectiveness of our time together. Not a day passes without sending love and thanks to my mentor of mentors, Dr. Leon Hammer.

31

Back to the Garden

"Man did not weave the web of life, he is merely a strand in it, such that whatever he does to the web, he does to himself."

—Chief Seattle

Though my continued schooling in traditional Chinese medicine affirmed a basic inherent understanding, my affinity grew ever stronger as I further explored its roots and, like my great grandmother, the "little doctor," devoted myself to understanding the healing effects of herbal remedies. I aligned naturally with the energetic practice of acupuncture, particularly my love of its poetic metaphors. However, I also recognized how I could expand my clients' treatment if, in addition to acupuncture and stories that intended to awaken an awareness of their inherent healing power, I could offer them complementary herbal remedies.

Growing up in the 1960s gave all those interested in good health and natural living a general introduction to herbal medicine. We learned that Echinacea and Golden Seal could ward off a cold or flu; Panax Ginseng could boost energy; Tang Kwai could aid in female reproductive problems; White Willow

Bark acted as a natural anti-inflammatory herb (from which aspirin was first derived), and Chamomile or Peppermint could settle the stomach. We tended to scoff at Western medicine and seek what the earth provided.

Rolling Thunder deepened my appreciation for the healing properties of herbs when he invited me to study with him, emphasizing how essential it was to understand the nature of each individual herb and how important it was for the herbalist to empower the herbs with prayer and intention. While studying the energetics of acupuncture it felt natural to extend my study to include a much more careful study of the healing power of herbs, completing a circle that Rolling Thunder had cast many years before.

My clients had often asked what they could do to augment their treatment. I would share my knowledge about healthy diet and lifestyle and advise their use of supplements to ensure their bodies received nutrients necessary to healing. Adding my knowledge of herbs offered them even more possibilities for nourishing and ultimately healing the body, mind, and spirit.

A Brief History of Healing Mind, Body, and Spirit with Herbs

The medicinal use of herbs likely began as far back as Paleolithic times, or 60,000 years ago. Even animals intuitively use and consume herbs to promote their own health. As early as 5,000 years ago, ancient cultures worldwide —Egypt, Greece, and China—recorded lists of plants and their medicinal uses. Women, the nurturers, most often shared the wisdom of healing with herbs for both therapeutic uses and spiritual qualities. It is worthy to note that across Europe between 1400 and 1700, during the Reformation and beyond, an estimated 70,000 women were executed for witchcraft when most likely their only crime was healing themselves and others. Some of them were living in New England in the 1700s.

Records used both in the East and West created the basis for medical treatment well into the 1600s, including work of the Greek physician, Galen of Pergamum during the Roman Empire, as well as St. Hildegard of Bingen's *Physica* in the 12th century, and *Culpeper's Complete Herbal* by the 17th century botanist Nicholas Culpeper.

Until the mid-1900s, herbal medicine generated the most prevalent compounds, even here in the United States. However, with the advent of super drugs, such as penicillin, steroids, and other hormonal medicines in the 1930s, the use of herbs fell into disrepute thanks to concerns about scientific substantiation of both efficacy and safety. The Western pharmaceutical industry became the future of medicine and healing. Regulation by the Federal Food and Drug Administration (FDA) further dampened public opinion on the medicinal use of herbal remedies. Nonetheless herbal medicine remains in strong use today, particularly in India and China, but also across Europe, most notably in Germany and Britain. Barbara Grigg's *The Green Pharmacy* provides a comprehensive reference for navigating herbal alternatives and complements to the pervasive pharmaceutical culture.

Western pharmaceutical medicines perform functions that the body may be struggling to perform itself. Granted, such medicines can save lives, but all too often at the physical, emotional, mental, and even spiritual expense of re-educating the body to resume its normal functioning. Herbs act as foods to encourage the body to heal itself. For example, synthetic thyroid hormone provides the body with thyroxin of which it is depleted or unable to produce. This can be life-saving in extreme cases, but the replaced hormone signals to the body that all is well, with the result that the pituitary gland does not produce TSH, the thyroid-stimulating hormone, which ensures the thyroid's effective functioning. This leads to more and more dependence on the drug.

I believe that the better approach is to support glandular functions with diet and herbs that can re-educate the thyroid gland to work more efficiently. The over-use of pharmaceuticals can produce many iatrogenic health problems, that is, disease and/or death caused by reactions to drugs, chemotherapy, or surgery. Such doctor-induced disease is one of the leading causes of fatalities in Western medicine. Recent statistics show that more than one out of every five hospital admissions is due to an iatrogenic reason. (Go to www.ahrq.gov/data/hcup/hcupnet. htm. for more information.)

Studying Chinese Herbal Medicine

During my second year of acupuncture school, Tri-State offered the opportunity to study Chinese Herbal medicine with Ted Kaptchuk, a master in the field. I learned that the qualities of the five elements had distinct flavors (Wood - sour, Fire - bitter, Earth - sweet, Metal - acrid or spicy, and Water - salty) and that yin represented cold natures and yang, hot. I deeply appreciated the poetic language of the categories of herbal classifications and how the language perfectly matched each one's pragmatic use, thus simplifying remembering each remedy's purpose.

I learned about herbs used to clear the surface and eliminate cold, thus treating the flu and common cold; herbs used to resolve dampness (phlegm) and to nourish the lung *chi* for addressing sinus or bronchial congestions. I learned about herbs to move toxic heat (dampness) from the joints for treating arthritis and inflammatory joint and muscle issues, herbs to clear heat from the blood to treat skin conditions, herbs to regulate the chi and harmonize the liver for treating acid reflux or digestive irritability, herbs to move and regulate the blood to address various menstrual symptoms, and herbs to nourish the heart and calm the spirit to treat anxiety, depression, or insomnia. Herbs can also invigorate the *chi* to support immune functions, fatigue, or to nourish the blood. The categories are endless, and, as you can see, the metaphors fit the use of the particular herbs.

We familiarized ourselves with hundreds of individual herbs during our work with Ted Kaptchuk, often journeying to Chinatown in lower Manhattan to purchase raw herbs—root, plant, or flower. I sometimes thought of Rolling Thunder on such outings. We would taste, smell, and touch the raw herbal material to truly experience it. Most of these herbs were grown in China and felt foreign to me, remembering what Rolling Thunder had shared about indigenous cultures using herbs that grew locally in their own backyards.

We learned that the Chinese believed treatment with individual herbs was inferior medicine and thus explored combining herbs into formulas, an honored practice that the Chinese respectfully considered essential to matching an individual with his or her particular symptomology. Much like choosing acupressure points in acupuncture, we learned to create formulas to match our clients' symptoms. We also offered them metaphors (or stories) to connect them to targeted systems in their body and to encourage them to focus on these areas to balance and to restore internal equilibrium, which will foster healing.

I carried 50 or so different herbs in my home office, storing them in clear glass containers for an exotic display. I made herbal combinations for my clients and instructed them to boil them into a thick concoction and to consume over the course of a few days. Such constitutional formulas were often intended to be taken for months, and in some cases, years. Most clients began their protocols enthusiastically, complying with the first batch, but the preparation would become tiresome, and they understandably began to prefer prepared herbal formulas that could be taken as tinctures or capsules.

concocting herbal formulas

Tinctures now offer the most flexibility. I can keep bottles of each herb in an alcohol base that guarantees potency as well as preserves the herbs forever. It has become a simple job now to combine the ingredients to match the formula for a specific individual. I delight in this process today, but it was not available to me with such ease when I began my practice.

Many of the traditional herbal formulas were available in pill form but it wasn't possible to add individual herbs necessary to concoct a proper formula to match an individual's needs. Nonetheless, the pills provided a simple means of ensuring compliance. Purity of imported Chinese remedies was suspect at this time, as additives had been discovered in them.

My practice grew steadily and soon people came to me as an acupuncturist, rather than a healer, with expectations of a cure for their symptom. I often used storytelling to invite them to look more closely at their symptoms as if branches of a tree when in fact the main problem resides in its roots. "We must look deeper," I would say. Those whose health improved quickly were usually on their way, but those who identified with the process turned to look more deeply at their lives and together we listened to the body for how to best navigate their way forward.

I realized too how much more I wanted to learn. I relished my intuitive approach when working with the herbs and their formulas and using storytelling to enhance my clients' understanding, but with such a wealth of information at hand, I felt I must better incorporate theoretical knowledge to balance my intuition. As Socrates could have said of this paradox: the more I was learning, the more I realized there was to learn!

My in-depth study with Ted Kaptchuk was richly informative and provided me the national certification that I needed for my practice, but it was my study with Simon Mills that truly deepened my understanding of healing with herbs.

Apprenticing with Simon Mills

During my final year of acupuncture school, Tri-State invited Simon Mills, the president of the Medical Herbal Association in Britain and a practitioner of Chinese herbal medicine, to teach a course in *Western* herbal medicine, his main area of expertise. He had formerly been trained as a physiologist and had served as director of research of the National Institute of Medical Herbalism. I had longed to study how to use our indigenous herbal allies and eagerly anticipated this new course. Mills was then working on a textbook on herbal medicine in Britain, and, it became apparent that he intended to try out his new curriculum, the synthesis of Eastern and Western herbal medicine.

I immediately connected with Simon. He had a soft-spoken, understated way about him but the stories he used to teach carried a profound knowledge. Our group of about 20 people intended to complete our course of study over two years, with weekend intensives in alternate months and homework in between. I would meet periodically with other acupuncture students between intensives to share how each of us used the new material with patients.

Simon was a walking encyclopedia. His course covered basic physiology, the organ systems of the body, and an introduction to Chinese energetic anatomy and physiology. Most of us naturally absorbed the Chinese component having been steeped in it, but Simon's synthesis of how the Eastern and Western herb systems could come together made seamless sense—science met metaphor—allowing us to well utilize our Chinese model while applying the biological and biochemical science of herbs. We dissected each herb to reveal its chemical constituents and to ascertain which were active and which were inert. We learned that the study of Western pharmacology was in effect the study of active constituents in an herb but in isolation from the plant and the chemical synthesis of active molecules. It eliminated the inert constituents deemed useless, and synthesized the remaining active chemicals into exact doses for each disease. A great theory, but only that, for in reality there is no such exact dose, as no two individuals metabolize in the exact manner, thus determining a treatment plan that matches a patient is an art, not pure science.

The discovery of digitalis to treat congestive heart failure is an interesting example of the evolution from traditional plant remedy to an extensively medical one. During the 1700s "dropsy," a disease characterized by fluid retention that begins in the legs and travels up the body, usually resulted in death. Physicians considered "dropsy" a kidney disorder and routinely treated it with diuretics, herbs that encourage release of fluids via urine, an approach often used today to treat high blood pressure. However, wise woman herbalists apparently had great success treating this disease. In 1785 Dr. William Withering, an English botanist as well as physician, visited some of these herbalists and analyzed their prescribed herbal remedy, noting the herb Foxglove (digitalis purpurea) as the main ingredient. Known as a poisonous plant, Foxglove, upon investigation, was also found to stimulate the heart. Dr. Withering isolated the part of the plant called "digoxin," the first step toward making congestive heart failure a treatable disease. This discovery led to the chemical synthesis of digitalis in modern day. When addressing some of the side effects of digitalis and returning to the foxglove to do so, scientists found that its natural constituents countered the side effects. In Europe, where it is legal, medical herbalists may treat congestive heart failure with the full plant and have done so successfully without side effects. Diuretics continue to be used to support kidney function and to foster elimination of excess fluid.

Simon guided us to assiduously analyze each herb, and we learned how each component part interacted within the body. During this process of discovery, it became all too clear that most industrial cultures sought the use of herbs to silence symptoms and get a person back to work. Bronchitis, pneumonia, or bad arthritis had to be controlled or eliminated, for if a person couldn't work his family couldn't survive. Thus, in the early days of modern medicine, the poisonous herbs, those richest in alkaloids, became most sought after, for they carried the strongest anti-microbial or anti-inflammatory compounds and therefore made the greatest impact. For example, to treat parasites, a common malady in those days, doctors used herbs such as wormwood that could kill the worms, or other parasites, hence its common use today. Ironically, these doctors most likely learned about the potent herbs from the wise women herbalists, but the establishment seldom heeded the women's dedication to patient nourishment and support, what Ben Franklin once wisely said, "an ounce of prevention is worth a pound of cure!"

Based on the belief that a healthy body, mind, and spirit was less likely to contract disease, many agrarian cultures in both East and West considered "tonic" herbs to be the most reliable treatment. Traditionally, a tonic is an herb or formula that supports overall health and vitality, but doesn't specifically address symptoms. In our Western culture today, it is not the acute infectious diseases that are the most prevalent, but the chronic, insidious diseases like autoimmune disorders that need attention. Doctors have a huge arsenal of weaponry to kill a pervasive disease but know almost nothing about nourishment, diet, or the use of natural agents to nurture. The recent use of the term "adaptogen" sheds light on a favorite story of modern herbal practice.

Siberian ginseng has been possibly the most studied herb in the world, dating back to the 1940s. In 1947, a Russian scientist, N. V. Lazarev, coined the word "adaptogen," while researching drugs that aided in the body's adaptation to physical and emotional stress. He found that Siberian Ginseng, which grows in northern Russia, was extensively prescribed through teas and direct ingestion to essentially treat whatever ailed the Russian population. Known by its Latin name, eleuterococus senticosus, it is no longer legal anywhere in the world to call it "ginseng" since the Chinese have fought and won to protect the word "ginseng" as part of the Panax family of herbs.

Over the course of a few years, the government gave all members of the Russian army Siberian ginseng, whether for combat, rest, or military exercises—to test its effectiveness. Half received supplements of eleutherococus and the other half were given a placebo. The eye-opening results found that Siberian ginseng supports the adrenal glands by producing adrenaline, when needed, and it also helps the body stop producing adrenaline when stressors have passed. Siberian ginseng could then address adrenal exhaustion or adrenal hyperactivity, and, in fact, temper an individual's response to stress, in general. This study led to the category of herbs called "adaptogens," and their supportive action now known as "adaptogenic."

Researchers returned to the laboratory with this information to explore which constituent within the herb was responsible for this adaptogenic function, and, surprisingly found that the glycosides, or sugar molecules, the "inert" and therefore useless parts, were responsible for relieving the stress. It's interesting to consider, in relation to the elemental properties of the Five Transformative Powers, that it's the inert herbal constituents that give them their sweet taste, the taste associated with Earth, the nourishing element.

In recent years many other adaptogenic, "tonic" herbs have been discovered, herbs that increase the body's resistance to a broad spectrum of dangerous stressors—physical and emotional—and support overall health.

Many such adaptogenic herbs have gained prominence in today's market as immune enhancers and energy tonics. They act as homeostatic mechanisms much as a thermostat registers too hot and brings the temperature down, and visa versa. Both the Asian and American forms of ginseng have been found to contain these same glycosides. Other adaptogens commonly used in herbal practice include Vitex for women's reproductive health, Hawthorn for regulating cardiac rhythm, and Rhodiola Rosea and Ashwaghanda for general as well as immunological vitality. All of these mentioned have been shown to be very safe, without side effects, and good for long-term use. In China, beginning in their forties people take these herbs for longevity and continue them for life!

After finishing the two years of study with Simon Mills and learning much more about Western herbal practices that enhanced my understanding of traditional Chinese medicine in conjunction with acupuncture, I invited Simon to visit us in

Simon Mills on my visit to Dartmoor, England

Woodstock, New York, for a weekend herbal walk. We explored the Catskill Mountains hunting for herbs in their natural habitat. Simon became the alchemist in charge. He excitedly pushed leaves aside to expose Wintergreen or Prunella spikes that we would use later that evening to fight off a participant's cold. His enthusiasm and knowledge of the natural world expressed his abiding relation with his herbal allies. On one of our long, exploratory walks my Black Bird appeared. Simon noticed my reaction, and I told him of my experiences with the Black Bird visitations. He smiled knowingly, having also had such visitors. My Black Bird visited again in Simon's presence near Dartmoor, England, the following year.

When I asked Simon to recommend a favorite book on herbal medicine, he smiled and suggested *The Way of Wyrd* by Brian Bates, an exploration of Anglo spirituality as it relates to the experience of "wyrd." This is not to be confused with weird as we know it, but "wyrd," meaning "that aspect of life which runs so deep, so all-pervasive, and so central to our understanding of ourselves and our world that it is inexpressible. At its essence it is the work of personal healing." I found *The Way of Wyrd* a fascinating and enlightening addition to my own spiritual path and return to it regularly. This book preceded Simon's own treatise on herbal medicine, *Out of the Earth, the Essential Book of Herbal Medicine.*

After finishing our course and our time together in Woodstock, Simon invited a few members of our class to apprentice while he attended patients at his practice in Exeter, England. It was a marvelous opportunity. We would sit with him in his office, listening and watching as he questioned the farmers and common folk, for he was their medical doctor. After gathering and assessing each patient's information, including pulse-taking and tongue-inspection, he would concoct an herbal remedy taken from hundreds of dark brown bottles that lined his office walls, each inscribed with its Latin name, choosing a combination of herbs that supported the patient as well as his or her symptoms. After the patient's departure, we would analyze why Simon chose which herbs and why. After reading *The Way of Wyrd* and spending considerable time with this alchemist-herbalist, I could imagine vapors rising as he poured an elixir for each client.

On many days we'd walk the moors, sometimes miles into the wilderness, where we'd come upon ancient henges, prehistoric circles with standing stones likely from Druidic rituals. We collected local herbs and tasted many to determine their qualities, and I came to understand why Simon had recommended *The Way of Wyrd*. It reminded me of Carlos Castaneda's books, which revealed through its narrator's journaling what it may have been like to be a sorcerer's apprentice in the Dark Ages. Based on detailed research on what life had been like when Christianity swept over Britain bringing it out of the Dark Ages, it tells the story of a Christian scribe whose life is forever changed while apprenticing with a Celtic shaman named Wolf. As the apprentice tells Wolf that he has read some of the Greek herbal literature, Wolf explained:

"'Plants of power are important allies for a sorcerer,'" he said as if reading my thoughts. 'With their aid I can influence the life-force of a person.'"

"The term 'life-force,' meant nothing to me."

"Wolf went on to say, 'Life-force permeates everything. It is the source of all vitality. In a person it is generated in the head, flows like a stream of light and into the marrow of the spine and from there into the limbs and crevices of the body. Power-plants help to control the channels through which the energy flows.'"

"I was puzzled by the term 'wyrd.' When used by monks orating poetry, it seemed to denote the destiny or fate of a person. I explained this view to Wolf and he hooted with laughter, sending the sparrows flapping from the shrubbery in alarm."

'To understand our ways you must learn the true meaning of "wyrd," not the version your masters have concocted to fit their beliefs. Remember that I told you our world began with fire and frost? By themselves, neither fire nor frost accomplish anything. But together they create the world. Yet they must maintain a balance, for too much fire would melt the frost and excessive frost would extinguish the fire. But just as the worlds of gods, Middle-Earth and the Dead are constantly replenished by the marrying of fire and frost, so also they depend upon the balance and eternal cycle of night and day, winter and summer, woman and man, weak and strong, moon and sun, death and life. These forces, and countless others, form the end points of a gigantic web of fibres which covers all worlds. The web of creation of the forces and its threads, shimmering with power, pass through everything.'"

On those walks through the moors I felt the wisdom of "wyrd" in the energy of the plants around us, the same plants that the shamans of old Britain had used in their medicine. I thought to myself: East meets West; science meets alchemy, and body and spirit unite in healing.

A year of acupuncture practice passed as I integrated herbal remedies more and more into my practice, prescribing herbs based on Chinese patents but also tonic combinations based on Simon's teaching of Western herbal medicine, a far superior approach when attempting to match a treatment to a person. I also created an herb garden of my own.

I returned to England the following summer to spend a few more weeks with Simon who had become a trusted herbal mentor and dear friend. I wanted to truly grasp his healing practice and particularly his relationship to the Earth and its healing gifts.

* * *

During my formal study at Tri State, I had often felt that my knowledge of acupuncture was limited by not engaging more fully in the emotional and spiritual aspects of the work. But, after my experiences with Simon Mills, I realized how my knowledge had expanded and that one can only share what one has truly experienced. Seeking deeper, more esoteric roots beyond the traditional Chinese training has made me a stronger, more sensitive acupuncturist, and this seeking nature has led me to my own healing and my ability to heal others.

When initially taught to use acupuncture needles, I methodically learned to turn the needle one way to energize the *chi* and another to drain excessive *chi* from a channel, but soon realized that when inserting the stainless steel needle into a particular acupoint, I could also feel my client's energy through the metallic handle of the needle. By clearly focusing my intention, I found that I could manipulate the energy through the needle and also through my hands.

A decade ago when asked to address an acupuncture school graduating class, I noticed that they used plastic rather than metallic-handled needles and asked, how they could possibly feel their clients' energy through plastic. I shared emphatically that I had learned through experience that stainless handles provided a conduit where the practioners could feel core energetic functions. Clearly by the puzzled looks on their faces, this concept had not occurred to them.

* * *

Not long after graduation, a priest from Iowa came in for treatment of an excruciating and debilitating condition called *ankylosing spondylitis*, a disease in which the whole spinal column fuses, causing excruciating pain and immobility. He had been unsuccessfully treated in Iowa, both with traditional Western medicine and alternative methods. He had taken a leave from his ministry to explore what he sensed were deeper psychological roots causing his affliction.

He had come for help to The Pathwork Center, in Phoenicia, New York, founded by John Pierrakos, my former therapist, and had been at the center for many months when he called me for treatment. When he walked through my office door, I saw a hunched-over, ashen man whose kidney energy was no doubt extremely depleted. Obviously frustrated, he told me his story, including how beneficial his stay at the center had been from a psychological perspective, but that he felt no relief from his symptoms. He had also sought treatment from numerous massage and physical therapists, all to no avail. I understood his underlying issues, but his case reminded me that old patterns, even when worked through emotionally and spiritually, might remain stagnant as physical obstruction in the body. I treated him with a combination of bodywork, acupuncture, herbs, and visualizations, all helping him feel better for a day or two, but the extreme symptoms sprang back almost immediately.

After a couple of months, I became frustrated myself and told him of the Plum Blossom treatment where a wand with seven tiny needles is gently hammered over the inflamed areas, in his case along both sides of his spinal column. After this procedure, the clinician places a glass suction cup over impacted areas. A small amount of blood releasing from the skin is normal. He agreed to go forward and when I put the cups in place I was startled to see that a large amount of black blood had been sucked into the cup. He likely heard me gasp, and I explained that the treatment was releasing stagnant blood and should give him some relief. Following that treatment he claimed to be 90-percent pain free, and remained so for years to come, confirmed by annual Christmas cards. Sometimes symptomatic treatments are called for!

My offices today have full herbal apothecaries with shelves very much like the ones I'd admired at Simon's so many years ago, holding hundreds of glass bottles filled with tinctures of herbs, most grown locally, but some sourced from around the world and organically grown. I smile at the alchemist in me as I concoct herbal tonics for my clients, imagining that I'm infusing the herbs with my love and intention for their well being and healing.

Recently I re-read Eliot Cowan's book *Plant Spirit Medicine* and related to his story. An acupuncturist who trained with J. R. Worsley in England, he apprenticed with a South American shaman and states, "Might it not be worthwhile to consider our relationship to plants? The most striking thing about this relationship is that we need them but they don't need us. We humans are utterly dependent on plants to cover all our needs: fuel, shelter, clothing, medicine, the petrochemical cornucopia, and, of course, food. (Even meat is made of plants.) In contrast, plant communities do just fine without people. We seem to offer plants nothing but suffering, destruction, and the threat of extinction."

32

Creating Space

"When you want to expand, you must first contract; when you want to be strong, you must first be weak; when you want to take, you must first give. This is called the subtle wisdom of life."

—Lao Tzu, *Tao Te Ching*

I've always resonated with the wave-like nature of the universe, in which one season seamlessly moves into another, night becomes day, and there is a time for doing followed by a time of being. Maybe Frank Sinatra had it right: Descartes said that to Be is to Do; Lao Tzu said that to Do is to Be; Sinatra said Do Be Do Be Do! Doing expresses the essential value in Western culture: the more we accomplish, the more we value ourselves or expect to be valued by others, yet I find being, my non-doing times, to provide the deepest satisfaction and my most profound connection to life.

After completing my years of training, I could fully open to the time for being, for integrating my learning and trusting that what I had learned would synthesize and find its truest meaning in the world. I knew that as long as I lived I would continue to learn and to consult, as needed, with colleagues on behalf of my clients, but I also wholeheartedly felt that I'd acquired enough information and needed time to absorb it. I had collected an abundance of information and experiential training from many masters—from psychology to bodywork, from psychic healing to meditation, from acupuncture to herbs, and the time had come to be still and to allow the integration to take place that I may live it fully. I felt the paradox of this keen awareness coupled with a still nagging discomfort.

During my years in India I had no goal, only an eternal now, but the thought of not being under the tutelage of a teacher or a student in a school somehow frightened me, confronting me with the old, haunting feeling that no matter what I achieved, no matter who I became, it was never enough. Whose voice precipitated this? It sounded like my own but surely I had not come into the world this way. Was it my perception of my father's disappointment in my choices? Had I failed to be the man he intended me to be? If I studied hard enough, trained long enough, expanded my knowledge, then would I be worthy, then would the man I'd become measure up? After deep reflection, I realized that as long as I continued to search for acceptance from any father figure, I'd feel the shame of not living up to their expectations. My mind could subdue these thoughts but when I was alone, self-doubt crept in and threatened to consume me. This doubt prompted me to do more, to learn more, to even *be* more, but inwardly I intuited that the acceptance I sought would be found in a gentle, receptive space where I could simply be who I was and in that I would always be enough. The sayings of Lao Tzu in the *Tao the Ching* comforted me:

Men are born and supple:
dead, they are stiff and hard.
Plants are born tender and pliant;
dead, they are brittle and dry.
Thus whoever is stiff and inflexible
Is a disciple of death.
Whoever is soft and yielding
is a disciple of life.
The hard and stiff will be broken.
The soft and supple will prevail.

During the week I saw clients and networked with other healing practitioners in the Hudson Valley. I had created an office wing at home and had made it a calming sanctuary, decorated with spiritual and healing art that I had accumulated from my travels.

Friends and clients regularly commented on the welcoming, warm energy that they experienced while there, and I felt grateful to share my work in such a special space.

Working a private practice from home, of course, has many perks, but it can also be isolating, and, with my wife in New York during the week, even lonely. Before and after work, I faithfully practiced my meditation, tended our abundant herb garden, and cared for our chickens. Life felt both full and simple.

Living in Woodstock, an energy vortex of sorts and a longtime artist colony, suited us. It attracted an eclectic group of individuals—devotees from a variety of schools of meditation, healers of every description, and artists across disciplines and genres. We had created real friendships and looked forward to building a life there.

My client sessions flowed with a natural rhythm and balance of energy work and acupuncture, with herbal remedy and lifestyle advice, all interwoven with effortless storytelling. The healing energy in the treatment room often reminded me of the ashram or  the Philippines. In India I had learned to channel Rajneesh's powerful energy; in the Philippines with the Elisaldes and psychic surgery I experienced a communal channel of a higher force field. In Woodstock, my training behind me, my busy thoughts could recede into the background, and I could once again align with the energy moving through me and direct it. I believe that this vibrational frequency, this reverberation with source, elevated the healing. Paradoxically, when I tried to be effective, to will the healing, I experienced interference, as in the call to save Vipassana all those years before. When instead I kept the channel open and simply received, the greater the healing energy that emerged.

I noticed also that when my practice was full, I felt on top of the world, riding a great wave, but when my client flow ebbed and the phone didn't ring, I heard the inner judge within putting me down, baiting me with "What's wrong with me?" or "My work isn't good enough!" old, worn-out tapes still triggered by shame or fear. Detaching enough to recognize the truth behind these episodes, I began to realize that I'd been forever complaining about not having enough time, and yet when time opened up I wasn't gracious enough to receive it.

This pattern continues intermittently to this day, but over the years I've discovered that by simply observing the old tapes, they disappear. I well know how such negative thoughts can diminish one's energy. I remind my clients of this fact regularly, calling this awareness technique the "psychology of the Buddhas," for the Buddhist approach simply brings awareness to old patterns, thus dissipating if not dissolving them completely. The mind acts, it seems, like a bio-computer, and the light of awareness, it also seems, can dissolve ancient negative thought patterns. Like an old vinyl record with a long, deep scratch in it, the needle sticks whenever that part plays, whenever the situation that triggers the tape occurs—rejection, shame, anger, and so on. By bringing awareness to such self-sabotaging inner responses, we theoretically place a sliver of wax into the scratch, so that the next time, the needle releases a little sooner than the last. One day, when the trigger signals its bio-computer, the pattern does not repeat and only in retrospect do we realize that we are no longer slaves to that particular belief. Life's mystery has its own rhythm, and I'm finally learning the meaning of "*Thy* will, not my will be done."

Each month a small group of acupuncturists from the Woodstock area met at one of our homes to review cases and to share feedback, but I missed the camaraderie of a group healing space such as I'd known at the ashram. Two friends who were both Jungian-oriented psychotherapists were looking for office space, and we decided that sharing space could be a great opportunity to work together and to learn from each other. We imagined sharing our expertise. They wanted to incorporate body awareness and energy work into their Jungian work with dreams and active imagination, and I wanted to learn more about the Jungian approach to therapy. We found a space in Kingston, New York, only ten miles from Woodstock, and opened the MindBody Center. Both meditators and excellent therapists, my colleagues and I shared much in common but when speaking about our healing work. I felt that my discussing clients from an energetic or Chinese medicine perspective as the "body worker," overwhelmed them, and I was less interested in a strictly psychological approach. We nonetheless enjoyed each other's company as well as sharing the space. They would often ask me to make an herbal tonic for a patient and provide a bit of background on its energetic properties. I would occasionally refer a client to them for psychotherapy.

Each time I noticed the array of bottles on the shelves in the waiting room, I thought of Simon and also "the little doctor." I'd wonder what her small cottage would have been like, imagining bottles just like my own lining her walls, the aromas of herbs rising into the room from decocting, or siphoning off the essence of their medicine.

My wife and I had agreed when deciding to marry that we would devote our lives to healing and meditation, but not have children. She'd often playfully ask, "Ready to have a kid?"

and I'd brush her couched request aside, as if it was an ongoing game. But one time in our early forties when she asked, I responded with a resounding, "Yes!" I stopped short just after I had said it, but it rang true. Yes, I was finally ready, and it was right. Entrenched in her residency and fellowship, she needed time to reflect, to be as sure as she could be.

We worked with a psychotherapist friend who guided us to explore our deeper feelings and acknowledge the potential joys as well as the inevitable responsibilities and commitment that having a child would entail. We were both clear about our decision to share the richness of our lives with a child, but it was also apparent that the time was at hand! He must have been waiting for the opportunity, because the first time we tried, he came!

We both agreed that we wanted to relocate from Woodstock to an area with excellent schools and resources. Northern Westchester provided a rural setting in close proximity to New York City. The commute to Kingston turned out to be too far. Fortunately, some friends and colleagues, a brilliant holistic optometrist and acupuncturist, Marc Grossman, and an amazing chiropractor, David Lester, were looking for a workspace in the New Paltz area, about half an hour closer to our home. We found a small house just outside of town, bought it, and created Integral Health Associates, today a thriving healing center that offers chiropractic care, acupuncture, herbal medicine, psychotherapy, holistic eye care, as well as homeopathy and bodywork. In the more than 20 years that we have run this center, the three of us have never had a major argument or disagreement—three men together who all honor their receptive, feminine energy.

Being at our son's birth was surely the most joyful experience of my life. I'd attended many births in India, but to see his light, our child, emerging into this life touched me to the core.

I commuted three full days each week to New Paltz but resisted building my Westchester practice because when home I wanted to spend all of my time with Adam, our son, seeing the world through his eyes.

My greatest learning through parenting has been the nearly effortless surrender that comes when a child is born. We perpetually consider what is best for them, not us. I had been seasoned in India for surrendering the ego, and here it was given to me to truly live. My surrender carried no regrets, no thought about what *I* could be accomplishing or enjoying but rather the simple joy of rediscovering the world through the rapturous eyes of my child. Perhaps this comes much easier for older parents; by age 40 we've likely played out many of our fantasies.

While raising Adam, my wife and I wanted to nourish in him a sense of tradition and also make it clear that he belonged to a larger circle of extended "family." We explored spiritual communities from the Unitarian Church to the Methodist to reformed Judaism, but nothing quite fit. Initially I related to the philosophy of Unitarianism, but in the end I found it too intellectual. Surprisingly, I realized that I wanted to connect Adam with my Jewish roots. The fact that the local synagogue had a woman rabbi, a loving feminist, and that the synagogue itself was built on the foundations of Isadora Duncan's old dance studio, somehow felt apropos as a means for both connecting to the traditions of my biological family while also revering the feminine way of being, which had long influenced my life.

This decision meant the world to my aging mother, having been the glue that had held any semblance of family tradition and connection together. "I know the family can't understand you or what you do, but stay connected for Adam's sake," she would say. My own "outsider" feelings had long held me back from restoring connections to my family, but I felt that my son could well benefit from such belonging, particularly since his mother's entire family lived in Europe.

Sadly, as Adam grew up he never felt welcomed into my ancestral family's traditions. We did our best to connect with them, especially on Jewish holidays or weddings, but he too felt like an outsider, which indeed he was. My wife and I encouraged him nonetheless to experience his Bar Mitzvah, a traditional rite of passage into manhood, but he resisted. Just as I had balked to my father long ago when struggling to learn Hebrew, Adam asked, "If God is all knowing, then he can speak English so why do I have to learn Hebrew?'" "When you are Bar Mitzvah, then you become a man. At that time you can decide whether to embrace Judaism or not," I replied, similar to my father's words to me, but less harshly. And indeed Adam and I both chose not to embrace it.

Adam often pointed out to me that I acted differently when with the extended family as if I was seeking approval or acceptance. "I love you and Mom," he would say, "We can talk about anything. I just don't fit in with them," and he was right. We surely learn from our children and many of his early perceptions have proven true. I've learned to trust his vision. We can feel love, even learn to forgive, but we need not subject ourselves to the judgment of others or give them the power to control us. I'm still humbly learning to free myself from such chains, heartened that Adam has such a good head start.

Ultimately we must embrace our own personal truth, even when we are alone. I experience such aloneness as the opposite of loneliness. Aloneness is being All-One. Loneliness often seeks wholeness through others. When we are whole within ourselves, we are free, free to love and accept others as they are including a family to which we don't truly belong.

* * *

One day when working with a client, she commented upon the intricate synthesis of my work and its deep effect on her and suggested that I write a book. The thought seized me with both excitement and fear. Yes, I would enjoy sharing the story of what I'd learned and offering others the tools to support their own healing, but I questioned my authority; there was so much that I didn't know. I witnessed again this familiar trigger of self-doubt and thought, "If not now, when?" I did indeed have much to share. I had acquired a wealth of information and the practical knowledge from many years of study in acupuncture, both Chinese and Western herbal medicine, and the unquestionable connection between mind, body, and spirit. But, more importantly I felt that sharing my own journey, its struggles and lessons learned along the path, might inspire others to better acknowledge the value of their own life experiences.

My client who was writing her own book introduced me to her agent, Janis Vallely. Janis came for a session and afterwards we met to discuss my idea of highlighting the power of teaching stories to engage individuals in their own healing processes. To my surprised delight, Janis became my literary agent. After much discussion, we decided that the book would be best geared to feminine healing supported by teaching stories from many traditions. It's true that I had much experience with healing women's health issues but, looking back, I realize that this focus also came naturally to me, partly due to my strong connection to my feminine lineage but also due to my receptive, open nature. We called the book *In The House of the Moon*. With my agent's guidance, I co-authored a book first on herbal medicine, *The A-Z Guide to Healing Herbal Remedies* (1995, Dell) while writing *Moon*. Realizing that a full time practice and fatherhood left little time for writing, my agent introduced me to Katherine Ketcham and over the course of five years we collaborated on two books: *In the House of the Moon* (now called *Feminine Healing)* and *The Five Elements of Self Healing* (now called *Chinese Medicine for Maximum Immunity*).

Birthing a book is a journey in itself, a journey to our core. Geared to the layperson, these three books required me to organize and express abundant and complex material simply and accessibly without watering down the information. I also wanted my books to inspire.

Writing opens an unexpected channel to a deep well where all life's experiences and learning coalesce until the essential truths rise to the surface to be shared. I found the researching and writing process enlivening and the synthesis that it called for also had a profound effect on my practice. The deep work necessary to write the books allowed me to more openly channel the flow of healing that moved through me—a testament to the sacred power of healing.

When the books were published, I was expected to promote them. I agreed to do television and radio interviews from New York City, phone interviews, and book signings, but I refused to go on the road. Believing I was not truly an author but a healer, my commitment to my clients and, of course, my family, came well before my books. The publishing executives did not appreciate this response and dropped my books like hot potatoes. The books nonetheless remain in print and I still derive a genuine joy from the occasional letters from readers who have experienced life-changing processes inspired from reading them. Another great benefit from writing my books has been the wonderfully tangible resource they provide my clients by re-iterating our common language expressed through the metaphors and stories that arise through our sessions together.

Coming now to the end of *this* book's journey, I am again heartened by the unexpected riches found through creative work. What is it, this communion with source, this regenerative energy? I call it resonance.

33

Resonance

We shall not cease from exploration
And the end of all our exploring
Will be to arrive where we started
And know the place for the first time.

—T.S. Eliot from *Four Quartets*

While researching and writing my books, my work with Eastern philosophies and their influence on Eastern healing modalities and my work with Western approaches, particularly in regard to Western herbal medicine and psychology, began to integrate as pieces in a puzzle. I confirmed what I'd intuited all along: an individual's beliefs essentially impact the healing process.

My research while writing *In the House of the Moon* introduced me to the field of psychoneuroimmunology, the study of how the mind affects both the healing and harming of an individual's health and well-being. My research directly affirmed that the teaching stories that I shared with my clients to awaken and engage their intentions to heal had a profound impact on a client's ability to get well. For years the medical community had insisted that if this was so, it was a mere placebo effect, un-proven, un-scientific, and irrelevant. Now, science had validated that attitude, belief, and intention could certainly impact a person's healing process, thus the hypothesis became undoubtedly proven, scientific, and relevant.

Until recently, science had been locked into the domain of Descartes, who insisted that mind and body were two fundamentally distinct realms. He posited that mind and body worked independently of each other and one had little or no influence on the health of the other. In Descartes own words he saw the body as a machine, like a clock "composed …of wheels and springs.... I consider the human being a machine." And this, since Descartes, has been the working hypothesis of Western scientific inquiry.

Modern physics points toward a totally different direction, provocatively in tune with mystical philosophies since ancient times. Our universe is a whole organism, a symmetrical web of relationships in which each subatomic strand contributes to the whole. The most brilliant scientific minds entertained and confirmed the ancient view of the universe as a sacred hoop. Albert Einstein's $E = mc^2$ explained that mass could be described as the movement of the atoms, or energy. Both rocks and humans are equally made of energy, but the movement of the atoms in a rock is significantly slower than in a person. Everything that exists is made of energy, and energy is sensitive to vibration. We are not a mind *or* a body; we are one mind-body. The effect upon one, equally affects the other. As Einstein pondered the universe as stated in *The Enlightened Mind*, edited by Stephen Mitchell, "A human being is a part of the whole that we call the universe, a part limited in time and space. He experiences himself, his thoughts and his feelings, as something separated from the rest—a kind of optical illusion of his consciousness. This illusion is a prison for us, restricting us to our personal desires and to affection for only the few people nearest us. Our task must be to free ourselves from this prison by widening our circle of compassion to embrace all living beings and all of nature."

For many years we've known that stress depletes the immune response, but we now have scientific proof that this is not only true, but that the impact of stress can also be measured by chemical fluctuations within our cells. When someone experiences love or even the thrill of a roller coaster ride, the body produces more *interferon*, an immune enhancer. However the same roller coaster ride for that person's friend might induce fear rather than thrill which depletes *interferon*, thus depleting immune functionality.

Our mind determines our body's ability to heal itself. In Bill Moyers groundbreaking PBS special, "Healing and the Mind," he asked neuroscientist Candace Pert to describe the mind. She discusses the activity of the neuropeptides, the strings of amino acids that function as information molecules allowing cells in different parts of the body to communicate with each other. "Intelligence is in every cell of your body," Pert explained. "The mind is not confined to the space above the neck. The mind is throughout the brain and body."

* * *

When scientists discovered that these neuropeptides appeared in cells throughout the body, influencing immune response in every cell, Dr. David Felton, whose contributions helped to establish the field of psychoneuroimmunology and lay the foundations for the physiological understanding of complementary and integrative medicine, exclaimed, "Mind is in the body."

The expression "I know it in my gut," becomes a scientific fact! Many studies support and refine these new realizations.

In the 1970s at Ohio State, a research experiment tested the effects of a high fat, high cholesterol diet on rabbits. As expected the result with the groups fed very rich diets had a higher rate of atherosclerosis than the less fatty diet, except for one group, where the rabbits fed this diets actually had a decrease in plaque. They repeated the experiment, but the results remained the same. They interviewed the researcher and discovered that she "loved" rabbits and petted them regularly. They repeated the experiment with petting as an active variable and found that the petted group had less plaque. We could deduce that love heals or at least declare the tangible effects of human contact.

Studies have shown again and again that the majority of initial heart attacks occur between 8 and 9 on Monday mornings. A study cited in *The Power of the Mind to Heal* by Joan Borysenko and Miroslav Borysenko and performed in Massachusetts confirmed that job dissatisfaction and a lack of joy were the two main variables for such attacks.

While working at San Francisco General Hospital in 1988, the cardiologist Dr. Randolph Byrd performed a study in which 400 patients who had been admitted to the coronary intensive care unit with a heart attack or suspected heart attack were assigned to one of two groups: standard intensive care only or intensive care, plus prayer at a distance. Groups of people met to pray, were given the names of the patients in the "plus prayer" group, and told briefly about each person's condition. Each patient had signed a consent form that specified that they had an equal chance of receiving prayer. Neither the patients nor the staff knew who was being prayed for. The results were impressive: the prayed-for group did significantly better than the other group on many counts. They were less likely to develop congestive heart failure or pneumonia, and five times less likely to require antibiotics.

Energy healer, Julie Motz, who worked with Dr. Mehmet Oz back in the 1990s, conducted an experiment using psychic healing in the operating theater, essentially directing energy to the patients during thoracic and cardiac surgery. Those patients who were sent "healing" during surgery recovered faster, had fewer post-surgical complications, and left the hospital sooner than a control group of people who did not receive direct healings. Both Ms. Motz and Dr. Oz wrote books about their experience and ultimately Dr. Oz got Oprah Winfrey's attention.

These studies reveal that energetic vibration, which can emanate from many sources, definitively influence healing. This could be the energy elicited through the interaction between therapist and client; the power of thought and/or prayer to align with peace and love; acupuncture or herbs that directly influence flow and vibrational levels, and, of course, more familiar substances such as food, sound, and light effect our cellular frequency.

My favorite form of healing comes through the timely use of teaching stories. Stories encourage us to suspend time, step beside our thoughts, and enter an alternative reality. Stories carry unique logic, and they help us to see ourselves through a fresh lens. For thousands of years human beings have turned to metaphors and images to reframe reality. Myths and stories create a subtle shift, gently guiding us to expand our boundaries, pushing out the edges of reality and helping us create a "home" — a place where we fit within the larger whole. When we listen to stories, the full impact may not be felt for days, or even years, for stories work like time-release capsules in which the wisdom seeps out in small doses, giving us time to adjust and adapt. Story medicine is powerful and long lasting.

When a client enters my treatment room, two of us are present; however, over time the boundaries between us begin to dissolve. We talk and tell stories at the beginning of each session and often within 15 or 20 minutes we both feel that the walls between us have lifted. It's only then that I invite my client to lie down on the treatment table. I put my hands above him or her and sense our energy fields connecting. I then hold her hand in mine and take her pulses. Many clients claim that they feel balanced after only my pulse-taking. This not only offers me information about their current condition but also establishes a reciprocal empathy between us. Often, standing next to them, taking the pulse, my mind empties and I receive information, not only from analyzing what I've learned from pulse reading, but also by tuning in and feeling the client's energy flow including their specific blockages. From this place, I perhaps use some bodywork to help them become aware of their physical holding patterns so that they may intentionally release chronically held muscle tension and allow relaxation.

With all of this information at hand, what I call "a poem" emerges, a treatment strategy with the appropriate acupuncture points to use to best balance their energy. For instance, to support the Kidney energy while taking heat out of the Liver channel, after inserting the needles I share the names and actions of these points and suggest that we meditate together to enhance the healing treatment. Then I will likely tell a story that relates to our intention perhaps adding music as different sounds vibrate different chakras and organs, usually Gregorian chants,

Buddhist chanting, or Tibetan bells. We create the healing field together so that the treatment may go deeper.

A new client may ask what to expect from treatments. I explain that we are opening the blocked channels to allow energy to move more freely to all parts of the mind-body, and that when old blockages are initially released, their exit may at first exacerbate symptoms before their true release.

Many clients come for treatment to relieve a particular symptom, such as a frozen shoulder, sciatica, or tennis elbow, which, of course acupuncture can address, but I explain that simply treating the branch will not change the root cause and that if not addressed, the cause will provoke the same or similar symptoms in the future. I will occasionally refer symptom-relief clients to colleagues who specialize in such, for the true purpose and passion of my work is to determine my clients' "home" vibration, that is, to be at liberty to attune to this, to create space for a deep, abiding healing. When a client chooses to take the longer, more arduous path, old, stuck patterns may temporarily re-emerge, but once exposed to the light of awareness, they usually dissolve for good.

My definition of healing is: **to be present in the presence of another in a state of love with mutual intent for the greater good**. This belief reminds me of "the little doctor," and I sense that 100 years ago she created a sacred space for those who sought her guidance and healing. Perhaps our mutual ancestors pointed the way and that is the root of my resonance with her.

Resonance is central to my work and to my life. Acupuncture developed through ancient observation that we are energetic beings, conduits, where each organ and every cell has its own vibration. By opening energy channels we attune to higher and clearer frequencies, and healing can happen naturally. All of the modalities that I've touched on in this book are rooted in my desire to help others move toward resonant states of being. Many factors affect our vibrational level, but most importantly is our ability to "let go" of all that separates us from the universal field from which we have come. If we can only let go of who and what we should be, who our parents, our clergy, our teachers told us we were, we can free ourselves to feel what moves us, what brings us fully alive. This is our true path to authentic and healthy living.

My realization and belief that allowing, not effort, creates a healing state first came to me during my brief study of aikido during one Esalen summer with Master Tohei. He seamlessly taught the concept and practice of the "unbendable arm." After first guiding us in "ki" exercises to connect us to our energy source, our root, we learned to extend this energy from the bottom of our spine, up, through the spine, through the arm, and out in space. When paired with a partner of equal strength, he instructed us to rest our wrist on our partner's shoulder, and, first by force, to prevent the other from bending our arm. Our partner would place both hands on the inside of our elbow. We struggled to resist, but usually our partner's strength would force our arm to bend. He called this our defeat. Then Master Tobei instructed us to rest our wrist again on the other's shoulder, but this time to keep the arm soft and to focus, as if the energy was moving, on extending our energy through our fingers into the wall on the other side of the room. We were not to resist our opponent's strength. Low and behold, we remained strong every time by staying focused and extending the moving energy, *not* by resisting. This lack of resistance reflected true power rather than force. This is the power of flow, and it is this power that moves in my treatment room.

In the Alexander Technique work, as discussed earlier, the practitioner comes to the client through the "uncommitted hand," where we meet the person where they are, through touch, without any other intention in our touch but to be there with their energy. Only after practitioner and client meet in this safe zone, can we allow the energy to move into higher vibrational levels. I have well learned that the healing happens through us. Every experience where I've *tried* to heal, enacting my will, the less the effect. But, the more I've surrendered, let go to the soft, the gentle, the flow, the outcome has always been more beneficial. Less is more. Easy is right. Water overcomes rock!

In his very simple yet profound book, *Power vs. Force*, David R. Hawkins Ph.D., M.D., states, "Force always moves against something, whereas power doesn't move against anything at all. Force is incomplete and therefore has to be fed energy constantly. Power is total and complete in itself and requires nothing from outside. It makes no demands; it has no needs. Because force has an insatiable appetite, it constantly consumes. Power, in contrast, energizes, gives forth, supplies, and supports. Power gives life and energy— force takes these away. We notice that power is associated with compassion and makes us feel positively about ourselves. Force is associated with judgment and makes us feel poorly about ourselves."

Hawkins claims to map consciousness based on levels of vibration and illustrates that the more evolved one becomes, the higher the vibrational energy they can emanate, and that healing directly relates to attuning to these higher vibrational levels.

Resonance being the central guiding principle of my life's journey, I'm acutely aware that we align with and then *echo* the very meaning with which we surround ourselves. Spending time with evolved or enlightened individuals creates a synchopatic dynamic where denser, heavier energy rises to merge with a more refined substance. All of the masters who I've sought out and studied have not only affected my energy but have also been instrumental in transforming it. I've repeatedly shared with my son how essential it is to sense how an individual affects his energy and to trust that those with whom he feels peace will elevate him and those with whom he feels dissonance will deflate him.

Since my experience with my son, Adam, at the Tenement Museum 13 years ago, my work has continually evolved, but not through further training or finding new teachers, rather through being present to life itself. My work has deepened. I no longer need to distinguish myself from others, to compare, to succeed. My work is a play, and the play is "foreverly now."

The Black Bird has stayed with me from my first visit to Esalen to the present. She is what the Native Americans call my ally. Her presence, each time she appears, wakes me up, when I am *not* present. One day, perhaps two years ago, while sitting at my Aunt Sulica's apartment, listening to her personal stories about "the little doctor," in her pile of old photographs, she found an old portrait of Esther, "the little doctor," dressed in her ubiquitous black garb with black headscarf worn in her time in Greece and Turkey. Her small, fine-featured face, her nose resembling a beak, told me she indeed was my black bird. I believe she has followed me to remind me to stay on my path.

One day about ten years ago, a real bird, a huge, brown owl who lives in the woods surrounding our home, flew directly toward my windshield as I drove down our small winding road. On my way home, I had advised my client to come into the waiting room if I had not returned by the time she arrived. The huge bird appeared as if it would crash through my windshield, when I realized that this was an owl, not my Black Bird. Moments before I expected it to crash into me, instead it gently glided to my left and landed on a tree branch, literally turning and staring directly at me from its perch. Every cell in my body tingled alive as I made my way into the office to meet my client, a clairvoyant woman who would often share her visions with me while on my treatment table. She gave me advice, wanted or not, but I knew she was often accurate. Before I asked her how she was, she declared, "I see birds around you, does this mean anything to you?" I shook my head in awe and shared the story that had just occurred, briefly mentioning my encounters with the Black Bird.

Later, while on the table, she added, "The owl has a message for you. She wants you to know that you are supposed to write the book!" I hadn't mentioned the book to her. This was three years after the experience at the Tenement Museum, and I had been arranging old photos, my old journals, and many of the books which directed my path across the years, and indeed when she said this I knew I had already begun this work.

> *[There was] a man who died and found himself in a beautiful place, surrounded by every conceivable comfort. A white-jacketed man came to him and said, "You may have anything you choose—any food, any pleasure, any kind of entertainment.*
>
> *The man was delighted, and for days he sampled all the delicacies and experiences of which he had only dreamed on earth. But one day he grew bored with all of it, and calling the attendant to him, he said, "I'm tired of all this. I need something to do. What kind of work can you give me?"*
>
> *The attendant sadly shook his head and replied, "I'm sorry sir. That's the one thing we can't do for you. There is no work here for you."*

To which the man answered, "That's a fine thing. I might as well be in hell."

The attendant said softly, "Where do you think you are?"

—From **Stories of the Spirit, Stories of the Heart,** edited by Christina Feldman and Jack Kornfield

In closing, although every ending is a beginning, I think of Adam, how parenting has been the most rewarding and difficult endeavor of my life. It has surely triggered my insecurities but it has also fostered my self-confidence. When I look at my son today, in spite of all my limitations, and grateful for my wife's clarity of vision when mine was obscured, I see an intelligent, loving young man. My wish for him is to stay true to his own path, which only he can walk.

I remember visiting Adam while a third-year student at the University of Vermont, studying philosophy and sociology, and playing drums in a fusion band. Over dinner he opened up to us, thanking us with great heart for allowing him to seek his passion. I had always encouraged him to do this, to find what moved him deeply, to be his own man. Affluence, I told him, follows congruity, for if you're doing what you're meant to do, the energy builds and attracts affluence. If you seek money or power as the goal, you will lose yourself. He looked me in the eye and said, "I know you've both encouraged me to find my passion, and I have, but you're not going to like it. I love music! It fills my soul, it connects me to something higher than myself." I responded, "perhaps you could find a passion which also generates a good income!" and we all laughed.

After graduating from university, Adam spent over two years working with emotionally disturbed children and found that using music with his students provided an amazing vehicle to help the children connect. Perhaps he is close to his calling. As I humbly observe him finding his path, following its thread, not knowing where it will lead, I realize that I am passing a torch.

I hope he will one day have many stories to pass on to his children.

* * *

How incredibly fortunate we are to have been brought up in a culture that offers us the choice to seek our truth, to follow our passion! In the old country, even if you couldn't make a living doing what you loved, you could learn to love what you must do—another kind of gift. I saw this principle lived in action all those years ago at the ashram, where we were taught that whatever job one we were given, we had an opportunity to become one with it, to bring it and ourselves to higher frequency, to be led by our better angels. This reminds me of one of my favorite books, *Jacob The Baker*, by Noah benShea. Jacob finds God in all that he does, loving everything that being a common baker gave him, every minute of the day.

> *Clearly Jacob was a man on his path in the process of this work (baking). He did not appear to be laboring. He was one with his efforts.*

> *Work for Jacob was, in many ways, like a prayer. It was a repetition, leading him out of himself and up Mt. Sinai with the grace of a soul not restrained by the weight of its own importance.*

painted by Emil Alzamora

Postscript

By Adam Elias

"The hardest part of a parent's task is to know when the task is done."
—Diana L. Paxson, from *White Mare, Red Stallion*

As I read my father's book and relive his incredible journey, I remember the many times throughout my childhood in which these stories helped me overcome obstacles and deepened my understanding of the constantly changing world around me.

I am forever proud to have a father who was able to free himself from societal constraints and follow an individual path, one that led him to all corners of the world and created a depth of experience that contributed to the man, the healer, and the good father he is today. His journey and his constant encouragement throughout my youth has inspired me to take risks and to step out of my comfort zones when led by resonance, those moments of flow when our longings and choices are affirmed. For this, I am eternally grateful.

As I write this, my life is in great transition. I began reading this book when I returned to my parent's house after six years of living in Burlington, Vermont and many months of travel. Returning to my hometown brought many old feelings and insecurities forward, and it felt daunting to take the next right step. Reliving my father's journey, his memories of both confidence and doubt, success and failure, helped me to put my own life into perspective and ultimately encouraged me to take the next step on my path — guided by what felt most resonant.

At the end of his book, my father defines his interpretation of healing: "to be present in the presence of another in a state of love with mutual intent for the greater good." As it happens I have chosen a similar path and resonate on a similar wavelength. I have just begun my graduate studies in Music Therapy, a form of expressive healing that has felt natural to me since the age five when I began to play drums on pots and pans. Music, whether played individually, with a group, or therapeutically, creates vibration, love, and resonance. This vibration generates a unique healing force that can be harnessed and utilized much like how my father describes the healing nature of acupuncture: "opening energy channels so healing can happen naturally."

Throughout my father's book, he hinted at his search for a good father figure, how his lack of communication and emotional connection with his own father had impacted his life. Without *my* father, I know I would not be the person I am today. In a world jaded by greed that too often teaches its young people that making money is the only real success, without my father's good example I would not have had the courage to pursue my calling.

I am deeply grateful for our relationship. He is not only a good father but also a good friend. The mirror he has given me to see myself, to trust myself, is invaluable. Words cannot adequately express my deep gratitude and full heart. It lives in the resonance between us.

APPENDIX

Relating to the Five Elements

The Five Element System takes special note of the intrinsic relationship between the cycle of the year's seasons and the transitioning seasons of the body's bio-energetic climate. Each season primarily echoes one of the five elements—Wood, Fire, Earth, Metal, and Water—and it is through the observation of these elemental dynamics within our self that we gain valuable insights into our physical ailments, emotional imbalances, psychological problems, and spiritual yearnings. In essence, when we deepen our awareness of how each season lives within us, and especially how we identify with a season's associated element, we more fully enter the delicate balance and indivisible harmony of life.

With each introduction of an element and its associated individuality and season, listen to your own body's vibration with that particular element and its associations. Your body knows.

WOOD: The Visionary and the Season of Spring

"If you want to be a great leader,

you must learn to follow the Tao.

Stop trying to control.

Let go of fixed plans and concepts,

and the world will govern itself."

—*Tao Te Ching*, translated by Stephen Mitchell

Who are you in relation to the element of Wood? Are you bold, ambitious, and fiercely competitive? If you are a Wood type, you are likely compelled to stay in motion, constantly seeking new challenges and adventures. It is your nature to be direct and forceful and to express your feelings clearly and effectively, using your abundant energy to remove any obstacles that might be in your way. Blessed with vision, insight, and solid planning skills, you are determined to carve a purposeful path.

Like a young sapling in the spring that sinks its roots deep into the earth while rapidly shooting up toward the sky at an astonishing rate, the power of Wood expresses itself tenaciously with pliability and adaptability. If you are a Wood type, you no doubt relate with the greening of spring, grounded in the awakened earth where you find your sense of self and "home," your place of belonging. Your deeply planted roots nourish unlimited potential while your attunement with the renewed vision of spring inspires you to commit to your goals and to bring your creative potential to fruition.

At its most potent and balanced the power of Wood energy is gentle, persistent, and filled with creative potential. It expresses the state of both being and becoming—being true to one's own nature and becoming more oneself by clearly expressing inner needs and desires.

Wood gently penetrates the Earth to bring forth Water, the source of all life. Drawing from your own "roots," you seek the energy to push forward with strength and firmness of purpose, always remaining supple, yielding, and true to your authentic nature. Wood restrains Earth by covering it, literally rooting it in place and preventing erosion.

Anger is the emotion most associated with Wood. In its balanced state, anger can be a healthy emotion, a natural reaction to stress, frustration, or injustice. When expressed with conscious control, anger acts like a thunderstorm that clears the air. Conscious, controlled anger can dispel tension and restore balance. An imbalance in Wood energy, however, whether excessive or repressed, usually manifests as "quick to anger," prone to volatile outbursts, irritability, and the tendency to judge others too quickly or harshly.

As a Zen koan states, "Sitting quietly, doing nothing, spring comes and the grass grows by itself." Sitting quietly runs contrary to those who resonate with the element of Wood and yet it can help to balance an overactive, overzealous Wood type.

This funny story illustrates such a predicament:

> *A man goes to the doctor with symptoms of flu. After examining the patient, the doctor agrees that he indeed has the flu and should rest, drink plenty of liquids, and consume extra Vitamin C.*
>
> *The man insists, "But doctor, I have no time for all that. Give me something to get rid of the flu!"*
>
> *The doctor advises him to take a cold shower, wrap a towel around himself, and run around the block three times.*
>
> *"But I'll get pneumonia if I do that," says the man.*
>
> *The doctor replies, "Yes, but for that I can give you a pill."*

Organs Associated with Wood include:

- **The Liver (Yin Organ)**, the body's largest organ and its master laboratory, stores and distributes nourishment for the entire body. It has hundreds of essential functions, including not only the formation of blood but also cleansing and filtering the blood to eliminate toxins and foster the body's vitality. In traditional Chinese medicine the Liver rules all "flowing and spreading," that is, the natural flow of energy and emotions throughout the body, mind, and spirit. **If you relate to the element of Wood**, you resist stagnation and inertia associated with all forms of disease.

- **The Gallbladder (Yang organ)** is a small organ that stores and intensifies the bile created in the Liver and pumps it into the body and bowel, as needed for digestion. In traditional Chinese medicine, the Gallbladder acts as Wise Decision Maker, utilizing the Liver's blood production an'd distribution to its best advantage to the body.

If you resonate with the element of Wood, you likely make wise decisions.

If your Wood energy becomes compromised, these physical symptoms are more likely to manifest:

- Muscle tension, proclivity for tendon and ligament injuries

- Sciatica (radiating pain from lower back into buttocks and down the leg)

- Headaches, especially migraines

- Irritability and outbursts of anger

- Visual disturbances

- Menstrual irregularities, PMS, fibroids

- Digestive disturbances, including heartburn (GERD), irritable bowel syndrome, ulcers

- High blood pressure, with tendency toward atherosclerosis

The Wood Element: Chart of Correspondences

Season	Direction	Yin Organ	Yang Organ	Emotion	Voice	Taste	Climate
Spring	East	Liver	Gallbladder	Anger	Shouting	Sour	Windy

FIRE: The Communicator and the Season of Summer

"He who stands on tiptoe

doesn't stand firm.

He who rushes ahead

doesn't go far.

He who tries to shine

dims his own light."

—*Tao Te Ching*, translated by Stephen Mitchell

Who are you in relation to the element of Fire? Are you enthusiastic, vivacious, and drawn to excitement? Do you love with your whole heart? If you are gifted with the radiant, passionate energy of Fire, you attract others to your warmth as a moth to flame. You enjoy people and work hard to create and sustain your relationships. Highly intuitive, you often know what your friends are thinking or feeling before they do. You yearn for union in love and remain steadfast and passionately loyal to those you love.

The radiance of the sun, the power of Fire, expresses itself most intensely during the summer when light illuminates our natural world and inspires our creative natures.

At its most potent and balanced the power of Fire is full of life, passionate in love and creative self-expression. It is also exceedingly compassionate towards others while benefiting from peaceful reflection. Wood feeds Fire, which burns to ash, nourishing the Earth. Fire restrains Metal by melting it, allowing it to be shaped and molded. Your passion can melt a rigid heart or soothe a broken one, but its flame can also burn out of control and turn your energy to ash bringing you back to solid ground.

Joy is the emotion associated with Fire. Balanced Fire expresses an overflowing enthusiasm for life. An excess of Fire can, however, create hyper-excitability and restlessness, while a deficiency of Fire can produce a lack of joy and a feeling of apathy.

Organs Associated with Fire include:

- **The Heart (Yin Organ):** In Western medicine, the small, muscular organ called the Heart is considered the center of the circulatory system. It serves as a pump that controls the flow of blood through the body. In traditional Chinese medicine the responsibilities of the Heart extend to emotional and spiritual realms. Ancient Chinese texts compare the Heart to a supreme monarch responsible for maintaining internal peace and harmony. Each of the elements in traditional Chinese medicine has a corresponding yin and yang organ, but the Heart is the supreme monarch attended by the Small Intestine along with the Pericardium and the Triple Heater.

- **The Pericardium (the Heart Protector)**: In Western medicine the Pericardium is the sac that surrounds and protects the heart. In Chinese medicine this strictly structural definition misses the true spirit of the pericardium, described in ancient texts as "the court jester who makes the king [Heart] laugh, bringing forth joy." Chinese medicine believes the Pericardium not only serves as a membrane that lubricates and protects the heart, but also acts as the gateway to the Heart, allowing entry to positive energies, while barring entry of negative energies, such as pathogens, into the its inner sanctum.

- **The Small Intestine (Yang organ)**: In Western medicine the small intestine supports digestion, assimilation, and elimination. In traditional Chinese medicine the purpose of the Small Intestine is "to separate the pure from the impure." Physically, it eliminates waste from our food and drink, leaving only the pure nutrients. Metaphorically, it separates the "nutritional" aspects of our daily interactions with others and eliminates the "indigestible" aspects from our consciousness, allowing for discernment in our relationships.

Within the traditional Chinese classification system, **the Triple Heater** is solely functional with no structural counterpart. Although the Triple Heater has no physicality, it is responsible for thermoregulation, heating and cooling the entire body, both essential to our health and well-being.

If your Fire energy becomes compromised, these physical symptoms are more likely to manifest:

- Excessive perspiration or lack of perspiration
- Rashes, hives, or skin eruptions due to heat
- Sleep disturbances, insomnia, and restless sleep
- Palpitations or an irregular heartbeat
- Restless, agitated, or explosive energy
- Inappropriate laughter
- Anxiety and irrational fears and phobias
- Inability to focus and to pay attention

The Fire Element: Chart of Correspondences

Season	Direction	Yin Organ	Yang Organ	Emotion	Voice	Taste	Climate
Summer	South	Heart	Small Intestine	Joy; Hyper-excitability	Laughter	Bitter	Heat

EARTH: The Peacemaker and The Season of Indian Summer

"The Tao gives birth to all beings,

nourishes them, maintains them,

cares for them, comforts them, protects them,

takes them back to itself,

creating without possessing,

acting without expecting,

guiding without interfering.

That is why love of the Tao

is in the very nature of things."

—***Tao Te Ching***, translated by Stephen Mitchell

Who are you in relation to the element of Earth? Are you naturally sympathetic and caring? Do have difficulty saying no, particularly to those in need? Blessed with a sunny disposition, patience, and the willingness to listen, you are a wonderful friend, a loving parent, and an eloquent spokesperson for peace and cooperation. Friends, relatives, and even complete strangers feel safe with you for you accept life in all its diversity and refrain from judging others. Kinship with other human beings is essential to your nature and you have a gift for creating loving communities.

At its most potent and balanced, your Earth energy evokes an image of a garden—fertile, solid, and forgiving. Those drawn to the power of Earth are natural mediators who thrive on harmonious relationships; discord and dissension unbalance them. Kinship and connection to others promotes their good health and happiness. Earth energy guides an individual to the center between opposites where differences and problems can find reasonable solutions.

The element of Earth is associated with Late or Indian Summer, that transitional time before the harvest comes due, when all life is at its peak, a time for slowing down and gathering energy. Indian Summer invites us to reflect upon where we stand, allowing for stillness. We consume the Earth's bounty—vegetables, animals, and water. Our bodies, our matter, becomes, in essence, what we consume. Earth energy embodies the process of procuring, absorbing, and converting Earth's food into living nourishment.

We find Earth at the center of life itself and everyone benefits from a share of Earth energy at the center of themselves so they can stand on solid ground. This center comforts us through our transitions and allows us to speak our truth. From this place, we know what we need—where we're lacking and where we're full. When we meet this center within, we recognize our strengths and our vulnerabilities. This humility allows us to empathize with others and to learn Earth's greatest lessons: to love and to serve.

Earth controls Water by absorbing it and forming dams and riverbanks to prevent it from overflowing its channels. Your Earth energy stabilizes your own and others' emotions. Earth provides a firm foundation and stable support for the mountains of Metal that rise upward toward the heavens. So too your Earth grounds inspiration that it may be fueled with balance and presence.

As Earth revolves on its axis, it relates to all the cycles of nature, central to the other four elements. In traditional Chinese medical theory, each of the other elements—Wood, Fire, Metal, and Water—represent the four seasons, the four directions, while Earth remains pivotal at the center, always the transitional point. In this way we recognize Earth not only as Late Summer but also Late Autumn, Late Winter, and Late Spring, where one season slowly becomes another. Symbolically, twilight and dawn evoke Earth energy.

Such imagery reminds me of a wonderful Zen teaching story:

> *The Zen master Hakuin was praised by his neighbors as one living a pure life. A beautiful Japanese girl whose parents owned a food store lived near him. Suddenly without any warning, her parents discovered that she was with child. This made her parents angry. She would not confess who the man was, but after much harassment at last named Hakuin. In great anger the parents went to the master. "Is that so?" was all he would say. After the child was born it was brought to Hakuin. By this time he had lost his reputation, which did not trouble him, but took very good care of the child. He*

obtained milk from the neighbors and everything else the little one needed.

A year later the girl-mother could stand it no longer. She told her parents the truth, that the real father of the child was a young man who worked in the fish market. The mother and father of the girl at once went to Hakuin to ask his forgiveness, to apologize at length, and to get the child back again.

Hakuin was willing. In yielding the child, all he said was: "Is that so?"

—From **Stories of the Spirit, Stories of the Heart**,
edited by Christina Feldman and Jack Kornfield

Sympathy and worry are the emotions associated with Earth energy. When balanced, Earth types express self-compassion and empathy for others. However, when they excessively take on another's pain, too much sympathy can be debilitating and over-worry can become obsessive compulsive. Alternatively, a lack of capacity for empathy, such as aloofness, also expresses an imbalance of the Earth element.

Organs Associated with the Earth include:

- **Spleen/Pancreas (Yin Organ):** The Spleen and Pancreas support the body's digestion and assimilation. The Spleen transforms our food into chi (energy) and blood by extracting essential nutrients from our food and eliminating the excess waste. In Western medical terms, the Spleen and Pancreas mediate sugar metabolism. On the other hand, Chinese theory goes beyond a physiological explanation to include the assimilation and absorption of spiritual qualities.

- **Stomach (Yang Organ):** The primary function of the Stomach is to "rot and ripen." Saliva in the mouth begins the breakdown of food before that food passes to the stomach where it is further transformed and sent to the Spleen, its yin counterpart, for assimilation and distribution throughout the body.

If your Earth energy becomes compromised, these physical symptoms are more likely to manifest:

- Excessive mucus, in nose throat and mouth
- Heavy feelings in the body, with achy arms, legs, and head
- Craving sweets!
- Bloating and indigestion, often with bowel irregularities
- Metabolic problems including hypoglycemia and diabetes
- Thyroid problems
- Lethargy and lack of energy
- Low self-esteem
- Chronic worry
- Craving love and affection

The Earth Element: Chart of Correspondences

Season	Direction	Yin Organ	Yang Organ	Emotion	Voice	Taste	Climate
Late Summer	Center	Spleen/ Pancreas	Stomach	Worry/ Sympathy	Sing-song	Sweet	Humid

METAL: The Artist and the Season of Autumn

When the ancient Masters said,
"If you want to be given everything,
give everything up,"
they weren't using empty phrases.
Only in being lived by the Tao
can you be truly yourself.

—*Tao Te Ching*, translated by Stephen Mitchell

Who are you in relation to the element of Metal? Are you drawn to life's core issues, essential structures, and guiding principles? Are you attracted to beauty, symmetry, and purity? Do art, philosophy, and religion inspire you? Do you thrive on intellectual discussions with like-minded people?

Autumn expresses the season of the Metal element. Its strength, endurance and tranquility is best symbolized by a majestic, snow-capped mountain, both reaching toward the heavens and profoundly grounded in Earth. Like the ore at the mountain's core, Metal energy runs deep, evoking our core issues, the most essential parts of ourselves, where we focus on existential reality, perhaps asking questions such as, "Who am I?" "What is my lifework?"

At its most potent and balanced, your Metal energy prefers quality to quantity. Disciplined and precise, strong-willed yet flexible, you search for higher truths. Your keen aesthetic sense and high moral standards guide you toward the true meaning of life. You seek to develop your character by devotion to ethics, morality, and knowledge.

Metallic ores and rocks underlie the river channels that give Water its direction, while minerals and trace elements give Water its nourishing riches. So too does your depth bring focus and clarity to your direction in life.

Grief or sadness is the emotion associated with Metal. As autumn bids farewell to the abundance of summer, Metal energy connects us with the ability to let go of the past and create space for the future.

Organs Associated with Metal include:

The Lungs (Yin Organ): The organs of respiration, the Lungs supply oxygenated blood to every other organ of the body and eliminate waste matter from the cells through expiration.

"Inspiration" connotes breathing in, the Lung's primary function, both physically and spiritually. The Lung reflects the spiritual nature of the autumn season, its letting go and its opening to receive anew. To be fully "inspired," we must not only release the stale air, the old ideas and preconceived notions, but also open to the fresh air, the new possibilities. In emotional and spiritual terms, the Lungs balance our ability to yield and to demand, to give and to take, to hold on and to let go. When the Lung (Metal) energy is out of balance, an individual will hold an extremely tight rein on order and discipline, including exhibiting controlling behavior and emotional inflexibility. The body too will stiffen up.

- **The Large Intestine (Yang Organ):** At first glance, the Lungs and the Large Intestine seem to have little in common, as one is involved with respiration and the other with digestion. But traditional Chinese medicine views things energetically rather then purely physically. The bowel is responsible for helping the body eliminate waste. Only when the body is cleansed of toxic matter can it receive the more refined energy brought in by its partner, the Lung. The Large Intestine makes distinctions between harmless and harmful elements, and it discriminates between the nutrients the body needs and those it must eliminate.

If your Metal energy becomes compromised, these physical symptoms are more likely to manifest:

- Bronchial infections and sinusitis
- Allergies are amplified
- Asthma and heaviness of the chest can appear
- Spine and joint problems, chronic stiffness and pain
- Eczema and/or psoriasis, sensitivity of skin

- Intestinal problems, constipation and/or diarrhea
- Fear of losing control
- Self righteousness
- Difficulty letting go of 'stuff'

The Metal Element: Chart of Correspondences

Season	Direction	Yin Organ	Yang Organ	Emotion	Voice	Taste	Climate
Autumn	West	Lungs	Large Intestine	Grief, sadness	Tearful	Spicy	Dryness

WATER: The Philosopher and the Season of Winter

Nothing in the world

is as soft and yielding as water.

Yet for dissolving the hard and inflexible,

nothing can surpass it.

—*Tao Te Ching*, translated by Stephen Mitchell

Who are you in relation to the element of Water? Are you called to a spiritual path? Are you drawn to the deeper meaning and mechanics of life through art, religion, ethics, and philosophy? Are you introspective, in perpetual search for knowledge and truth? If Water speaks to your nature, you like to retreat into a quiet, still place where nothing distracts you from thinking about the mystery of life. Insatiably curious and blessed with a vivid imagination, you are an intellectual and perhaps a philosopher. The world of logic and analysis appeals to your reflective nature.

Water, the most yin of the five elements, is associated with winter, effortlessly changing shape and yet never losing its essential character. Water freezes into icicles, melts come morning, falls again as snow overnight, and dissolves in the sun-warmed morning mist.

Like a stream flowing down a mountain, at their most potent and balanced Water types hold firm to their course in life, refusing to fret over setbacks or worry about past defeats. Water energy is fearless and directed—it knows where its going, and has the inner driver to get there. Every action Water takes, even the non-action of pooling and reserving strength evokes readiness to continue onward, yet Water knows its limitations. It yields, refusing to waste energy in vain pursuits. When you resonate with Water, you likely know who you are.

Water irrigates the fields and forests so that Wood can grow just as your spiritual awareness softens Wood's relentless tendency. Water controls Fire by quenching it as clear, fearless awareness can snap a Fire type out of its hyper-excitability.

Fear is the emotion most associated with the element of Water. In a healthy way, fear moves and directs us to remain alert and attentive to our surroundings and situations. When confronted with danger, constructive fear can both caution and restrain us, inviting a readiness and courage to face a dangerous or very complicated situation. When Water energy is out of balance, fear can stop us short but also unground us, as adrenalin soars and our heart races.

Organs Associated with Water element include:

- **The Kidneys (Yin Organ)**: According to Western medicine, the Kidneys regulate water metabolism and stabilize the heart and blood pressure, maintaining homeostasis, a dynamic, continual rebalancing within the body. Traditional Chinese medicine teaches that excess fear injures the Kidney (Water) while a Kidney dysfunction further increases our fear. The Kidneys elicit a vital yin force that cools and lubricates all body structures. This keeps the body and mind flexible and prevents the build-up of unnecessary, excessive friction.

- In traditional Chinese medicine, Kidney (Water) energy supports healthy teeth, bones, and bone marrow. In fact, ancient Chinese medical scholars considered the brain and spinal cord to be extensions of the bone marrow, concluding that the Kidney rules the skeletal structure and functioning and, therefore also intelligence, reason, perception, and memory. Contaminated aspects of Water move to the Urinary Bladder for storage and elimination while the pure aspects transform into a mist that circulates freely throughout the body.

- **Urinary Bladder (Yang Organ):** The Urinary Bladder, described in Western medicine as a hollow container with muscular walls, joined to the kidney by the ureters (tubes that propel urine) and to the body's exterior by the urethra where every few seconds urine passes from the Kidneys to the Urinary Bladder, where it is stored until eliminated. Traditional Chinese medicine compares the Urinary Bladder to a reservoir where the Waters of the body collect. When the Urinary Bladder leaks or is not functioning properly, the entire body can dangerously absorb toxic wastes. Such imbalance of Water creates depression, fatigue, difficulty adapting to new circumstances, and a general sense of foreboding.

If your Water energy becomes compromised, these physical symptoms can more likely manifest:

- Lower back pain—chronic or acute
- Knee pain and weakness

- Problems with urinary retention

- Fatigue and shortness of breath

- Vertigo or dizziness

- Sexual problems, including lack of excitement, premature ejaculation, vaginal dryness

- Anxiety and excessive fear

- High blood pressure and/or occipital headaches

- Inflexibility and resistance to change

The Water Element: Chart of Correspondences

Sea-son	Direction	Yin Organ	Yang Organ	Emotion	Voice	Taste	Climate
Winter	North	Kidney	Urinary Bladder	Fear	Moaning	Salty	Cold

The metaphors for each of the Five Transformative Powers have immeasurably enhanced my ability to help my clients heal, particularly by engaging their participation in that effort and ultimately encouraging them to embrace the metaphors themselves. Our mutual resonance with the Five Element System expands healing awareness and encourages each client to look more deeply within, to listen and learn from challenges, and to seek balance within to live a more peaceful, healthy, and joyful existence.

Acknowledgements

Having lived long and well with many rich encounters and learning experiences, I have a multitude of individuals to acknowledge for their grace, wisdom and generosity. In keeping with my love of stories and their subtle teachings, I remember the Ramayana myth, the tale of Rama (my sannyas name) who is called to reclaim his feminine half, Sita. She had been captured by the evil Ravana and taken to his domain in Sri Lanka. Rama was charged with defeating this potent enemy to bring Sita home to India. The Hindu holiday Diwali symbolizes this return home and is known as the Indian Festival of Light, where all homes in India place candles or light outside of their homes to guide and welcome back their divine presence. The lights that have served as my guides, are the many teachers and friends who have shared their wisdom with me on the crossroads, the thresholds, and beyond. To them I am eternally grateful.

Writing this book has been a journey in and of itself with the greatest gratitude to my dear editor, writing coach, and guide, Catharine Clarke. This book would not exist without her indispensible presence.

Dr. Stephen Larsen, thank you for your friendship, support, and your generous foreword.

I would also like to thank Jone Miller for seeing the "black bird" as the thread, which connected me to the "little doctor," and Renee Pastolove for helping me to envision the form of the book as stories within stories as well as for her editorial feedback. Olivia Buehl, Steve Cole, and Janet Hariton also added value to the manuscript. And thanks to my cousin, Isadore Elias, for his support with family history and its roots. Additional editorial support came from too many of my dear friends to mention.

* * *

My partners at Integral Health Associates, Dr. Marc Grossman and Dr. David Lester, longtime friends, support my work unceasingly. Our partnership exemplifies the saying, "things can flow effortlessly when the parts disappear into the greater good." A warm thanks also to my office manager, Lori Baczynsky, for her continual support; to Mikio Kennedy for his graphic genius and invaluable guidance and maintenance of the fiveelementhealing.net website, and to Joan Forlow for her gift of the painting of the bird and the saint that closes this book.

I deeply appreciate my family—past, present and future— with a special nod to the "little doctor" and her ancestors as well as to my parents. Finally, to my beloved wife, I am particularly indebted for her continual loving support, her compassionate editorial critique, and her abundant patience.

And, finally to one of my greatest teachers, my son Adam, life with you is all about love.

About the Author

Jason Elias is a healer. Through trust in resonance, that knowing within each of us, he has lived a life of seeking and learning. He believes stories carry true meaning and share universal principles across cultures, races, genders, and creeds to shed light on dark places.

He practices acupuncture and herbal medicine in New York state where his journey toward healing and wholeness continues.

For more information about his work, contact: fiveelementhealing.net.

CPSIA information can be obtained at www.ICGtesting.com
Printed in the USA
BVOW05s1042121115

426785BV00007B/29/P